Gender in the Market Economy

Gender in the Market Economy

Edited by
Sudeshna Mukherjee

RAWAT PUBLICATIONS
Jaipur • New Delhi • Bangalore • Guwahati • Kolkata

ISBN 978-81-316-0705-3

Published by
Prem Rawat for **Rawat Publications**
Satyam Apts, Sector 3, Jawahar Nagar, Jaipur 302 004 (India)
Phone: 0141 265 1748 / 7006 Fax: 0141 265 1748
E-mail: info@rawatbooks.com
Website: www.rawatbooks.com

New Delhi Office
4858/24, Ansari Road, Daryaganj, New Delhi 110 002
Phone: 011 2326 3290

Also at *Bangalore, Guwahati* and *Kolkata*

Typeset by Rawat Computers, Jaipur
Printed at Nice Printing Press, New Delhi

Dedicated
to
My Mother and **Grandmother**
the women behind me

Contents

Section II
Market Economy of Marriage

Section III
Market Economy of Gender and Health

Foreword

I have known Dr Sudeshna Mukherjee for the last few years and have been impressed by her understanding of political economy and gender issues. Coming from a background of sociology, her conceptualization of how under a capitalist economy there is an inherent tendency towards not only commoditization of many areas of life, but also simultaneously commercialization of public goods, making for increasing inequality between classes and gender, is well illustrated in this book. The book captures how much of our social life, hitherto shielded within a private realm and subject to tradition, now has increasingly become buyable and saleable 'product'. As a result, human relations and institutions have not escaped the onslaught of the market. What is unique in Dr Mukherjee's innovative approach is the way she demonstrates how not only individual aspects of social life are commoditized, but they are also interlinked, in other words each area of life is interlinked to others though commercial ties – be it marriage, entertainment, health care, drugs or weapons. Public goods like water and nature are also within the ambit of the cash nexus. The new economic forces in alliance with existing patriarchy, deal a particularly insidious victimization of women in India. It is worth quoting her from her concept note:

> Market transactions cannot be disembodied from social and geographic relations. Each economic act or transaction occurs against and incorporates a geographically and culturally specific complex of social histories, institutional arrangements, rules and connections.

The articles she has included in the book reflect the significance of the above statement. Women are tied to domestic work but what kind of identity of respect accrues to one depends on where one is working, says Nitya Rao. Considered the bottom of the heap in India, ill paid, much exploited, without social security or unionization except in a few towns – in advanced economies, these 'maids' have a better deal. I remember during my sojourn in the USA, maids have to be registered, paid social security, have regular working hours and often come in an automobile, with gadgets that ease the arduousness of cleaning jobs. Yet even this protected work is going, with migrant women taking up these jobs without these perks. Even in the cinema, women are more vulnerable workers (Nirmala M.N.). Not just domestic work of cleaning but caring for the sick, elderly, infants and children get assigned to women – thus enforcing women's stereotypical status in the economy (Vinita Singh). Working in isolated houses, it is difficult to mobilize these domestic workers. Women workers in a hybrid capitalist economy like India, find place mainly in the so-called unregulated informal economy (Jasbir Singh).

The most interesting articles are on how marriage has become commoditized (Namratha Mogaral, Moly Kuruvilla). There was a time when marriages were arranged, through known intermediaries, between families within the same location – by the broker or family friend. Today, however, marriage bureaus, internet information called matrimony-channel have arisen; newspapers are used to advise desirable bride or groom in a given caste, etc.; arrangements for marriages can be given to contractors; beauty parlours do the decoration of the bride and groom; astrologers use the media (Madhurima Mukhopadhyaya). Scores of industries proliferate as suppliers for a marriage.

The several articles on health (Kalpana Mehta and Nalini Bhanot; Heena K. Bijli) highlight health care becoming highly iniquitous with privatization, bypassing the needs of poor women. Reproductive technologies further increase inequality with womb-hire; pre-sex selection, etc. (China T. Mills; Sudeshna Mukherjee, Heena K. Bijli). The mental health of sex workers have not been given any importance (Suneha Kandpal).

The selected articles and the themes addressed, cover a gamut of issues but are germane to the gender polarity accentuated by the market economy. Women's subordination which we term 'patriarchy' has found a willing and useful ally in capitalism. Years ago, Meivat Hatem (Hatem, Meivat, 1987, *Class and Patriarchy: Competing Paradigms,* Contemporary Studies in Society and History, Vol. xxix) wrote about Class and Patriarchy being competing paradigms. While the book's concept note mentions that these issues are contested and struggle against, there is no reference in the articles themselves about this. Altogether, a welcome book for teaching, and for research in Women's Studies and, most of all, as a pointer to the women's movement on our continuing agenda.

Maithreyi Krishna Raj

Acknowledgements

This book is an initiative towards the collection of select research papers presented in the Indian Association of Women's Studies (IAWS) Conference held in Wardha during 2011. Papers were presented in one of the sub-themes on 'Women in Emerging Market and Interlocking Inequalities'. The title was suggestive and presenters were given liberty to explain the issue from their points of view. Rewriting and revisions were done on the basis of criticisms received during the conference. So, my sincere thanks go to the contributors for their perseverance and patience as the project took quite some time to materialize and, of course, to the critics for their constructive criticisms.

I am indebted to the IAWS and especially Sumi Krishna, former President of IAWS for entrusting the responsibility of coordinating this research group. I profusely thank Sumi, for all her support and encouragement to bring out this volume. My heartfelt gratitude goes to Maithreyi ma'am (Dr Maithreyi Krishna Raj) for always being a support and her prompt acceptance in writing the wonderful foreword. I also would like to thank Suparna for her support during the conference. Thank you Dr Vinita and Dr Jha for your professional advice and help when I needed them the most! I also acknowledge the technical support of Veena, my research student during the final stage of the book.

Last but not the least, my parents and Soumendu provided me much needed space and mental strength to face all odds. Samadrito and Sampoorno, my children were my stress busters. Finally, I also would like to thank Rawat Publications, especially Mr Pranit for his support to make this project a reality.

Sudeshna Mukherjee

Contributors

Anwesha Ghosh, were has been working as a Research Associate in United Nations Research Institute for Social Development (UNRISD), Sponsored Project from Indian Social Studies Trust (ISST), New Delhi.

Bikram Keshari Mishra, Reader in Sociology, Ravenshaw University, Cuttack, Odisha.

China T. Mills is a Research Officer at the Oxford Poverty and Human Development Initiative (OPHI), at the University of Oxford.

Dilshad Valasseri, Research Scholar, Centre for Women's Studies, University of Calicut, Malappuram, Kerala.

Heena K. Bijli is Associate Professor, Community Resource Management and Extension, School of Continuing Education, Indira Gandhi National Open University, New Delhi.

Jasbir Singh is Professor of Economics, University of Jammu, Jammu, J&K.

Kalinath Jha, Associate Professor, Department of Sociology, Sagar University, Sagar, Madhya Pradesh.

Kalpana Mehta is well-known Social Worker with Manasi Swasthya Sansthan, Indore, Madhya Pradesh.

Madhurima Mukhopadhyaya is Guest Faculty, Department of Comparative Literature, West Bengal State University, Kolkata.

Moly Kuruvilla, Associate Professor, Centre for Women's Studies, University of Calicut and Member, UGC Working Group for Capacity Building of Women Managers in Higher Education.

Nalini Bhanot is associated with Manasi Swasthya Sansthan, Indore.

Namratha Mogaral, Associate Professor, Department of English, Kuvempu University, Shimoga, Karnataka.

Nirmala M.N. is Doctoral Student, Department of Film Studies and Visual Communication, The English and Foreign Languages University, Hyderabad.

Nitya Rao is Professor of Gender and Development, School of International Development, University of East Anglia, UK.

Sudeshna Mukherjee is Assistant Professor, Centre for Women's Studies, Bangalore University, Karnataka.

Suneha Kandpal is Consultant (Research), International Centre for Research on Women (ICRW), New Delhi.

Vinita Singh is Associate Professor, Department of Sociology, Ranchi Women's College, Ranchi, Jharkhand.

Introduction

Gender as a social construct and culture as a set of material practices are rooted in society, shaped by political and economic forces. One way of understanding how hegemonic patriarchal forces structure gender relations is in terms of interlocking exploitations in the markets. In mainstream economics, the concept of market signifies any structure that allows buyers and sellers to exchange any type of goods, services and information. Under Capitalism's inherent tendency of commodification, markets permeate and commodify all human relations and institutions under an integrated, all encompassing and cohesive global capitalist economy. Market relations lead to undue exploitation of labour and of women in the market economy. Women particularly are the victims of both capitalist commodification and patriarchal subjugation.

Market transactions cannot be disembedded from social and geographic relations. Each economic act or transaction occurs against this backdrop and incorporates a geographically and culturally specific complex of social histories, institutional arrangements, rules and connections. Thus, market exchanges of any kind involve a history of struggle and contestation. The present book invited papers that dealt with the ways in which the hierarchies, inequalities and disembeddedness of markets, from the local to the global, impinge on women. It explores and tries to understand how women are contesting, resisting, and negotiating in the new markets.

In the recent past, especially since 1990s the world economy has undergone tumultuous changes. In the less developed or developing countries like India, economic transformation has been associated with the attempt to generate higher rates of economic growth. Following the Chinese model, other Asian, Latin American and African developing nations, under the aegis of International Monetary Fund and World Bank-driven 'Structural Adjustment Programmes', abandoned import substitute strategies and attempted to integrate their economies into the global marketplace. The shift was perceptible from state planning to market-driven decision-making in public policies (Aslanbeigui, Pressman and Summerfield, 2013).

Under the influence of structural adjustment programmes, different forms of privatization of infrastructure and services, which were previously the responsibilities of the state, have created hybrid private-public formations and graded degrees of commodification, commercialization and privatization. Under such a variety of hybrid institutional orderings, a plethora of 'new' markets (or new twists to old market relations) have emerged – marriage, entertainment, health care, education, drug, weapon, etc. besides markets in carbon trading, pollution rights and even new markets for basic common goods like water.

Market economy may have expanded the choice in selection of goods and services for the middle and upper middle-class population but have miserably failed in meeting the aspirations of the have-nots. Studies show that, for women, job opportunity has widened but sex segregation in employment under patriarchy, relegated women to low-paying jobs, often reproductive in nature. Increased economic opportunities undoubtedly increased bargaining power and decision-making rights within the household but economic crisis due to 'volatile capital' has further accentuated vulnerability of women in the globalized world. In developing countries like India, women's lack of access to property, lack of political voice and near absence in policy-framing lead to their increased exploitation in the all-encompassing market economy.

Substantial economic reform, however, never affects everyone in the same way. Change in distribution of economic rewards change the definition of winners and losers in the market. Regardless of the country, studies show – regardless of whether per capita income has increased, stagnated or decreased – women have been over-represented among the losers and under-represented among the winners (ibid.).

For instance, India has a vast pool of both skilled and unskilled labourers, of which only about 9 per cent are in the organized sector. The majority of women labourers are unskilled and, therefore, in the unorganized sectors. There is considerable literature on the gender and class-specific issues related to the unskilled, unorganized market. In this book, we would like to extend the debate on how new labour markets have impinged upon women's health, marital situation, etc. Prof. Jasbir Singh, in his paper titled *Gender Discrimination and Inclusive Growth: A Study of Informal Labour Market in India,* opines that women form one of the most vulnerable groups and the largest minority among the socially discriminated sections of population in India. Liberalization and later on, inclusive growth in India was expected to increase women's participation in labour market. Though this did happen but demand for women labour increased only in those sectors where it was cheaper than male labour, and in low paid and low skilled areas. Women are often under-represented in higher-income activities and over-represented in low-income activities. The contribution of women in the formal sector to total GDP is greater than the share of employment in the informal sector. This is because more women than men engage in multiple activities including unaccounted activities in the informal sector. About 60 per cent or more of women non-agricultural workers in the developing world are informally employed. The vast majority of women in the informal sector are home-based workers or street vendors.

New economy has indeed expanded the work opportunities for the urban middle and upper middle-class educated women but their going out of the house has never been substantiated by calling 'men' in the sphere of domesticity. Doubly burdened professional working women from nuclear families relied more and more on the services of the domestic helps to manage the show and this has resulted in the proliferation of market for migrant domestic workers from the relatively poorer states to the metropolitan cities with more white-collar working women. This situation is brilliantly captured by Nitya Rao, in her paper titled, *Social and Spatial Meanings of Respect: Migration and Identity of Women Domestic Workers in India*. The focus of this paper is on the changing context of domestic work in Delhi, with an apparently growing demand for female, ethnic minority, migrant strangers, as well as the experience of that domestic work by these women, highlighting women's agency in dealing with some of the contradictions they face between earning incomes and gaining respect. The paper focuses on unpacking the social and spatial expressions of respect across the urban and rural worlds which the workers stride. The experience of migration for the domestic workers is contingent on a range of factors – personal attributes such as age, marital status and education, but also the larger institutional context both at home and at the destination (including the nature of mediating agency). The role of education in shaping women's agency is explored, especially in terms of generating political voice to legitimize the social value of domestic work. The paper is based on empirical material collected from a village in Jharkhand State, eastern India, which has witnessed increasing migration of women as domestic workers to Delhi over the last two decades.

In another paper titled, *The Emerging Market of Care Work: Issues and Challenges* by Vinita Singh and Kalinath Jha describes how the concept of market signifies the presence of potential buyers and sellers exchanging goods and services in the field of caregiving, a traditional strong domain controlled by women in the house. Market permeates to commodify all human relations. Due to New Economic Policy (NEP) and Structural Adjustment

Programme (SAP), a hybrid of institutional orderings or what may boldly be addressed as New Markets, that are being established and the emergence of care service as a new market in India has become very significant for researchers. The notion of 'care' and caregiving practices are the prime responsibility of women. The present paper will like to see how inequality and disembeddedness of market impinge on the women, that is, how women caregivers are being affected in the presence of the market of care in relation to the changes in macro-structures and the manner in which they impact on women. It would also see how the market of paid-care, works to deepen the pre-existing inequalities of class, gender, ethnicity in urban India. It will also focus on paid-caregivers who are contesting, resisting and negotiating from their marginalized position vis-à-vis the new markets. It will look into the sites of oppression, the forms of domination and exploitation, the process of resurgence and assertion among the paid-caregivers in the new market of care. The paper looks extensively into the 'supply and demand' aspect vis-à-vis migration among those who work as care-providers in the cities which are the chief centres of the supply of paid-care. It also looks into the role of placement agencies in providing care jobs to the new arrivals and the costs they bear for caregiving. The paper concludes that the goals of gender equity and development cannot be realized until and unless care-work is made more valuable.

Nirmala M.N. in her paper titled *Feminine Representation and Identity as the Vulnerable Workforce in the Indian Cinema Industry*, looks at the representation and identity of women as vital workforce in another, large unorganized sector – the Indian film industry. The hierarchical division of labour and of social space constrains feminine activity and expression and projects women as dependent on men. In this case, the implication is that women should fight for the right to enter into these domains from which they were previously excluded and to ensure that their formal legal rights are actually availed of. The arguments, that of women are unrecognized, or that they are excluded are not usually interrogated. Women have been and still are excluded from the production of and representation in cinematic activities, but even when they are included they do not receive their due recognition. In many genres of representation, however, women are not only visible, they are prominent objects of attention. The issue is then transformed into one of the correctness or incorrectness of the representation. While the representation of women on screen are seen as instancing two processes, the commoditization of women and the trapping of the feminine, within an overall cultural context that is both homogenizing and hegemonizing and, off screen, due to lack of social security, absence of work ethics – junior artists in the industry, mainly female junior artists are subjected to abuse and exploitation. While the abuse, attack on the female lead actresses are buried as gossip, the exploitation of female junior artist off/on screen are rarely voiced. The paper looks at the patriarchal influence in Indian cinema industry and its impact on the women.

A next set of papers aims to uncover the permeation of market in marriage relations. In India, the links between 'marriage and market' have been very strong for centuries. Becker's theory defines marriage as an arrangement for non-market transactions, and the centrepiece of his view on marriage is the production of children; most other transactions associated with marriage regarding sex, household upkeep and the like could be provided for, in the market, but the production of one's own children, Becker calls the distinguishing characteristic of marriage (Becker, 1973: 813–846). Marriage and market should have no relation, whatsoever, but unfortunately in our country they are not only strongly related but held centre stage for all these years. Any market anywhere should follow the main principle of demand and supply but in Indian marriage market in spite of having abysmal sex ratio (940 as per Census 2011) several other factors come into play, and they have been changing the market economy of Indian marriage rapidly.

Every culture has specific rules governing the formation of marriage, which define the pool of eligible spouses (Eckland, 1970). For example, marriages in India are arranged by the parents of the prospective spouses, are subject to certain rules of caste, kinship, religion and geographic region and require the bride's parents to provide a dowry to the groom and his household (Banerjee, 1999). This aspect of marriage has always been traditionally related to the market, where 'choice' plays an important role in selecting a suitable bride or groom. The intermediaries play a significant role as mediators of this choice. Madhurima Mukhopadhyaya in her paper titled *Ghataks, Marriage Bureaus, Astrologers: Studying Intermediaries in the Kolkata Marriage Market*, explored how in Kolkata, intermediaries like the Ghataks (matchmakers), marriage bureaus and astrologers are commonly used by parents of eligible young men and women to find a suitable match for their wards. This paper intends to study how these intermediaries differentiate between a prospective male and female client in three categories of 'never married', 'divorcees' and 'late marriers'. It also seeks to investigate further the negotiations between these intermediaries as they coexist in the 'marriage market' facing competition from global intermediaries like the matrimonial websites. Lastly, how they modify their functioning, in keeping with the 'modern' needs of the clients, retaining traditional practices and norms. The intermediaries coexist catering to different age-groups and economic-classes. Ghataks are more used by the low income groups. Marriage bureaus and astrologers are visited by the middle and the upper-middle classes. These intermediaries in their own ways negotiate traditional practices while introducing 'modern' practices. The Ghataks ensure that the bride and the groom 'date' each other before marriage and find each other compatible. Most Ghataks emphasize this practice since marriages are 'breaking easily nowadays'. To keep up with the competition from local and national matrimonial websites, marriage bureaus offer the facility of matchmaking via the internet, whereby a website which contains their bureau's database is monitored and their clients can log in with a password and search the database of the bureau for a suitable match.

The custom of arranged marriages has been a part of Indian culture since the fourth century. The practice was begun primarily to maintain and pass on the family traditions from one generation to the other. It is still prevalent in both rural and urban parts of India, former being more inclined towards the system. In this context Namratha Mogaral's paper titled, *Internet Arranged Marriages: Passions of the Indian Eve* explores how the tradition of arranged marriage in India has taken a new fillip with the advent of online-matchmaking sites. This culture has especially caught the wannabe middle-class marriage market, which in India today is an ever-burgeoning stratum. A diversity of websites has emerged in the last six to ten years, which one can access either individually or via an agent for no great cost. Under the umbrella label of matchmaking for marriages, these websites offer a range of services what may be best called as 'sex related' services. The more adventurous of them offer daring short-term liaisons from purely platonic dating to hot one-night affairs. Others offer fully fledged relationships described conventionally. Most of these websites claim to cater to individualized needs and choices. For instance, a woman wanting to upload her biodata with a view to locating a suitable match is at liberty to express her needs including the traditional categories like caste, class and horoscope or she may forgo all these and project as a liberal free individual.

As actual experience will reveal that undertaking a liaison of such kind with the help of these websites is a package affair that ties up with a range of other goods also being sold online, such as fashion, food, entertainment (like partying at a restaurant or a short holiday during courtship, or a beauty pageant for a group of prospective couples) and housing goods. A marriage so contracted may cover, if one is willing to shell out the money, counselling for modes of courtship, beauty tips for the couple involved, with follow up on family planning and setting up house. Themes are offered for the actual marriage ceremony with readymade venues and honeymoon spots. The new media has been at the outset characterized as a free and liberal cultural space not bound by traditional biases, prejudices, oppressions and inequalities. The internet is supposedly a plastic space of freedom, in which one can shape one's identity and future as one wants. In this context, her paper seeks to explore the various dimensions of the cultural space created by online matchmaking.

However, with the changing time, people in India have accepted the concept of love marriage, which is otherwise considered against the Indian culture. Therefore, both arranged and love marriage find equal importance in the wedding scenario of India. People with an orthodox or conservative outlook of life are still firm about marrying within the same caste, community and religion. Contrary to this thought, people in the present time do believe in solemnizing weddings of two different individuals belonging to different family background and culture.

One of the important social functions of marriage is formalization of sexual gratification. For ages, women from lower-castes have been regularly trafficked for the purpose of sex work. Most of these women live in brothels and are oppressed and exploited against their will. Most trafficked women are conscious of their terrible condition and would want to change their fate. In most cases, they would definitely want to change the fate of their children and make sure they do not follow their mothers into a similar fate. As such, in recent years there has been a lot of support from civil societies to hear their voices and there has been a consensus towards strengthening their rights.

In case of caste-based sex work, however, there is no such consciousness of oppression on part of the women sex workers. Sex-work is considered a way of life and is part of the community structure. The women, hence, in this case are neither 'choosers' nor 'victims'; they become 'destined' by virtue of birth to follow their caste-occupation of sex work. In this context Anwesha Ghosh's paper titled, *Caste-Based Prostitution: Caste, Marriage and Prostitution* would be dealing with the phenomena of caste-based sex-work known to be practised in various pockets of northern India. Since the phenomenon is rooted in tradition and caste ascription, it is very difficult to break the modus operandi of this form of prostitution. This paper, in particularly, will be focusing on one such community (caste) called the 'Pernas', found on the fringes of Delhi, who practise their age-old caste occupation of prostitution. Interestingly, amongst the 'Pernas', it is the daughter-in-law who works as a sex worker. Hence, the idea of the sanctity of marriage as we know it in the Brahminical Hindu ideology is turned on its head in this otherwise Hindu community following its caste occupation. Hence, the paper would be examining the functionality of such an arrangement, as well as, the challenge it throws to the hegemonic idea of sanctity of marriage. It would also be examining how materialism through means of mass communication such as cable television, continue to strengthen the trade, further endangering future generations of such communities.

Now, novel marriage markets are emerging (even as caste, class, religion and region continue to hold sway). The conception of the ideal bride in matrimonial advertisements has evolved through every decade from the 1960s. By the 1990s, the demand was for professionally qualified and physically perfect working women. 'Dowry' in its globalized consumerist avatar continues to control supply and demand and has given birth to scores of ancillary industries like fashion, jewellery, household accessories, and beauty products and so on. Even seeming equality in the access to education may mask deeper inequalities, such as education being used only to enhance the product's brand value in the marriage market. Indeed, even some religiously sanctioned and legal marriage systems may be just a way to procure cheap sexual and physical labour.

Dowry plays a very intrinsic role in Indian marriage. It is the root cause of various other oppressions meted out to the Indian women under the aegis of patriarchy. Dowry commodifies the sacred relations of marriage to market transactions. In the yesteryears, the ceremony was a brief affair, confined to an economical budget. On the contrary, in the present time; the occasion is generally celebrated in an elaborate way, with number of rituals that are conducted before, during and after marriage. A long guest list, colourful and extravagant venue, lavish feast and a series of rituals are the key ingredients of the 'big fat Indian wedding' in 'Bollywood' style. While for 'grooms', education and economic status is the main determinant of his market value; for 'brides' beauty, looks, docility, adherence to so-called Indian value system and parental capacity to pay dowry, ruled her market value. Of late, for educated women, their earning potential has become another determinant without compromising the previously mentioned ones.

In the days immediately after Independence, the landed property of the groom played the dominant factor. Dowry ruled the roost. The Zamindari system took some time to get extinct and gave birth to the second stage, in which the grooms holding a good government job, which provided complete job security and status held the centre stage. In the 1950s the only jobs available were in the government. The grooms with better jobs attracted more brides and dowry. This practice of dowry was initially confined to the so-called upper castes but quickly spread to all castes, communities and religions. The third stage was linked with corruption. The under-the-table income came into sharp focus. The intermediaries who arranged the alliances specifically mentioned this aspect while giving the particulars of the groom to be. The fourth stage occurred when some professions started paying very good salaries/compensation packages. The Airlines staff and people in Mercantile Marine started getting good pay packets and perks which attracted the attention of the parents of the girls. The next stage came when the opportunities abroad started opening up. A boy employed in USA, earning dollars and enjoying a good lifestyle earned the pride of place among the eligible bachelors. A Non-Resident Indian (NRI) son-in-law became not only an attractive proposition but also a status symbol. The girls too left the shores of India with stars in their eyes and pride.

In this context paper by Moly Kuruvilla and Dilshad Valasseri titled, *Mysore Kalyanam: An Event Where Violation of Women's Rights are Legitimized* throws light on a particular interstate marriage practice conducted for the want of dowry, happening in certain specific regions of Kerala. In Kerala, interstate marriages such as Mysore marriages are quite rampant. 'Mysore Kalyanam' means the specific type of interstate marriage in which the brides from poor socio-economic background and belonging to rural remote areas of Wayanad or Malappuram districts of Kerala are married to bridegrooms who are residents of Mysore (Karnataka State) and which involves comparatively low dowry. The issue of dowry is the major cause for these interstate marriages. Once a girl reaches the age of 20, she is considered as overage for marriage in certain regions and certain communities, which in turn leads to higher dowry demands for an alliance within the state of Kerala. Hence, the parents are compelled to take the painful decision to marry their daughters to bridegrooms from the neighbouring state with comparatively lesser dowry demands and send her to a totally strange, far-off place. Women in interstate marriages have to face serious problems like the unfamiliar language, culture, poor life situations, economic dependence, domestic violence, etc. Though most of them are deserted and back in their parental homes, they are neither legally divorced nor getting any support from the husbands for their survival. At the same time, most of them do not expect or wish a rejoining with their husbands. In spite of all these, the occurrences of Mysore marriages are still rampant in the backward regions of Kerala, highlighting the helplessness of rural women in the face of compulsory marriage. The paper is hoped to be an eye opener to the grave situation of rural women in certain pockets of the glorified state. There are other types of interstate marriages like Mali, Mangalore and Haryana marriages occurring in different places of Kerala that share similar characteristics with regard to their causes, gender issues and the impacts on women's lives. Since 100 per cent of the aggrieved women in Mysore Kalyanam belong to the Muslim community, the social backwardness of the specific community should be addressed politically. Strategies are to be evolved to eliminate the notions regarding compulsory marriage in the lives of women and to correct the misconception that marriage is the life goal of women.

Final section of the book is concentrating on the issues pertaining to the 'Market Economy of Gender and Health'. Health is one of the fundamental human rights but understructural adjustment's policies, government disinvestment and growing privatization have transformed wellness and health care into a swiftly burgeoning commodity market. Affordable health care is still a mirage for the vast majority of poor Indians, and particularly poor women, since the health and pharmaceutical sectors are essentially 'corporative' in nature. Reproductive health of women continues to be the primary focus of the state and governmental policies, as if women only die during childbirth, and other diseases and health problems do not affect women's well-being. The sub-theme seeks to explore how inequalities in the health market interlock with other markets and impinge upon women's wider burden of disease, mental health issues, ageing and so on.

Health care is one of India's largest sectors, in terms of revenue and employment, and the sector is expanding rapidly. During the 1990s, Indian health care grew at a compound annual rate of 16 per cent. Today, the total value of the sector is more than $34 billion. The health care industry in the country, which comprises hospital and allied sectors, is one of the fastest growing markets. The growth in the sector would be driven by health care facilities available in private and public sectors, medical diagnostic and pathlabs and the medical insurance sector. The private sector accounts for more than 80 per cent of total health care spending in India. India's thriving economy is driving urbanization and creating an expanding middle class, with more disposable income to spend on health care. More women are entering the workforce as well, further boosting the purchasing power of Indian households. Between 1991 and 2001, the percentage of women increased from 22 per cent to 26 per cent of the workforce, according to the 2001 Indian Government Census. If the economy continues to grow faster than the economies of the developed world, and the literacy rate keeps rising, much of western and southern India will be middle class by 2020. Another factor driving the growth of India's health care sector is a rise in both infectious and chronic degenerative diseases. This troubling trend can be attributed, in part, to substandard housing, inadequate water, sewage and waste management systems, and a crumbling public health infrastructure. In this context Heena K. Bijli's paper titled, *New*

Market Economy and Problems of Women's Health in India discusses recommendations initiated at the Programme of Action, International Conference on Population and Development (ICPD), Cairo, (1994). It was that population programmes should provide comprehensive reproductive health (RH) services that are integrated and coordinated with each other and with other health services. Today, the underlying conditions determining women's health and childbearing are only deteriorating. Economic reforms have been to the detriment of women's health more generally, not just to the health services they need. Since women tend to be more economically disadvantaged than men, they suffer from poor access to food, clean water, sanitation, decent housing, livelihoods, quality education, and a healthy working and living environment. In the absence of any other form of social security, women are the worst affected when neo-liberal economic policies and trade agreements are implemented. A large proportion of maternal deaths in India, is attributable not to lack of contraception, or even to little or no access to quality health services, but to undernutrition, anaemia and communicable diseases stemming from lack of food, poverty and inequity. The recent National Rural Health Mission (NRHM) report reveals that nearly 85 per cent of the country's primary health centres do not have a doctor. The condition of community health centres is equally appalling. Putting RH and rights at the centre of population policies has encouraged policy-makers to continue to think of women only as wombs to the neglect of the wider economic and social roles, and of the conditions that could advance the health of women. Neo-Malthusian or populationist thinking in population and development programmes and institutions, restricts women's ability to exercise their reproductive and sexual rights. This thinking is also detrimental when it acts through institutions that formulate and carry out economic development policies. Population policies should not have an ultimate goal of 'population stabilization', in which they regard women's empowerment and the elimination of social, cultural, political and economic discrimination against women, mainly as prerequisites for low fertility. The need to separate the women's agenda of empowerment and self-determination from the population agenda of mass fertility control is as important today, as it was in 1990s. We as thinkers and activists need to build up networks and alliances with each other. We need to pave the way for Reproductive and Sexual Health and rights to be incorporated within the larger agendas of other social movements and of society in general.

Paralleling the rise of disease is the emergence of a robust pharmaceutical industry in India. It is an ongoing challenge to balance the commercial interests of pharmaceutical companies with the broader social objective of curing disease and preventing epidemics that could decimate the Indian population. India's health care infrastructure has not kept pace with the economy's growth. The physical infrastructure is woefully inadequate to meet today's health care demands, much less for tomorrows. While India has several centres of excellence in health care delivery, these facilities are limited in their ability to drive health care standards because of the poor condition of the infrastructure in the vast majority of the country. The lack of drug research and development for 'non-profitable' infectious diseases will require new strategies. No sustainable solution will be forthcoming for diseases that predominantly affect poor people in the South without the establishment of an international pharmaceutical policy for all neglected diseases. Private-sector research obligations should be explored, and a public-sector not-for-profit research and development capacity promoted (Trouiller et al., 2002). Kalpana Mehta and Nalini Bhanot, in their paper titled, *Unbelievable: The Case of HPV Vaccines* investigates how we have witnessed in the case of Gardasil and Cervarix, although these are not consumer products but vaccines; they are being promoted among 9 to 14-year-old girls in more than a hundred countries. Some of the moves are outright illegal and some others are condemnable but nothing befitting a product which is meant to prevent women from getting cervical cancer. India is getting out of the license-permit Raj, centralized governance and is either handing over production and import to the private sector directly or is sharing its revenues and advantages with the private sector through the now popular buzz word Public Private Partnership (PPP). Social sector spending was curtailed in the early nineties with structural adjustment imposed by the IMF and the World Bank. Despite promises to the contrary and much discussion around adjustment with a human face, the situation is that India has one of the most privatized health care systems in the world. A recently released report by the World Health Organization (WHO) has shockingly revealed that even in 2008, general government expenditure on health was a mere 32 per cent of the total expenditure on health in the country. This is lower than the average for low income countries (40.5%) and also lower than the average for the South-East Asia region (41.3%). In India, about 68 per cent of the total expenditure on health is paid for, by people from their own pockets and this expenditure is pushing them, especially the poorest, below the poverty line. The government is ready to let the private sector benefit at the cost of the larger good. Needless to say, with doctors diverted towards the rich-paying clientele and drug companies' research agendas, the poor will have reduced access to them. Medicines and treatment costs are spiralling and people will now be doubly exploited to become trial subjects and surrogate mothers.

When it comes to health care, there are two Indias: the country that provides high-quality medical care to middle-class Indians and medical tourists, and the India in which the majority of the population have limited or no access to quality health care. Today, only 25 per cent of the Indian population has access to Western (allopathic) medicine, which is practised mainly in urban areas, where two-thirds of India's hospitals and health centres are located. Many of the rural poor must rely on alternative forms of treatment, such as Ayurvedic medicine, Unani and acupuncture. There is a clear divide in health care sector. There is a lack of effective, safe, and affordable pharmaceuticals to control infectious diseases that cause high mortality and morbidity among poor people in the developing world.

Mental health problems affect women and men equally, but some are more common among women. Abuse is often a factor in women's mental health problems. Treatments need to be sensitive to and reflect gender differences. The same numbers of women and men experience mental health problems overall, but some problems are more common in women than men, and vice versa. The positive association between poverty and mental health problems is one of the best established in all of psychiatric epidemiology. Research has documented consistently that low income and low socio-economic status are associated with high rates of mental disorder. With the prevalence of poverty itself, now on the rise in our country, particularly among women, children and those from minority groups, increased attention must be paid to the mental health risks that accompany poverty. In this context, Suneha Kandpal's paper titled, *Mental Health: A Fringe Issue in the Prostitution or Sex Work Debate* deals with how in the public health debates and literature on prostitution/sex work, there has been a major focus on HIV or Sexually Transmitted Diseases (STD) which tends to exclude discussion of mental health, critical to the question of prostitution/sex work. The present paper discusses the mental health implications of prostitution/sex work and an abysmal response to it in the public health discourse. The paper will also provide an overview of the existing literature/research and field experiences in context of the mental health issues on women working in prostitution/sex workers. There is a real dearth of research in this particular area, particularly, in India. We need intensive, longitudinal, ethnographic studies to find out what affects their health and mental health over a lifetime as they either stay or leave prostitution/sex work. This also raises pertinent questions on, the extent to which psychological harm of prostitution can be/are controlled or decreased by decriminalization or state regulation. Since there have been studies which, in fact, show that there is no difference found in the incidence of Post Traumatic Stress Disorder (PTSD) and depression in the legalized and 'street' types of prostitution, suggesting that the emotional experience of prostitution is intrinsically traumatizing, regardless of its location and decriminalization. Hence, regardless of legal status, prostitution/sex work has devastating effect on women's overall well-being, especially psychosocially.

Although the traumatic effects of rape and other violence to women who are not in prostitution are well established, the same trauma is not well understood among women in prostitution/sex work. Domination is the central theme of prostitution where one person socially, legally or economically enjoys the right to employ the other person, mostly women to be an object sexual gratification. In addition, as a result of trauma of prostitution/sex work, multiple psychological dysfunctions are experienced by these women, which inadvertently also spill over to their overall functioning and well-being. Most women who have been in prostitution/sex work for any length of time experience sexual dysfunction, have a distorted view of self, their sexuality, and their attitude toward men. Dissociation, depression, and other mood disorders are common among prostituted women in street, escort, and strip club prostitution. The constant objectification, dehumanization over years, instils learned helplessness which restricts their ability to think for themselves. Eventually, they begin to view their body as a commodity/object, which in turn normalizes various kinds of violence. Trauma and torture survivors commonly experience this profound disconnectedness. Unfortunately, due to the lack of in-depth understanding of mental health issues, closely entwined with human rights, legal and public health discourses, translates into grossly inadequate or absent laws and services for this marginalized population. This becomes even more emphatic when we talk about empowerment of sex workers and achievement of political or legal rights while ignoring the psychological rights of the women. If the voices of the silenced must be heard, then mental health must not become a fringe issue in the whole prostitution vs sex work debate.

China T. Mills, in her paper *Colonizing Distress: The Violence of Normalization and Normalization of Violence* drawing on her own research with children, discusses how coherent responses to the material and discursive violence performed on children who do not 'fit' are dominant frameworks of the 'normal'. It tenuously explores how facets of the colonial relation are enacted within psychiatric intervention with children, particularly how children framed as 'mentally ill' occupy 'quasi-colonial status' (Du Bois 1970).

Pharmaceutical colonization and medicalization of children's everyday lives is particularly worrying because the huge commercial incentive to construct particular experiences as 'mental illness' changes our view of what it means to be a child, and ultimately to be human. Here, the desire 'to be yourself' and to 'get your child back' is increasingly being mobilized, acting as both an exploitable and marketable desire. These dominant pharmaceutical schemes of intelligibility, normalize the absence of children with mental illness and pathologize their presence within psychiatric discourse and legislation. Currently, the pharmaceutical industry operates as a monopoly of possible frameworks for understanding children who hear voices, governing and delimiting the emergence of non-medicalized and non-pathological frameworks for understanding children's experiences and distress.

Psychiatry's construction of children who hear voices as 'psychotic', 'irrational' and 'schizophrenic', establishes parameters of what can be justified under the guise of 'treatment', meaning that these children are subjected to 'treatment' that would, in other circumstances, be constituted as legal battery and child abuse. Mills has explored how it is on the body and in the minds of those children, framed as mentally ill, developmental psychology, psychiatry and bio-power converge and interweave. A technology of normalization is translated into material violence. This paper will read children's experiences and resistance through a post-colonial lens, drawing particularly on the work of Homi Bhabha. Here, we can glimpse how the hidden transcripts of resistance can enable political subversion through frustrating any voyeuristic desire for fixity as categorized subjects, changing the terms of recognition of what it means to be a child.

Medical tourism is one of the major external drivers of growth of the Indian health care sector. A Google search of 'India medical tourism' turns up more than two million results. The emergence of India as a destination for medical tourism leverages the country's well educated, English-speaking medical staff, state-of-the art private hospitals and diagnostic facilities, and relatively low cost to address the spiralling health care costs of the western world. India provides best-in-class treatment, in some cases at less than one-tenth the cost incurred in the US. India's private hospitals excel in fields such as cardiology, joint replacement, orthopaedic surgery, gastroenterology, ophthalmology, transplants, urology and artificial reproductive technology with surrogacy practices. My (Sudeshna Mukherjee) paper on *Reproductive Technologies: New Market and Emerging Inequalities* emphasizes how, since the advent of the feminist movement, one of the most important issues confronted by the feminists is their attempt to gain control over female body. For centuries, their bodies and reproductive capacities were used to control and oppress women. Feminist movement led by Radical feminists sought to liberate women from being prisoner of their bodily capacities. Right to abortion was an important step towards this end. Radical feminists like Shulamith Firestone believed that women with the help of the emerging new reproductive technologies can exercise more choices and will liberate themselves from oppressive and restrictive reproductive practices. But many believe these choices, especially in case of surrogacy, opens up newer areas of patriarchal, capitalistic, societal control and exploitation over women through their reproductive capacities. In this light, my paper would like to make a critique of the Artificial Reproductive Technology Bill (Draft) tabled before parliament on 2010 and to study India's emerging status as soft reproductive tourism destination. Recently, in number of cases (especially in the case of Baby Manji) we have come across a lot of legal and ethical issues associated with surrogacy but plight of the surrogate mothers, who often hails from impoverished background, has often gone unnoticed. IVF (in vitro fertilization) clinics also maintain utmost secrecy on the details of surrogate mothers. Thus, this paper tries to locate how aided by technology, market is widening the inequality in the areas of women's reproductive health.

Marketization of health care facilities extended to the concept of body images. Body image is a complicated aspect of the self-concept that concerns an individual's perceptions and feelings about one's body and physical appearance. Females of all ages seem to be particularly vulnerable to disturbance in this area; body dissatisfaction in women is a well-documented phenomenon in mental health literature. Researchers have called female's concerns with their physical appearance 'normative discontent'; implying that body dissatisfaction affects almost all women at some level. Socio-cultural standards of feminine beauty are presented in almost all forms of popular media, barraging women with images that portray what is considered to be the 'ideal body'. Such standards of beauty are almost completely unattainable for most women. In the light of this Bikram Keshari Mishra's paper on *Beauty and the Market: A Critical Perspective* explores how woman's body continues to be a terrain of perpetual battle in contemporary socio-political milieu. It is not surprising that while thinking of woman, the ideas that ineluctably strike one's imagination irrespective of her achieved/ascribed positions are 'body' and 'beauty'. In fact, there is a tendency among people to ascertain woman's worth in terms of her skin-centric physical appeal. The notion of physical beauty predominates one's consideration while judging the entire personality of a woman. The market treats her body as a commodity that can be advertised, shaped, reshaped, used, consumed, exposed and sexualized in accordance with the tunes of the market economy and that of patriarchy. No wonder, the entire business in the public sphere seeks to use feminine 'body' in order to maximize its gain. Even the domain of electoral politics is no exception. The reason why political parties aggressively induct sexually appealing beautiful actresses/female icons into their organizations is explicitly understandable. Woman's physical body is increasingly viewed as the birthplace of appealing 'beauty'. Market has discovered a new industry in this beauty, to cash in on. Correspondingly, woman's body has become a terrain for the practice of experimentation as well as commerce in order to expedite the running of the beauty industry and foster the cult of 'beauty-worship' in society. Thus, the entire understanding of woman's 'body politics' gives rise to a series of conundrums.

Thus, from all the papers these facts are quite evident that:

- New economy has widened the work opportunity for women as capitalism-driven market economy and patriarchal family require their cheap labour for their further expansion and proliferation.
- These new markets, undoubtedly, increased work opportunities for women across the category but have differential access and impact on women belonging to different categories, and majority of them, across the globe, are at disadvantageous conditions.
- Their nature of work in the market economy is often the further extension of reproductive activities back home, with some monetary incentives which only helps in meeting practical gender needs, and far from empowering them to achieve strategic gender needs.
- Defying the notion of universal sisterhood, there is emergence of a category/class of women who need to exploit their poorer sisters (in terms of domestic help, caregiving, surrogacy and so on) for their prosperity.
- There is a demand for much broad-based intersectional analysis to understand subjugated position of women in the market and providing solution for their amelioration.

References

Aslanbeigui, Nahid, Steven Pressman and Gale Summerfield (eds), *Women in the Age of Economic Transformation: Gender Impact of Reforms in Post-Socialist and Developing Countries*, Routledge, London, 2013.

Banerjee, K., 'Gender Stratification and the Contemporary Marriage Market in India', *Journal of Family Issues*, Vol. 20, 1999: 648–676.

Becker, Gary S., 'A Theory of Marriage: Part I', *Journal of Political Economy*, Vol. 81, July/August 1973: 813–846.

Belle, Deborah, 'Poverty and Women's Mental Health', *American Psychologist*, Vol. 45, No. 3, March 1990: 385–389.

Cash, T.F. and T. Pruzinsky (eds), *Body Image: A Handbook of Theory, Research and Clinical Practice*, Guilford Press, New York.

de Arellano, Annette B. Ramirez, 'Patients without Borders: The Emergence of Medical Tourism', *International Journal of Health Services*, Vol. 37, No. 1, 2007: 193–198.

Du Bois, 'Speak: Speeches & Addresses', Pathfinder, New York, 1970.

Eckland, B.K., 'Theories of Mate Selection', *Eugenics Quarterly*, Vol. 15, 1970: 71–84.

Lin, L.F. and J.A. Kulik, 'Social Comparison and Women's Body Satisfaction', *Basic and Applied Social Psychology*, Vol. 24, No. 2, 2002: 115–123.

Sharif, Abu Saleh and Maithreyi Krishna Raj (eds), *States, Markets and Inequalities*, Orient Longman, New Delhi, 2007.

Trouiller, Patrice, Piero Olliaro, Els Torreele, James Orbinski, Richard Laing and Nathan Ford, 'Drug Development for Neglected Diseases: A Deficient Market and a Public-Health Policy Failure', *The Lancet*, Vol. 359, No. 9324, 22 June 2002: 2188–2194.

SECTION I

Gender in Labour Market

CHAPTER 1

Gender Discrimination and Inclusive Growth

A Study of Informal Labour Market in India

JASBIR SINGH

Inclusive growth has been the main mantra of 11th Five-Year Plan, which is aimed at providing an opportunity to restructure policies, to achieve a new vision based on faster, more broad-based and inclusive growth. It is designed to reduce poverty and focus on bridging the various divides that continue to fragment our society. It also aimed at putting the economy on a sustainable growth trajectory with a growth rate of approximately 10 per cent by the end of the Plan period. During the Plan period, efforts were to be made to reduce disparities across regions and communities by ensuring access to basic physical infrastructure as well as health and education services to all. It has to recognize gender as a cross-cutting theme across all sectors and commit to respect and promote the rights of the common person. The 11th Plan strategy for gender equity was expected to pay attention to all aspects of women's lives. It must ensure that women live with dignity. It must examine everything from generic problems like freedom from patriarchy to specific issues such as clean cooking fuels, care for pregnant and nursing women and dignified spaces for violated women, and toilets for women and girls, crèches at work places, etc. The Committee suggested that all chapters of the Plan document need to include analysis of women's location in each sector, so that women's perspectives are explicitly recognized and integrated into sectoral programmes and policies (Committee of Feminist Economists, 2007–2012).

For gender equity the Approach Paper to 11th Five-Year Plan expected to have adequate provisions in policies and services across Ministries and Departments. It also entails strict adherence to gender budgeting across the road. All had to be complemented by campaigns for public awareness that educate men and women – both are gripped with patriarchal values – about emerging social and economic realities. Special measures for gender empowerment and equity were made an essential component of the 11th Plan. The Plan started with special focus on four aspects – violence against women (VAW), economic empowerment, political participation and women's health (Government of India, 2006).

Gender Discrimination

Gender-related segregation in occupations is done pertaining to the prominent and endurable aspects of labour market, the world over. This phenomenon exists in two different forms, namely, horizontal segregation and vertical segregation. The former refers to concentration of women and men in different types of jobs without reference to job hierarchies, while the latter concerns itself with concentration of men in higher-level jobs and women in lower ones, both within and between occupations and industries (Talwar and Bulla, 2009). The tasks performed by women are also influenced by the traditional gender division of labour. The domestic responsibilities extending to labour market contexts constitute the most common jobs including maids, cooks, tailors, nurses and more culturally accepted job of a school teacher. These jobs may help them to find professions, like cooks and maids may move on to become chefs and housekeepers, nursing to medical technicians, tailoring and sewing may be utilized for garment-making jobs.

The 2004–05 (61st NSS round) data show that the women workers are engaged in a large number (more than 40%) in occupations like maids and housekeeping services, tobacco preparers and bidi-makers, farmers other than cultivators, housekeepers, matrons and stewards, nursing and other medical and health technicians and teachers, while 30 to 40 per cent of them are engaged as agricultural labourers, production related workers, launderers, plantation labourers, social scientists and related works, building caretakers, sweepers, cleaners and related works, spinners, weavers, forestry workers, tailors, dress makers, sewers and cultivators.[1]

The labour force participation and worker population ratios are in general very low in India due to high dependency of children, elderly and other members of the family who do not work. Labour force participation measures the proportion of men and women who are willing to engage themselves in the economic activities which are included in the system of national income accounting. Labour force consists of those who are employed and those who are unemployed but looking for work. The work participation rate shows only those who are employed as a proportion of the total population. Both these measures reflect women's participation in economic activity compared to that of men (Kaur and Kaur, 2009). The situation in rural areas has undergone a change like in 2004–05 (61st NSS round), higher percentage of women were self-employed than men in rural areas. About 63.7 per cent of rural women workers were virtually unpaid workers in self-employed category in 2004–05. Regular wage and salaried employment was much higher for men than women. There were only 3.7 per cent women workers in regular employment, slightly increased for both men and women in rural areas. About 32.6 per cent of women workers in rural India were casual labour in 2004–05. Thus, the category of employment available to women in rural areas is self-employment and casual labour employment.

Gender bias is deeply ingrained in our social psyche and this is reflected in indicators such as sex ratios, literacy, health gaps of boys and girls, maternal mortality rates, etc. These data, however, do not fully reflect the discrimination against women. The 11th Plan strategy for gender equity must pay attention to all aspects of women's lives. It must ensure that women live and live with dignity. It must examine everything from generic problems like freedom from patriarchy to specific issues such as clean cooking fuels, care for pregnant and nursing women and dignified spaces for women victims of gender-based violence, toilets for women and girls, crèches at work places, etc.

Informal Sector

In economic parlance the term informal sector is commonly used interchangeably with unorganized sector. The term was used to define informal economy which includes all forms of informal employment, i.e. employment without labour protection and social protection, both the cases of self-employment and wage employment.[2]

Indian informal sector accounts for 92 per cent of the total workforce. Informal employment has increased from 361.7 million to 422.6 million, whereas formal employment has declined from 35 million to 34.9 million between 1999–2000 to 2004–05. Informal employment is normally a larger source of employment for women than for men in the developing world. When material deprivation dictates poor women to contribute to the household survival, it is the informal sector that comes to their rescue. About 60 per cent or more of women workers are in informal employment outside the agriculture sector. They work as contract workers in manufacturing, unpaid family workers, construction workers, petty venders, hawkers, domestic workers or as casual workers. Women earn less than men and are poorer than the males working in this sector and face gender-based discrimination. In spite of inclusive growth as main objective of the 11th Five-Year Plan, women, a major chunk of population, have been left out which has badly affected their education and health.[3]

Trends in Employment

The National Sample Survey (NSS) data show that about 25 million women workers (both principal and subsidiary status) have added to the workforce between 1993–94 and 2004–05. The increase in the number of women worker is more in rural areas as compared with urban areas. Such an increase was 17 million in rural and 7 million urban areas during the same period. Large numbers of additional women workers were reported to be in principal status with only 3 million being incremental in subsidiary status. The incremental additions during this period comprise nearly one-third of the urban women workers in 2004–05 (Rustagi, 2010).

The gradual upward increase reflected in the employment over the last quinquennial period of 1999–2000 to 2004–05 could have been interpreted as the overcoming of the jobless nature of our economy. This trend has been welcomed by some as the inevitable outcome of the high growth rates in the economy, but researchers like Mazumdar and Sarkar (2008) and Narain (2006) argued that most of the additional employment is perhaps that of women as subsidiary workers with very marginal gains as principal workers. It is also noted that an increase in the women's participation in work is not only an outcome of the increasing availability of persons to undertake work and their willingness to do so, but also partly due to the enhancement of work opportunities. Data also show that a large number of women remain occupied in the primary sector, especially in the rural areas as cultivators and farmers more than agricultural labourers. This trend continues, with the additional factor being that the relatively older women in the post-reproductive years are concentrated in agriculture and not the younger women or men for that matter. The latter are, in fact, shifting out of agriculture, which is leading to the feminization of agriculture, in that women's share is increasing, though in actual magnitude the total number of women registered a decline over the period 1993–94 to 2004–05 (Srivastava and Srivastava, 2010).

The sector-wise data show that women are shifting to manufacturing as well as service sector while majority of these jobs are informal, low paying and offer no social security, though some of them are actually regular employment. To quote Rustagi (2007), casual workers have been on the decline and a shift into self–employment has been noted. For women, this signifies a shift away from the paid to the unpaid employment categories and may not necessarily result in economic empowerment.

The percentage distribution of workforce by gender in Table 1 shows that during the period 1999–2000 to 2004–05 women workers were found to be in higher percentage in self-employed and casual labour category both in rural and urban areas. This also shows that women participation was far less in regular wage/salaried class during the period mentioned above.

Table 1

Percentage Distribution of Workforce by Gender

Area/Gender	*1999–2000*			*2004–05*		
	SE	*RWS*	*CL*	*SE*	*RWS*	*CL*
Rural Male	55.0	8.8	36.2	58.1	9.0	32.9
Rural Female	57.3	3.1	39.6	63.7	3.7	32.6
Urban Male	41.5	41.7	16.8	44.8	40.6	14.6
Urban Female	45.3	33.3	21.4	47.7	35.6	16.7

Notes: SE= Self Employment; RWS = Regular Wage/Salaried; CL = Casual Labour.

Source: Rangarajan et al. (2007); Statement 5.7 of NSS Report No. 515.

The data compiled from different NSS rounds (Table 2) clearly show that Worker Population Ratio (WPR) for women have always been higher for women in rural areas as compared to urban areas. The data in 1993–94 show that Woman Population Ratio for rural men and women was 55.3 per cent and 32.8 per cent respectively in 1993–94, while it was 54.6 per cent and 32.7 per cent for men and women respectively in rural areas in 2004–05 under UPSS (Usual Status).

Table 2

Worker Population Ratios – India (%): Usual Status (UPSS) and Principal Status (UPS)

	UPSS			UPS		
Sector	*1993–94*	*1999–2000*	*2004–05*	*1993–94*	*1999–2000*	*2004–05*
Worker Population Ratios						
Rural Male	55.3	53.1	54.6	53.8	52.2	53.5
Rural Female	32.8	29.9	32.7	23.4	23.1	24.2
Urban Male	52.1	51.8	54.9	51.3	51.3	54.1
Urban Female	15.5	13.9	16.6	12.1	11.7	13.5

Source: Rangarajan et al. (2007).

In urban areas, Worker Population Ratio under UPSS was very low for women. It was 52.1 per cent and 15.5 per cent for men and women respectively in urban areas in 1993–94, while it was 54.9 per cent for men and 16.6 per cent for women in 2004–05, respectively. Under UPS the WPR was also not in favour of women both in rural and urban areas. The data show that in rural areas WPR under UPS was 53.8 per cent for men and 23.4 per cent for women in 1993–94, respectively; while it was 53.5 per cent for men and 24.2 per cent for women in 2004–05, respectively. On the other hand, in urban areas it was 51.3 per cent for men and 12.1 per cent for women in 2004–05, respectively.

Labour Force Participation Rate for women in NSS data has also not been in favour of women. It is much below the Labour Force Participation Rate for men under UPSS and UPS during the period between 1993–94 and 2004–05. The Labour Force Participation Rate under UPSS was 56.1 per cent for men and 33.1 per cent for women in 1993–94 while it was 55.5 per cent for men and 33.3 per cent for women in 2004–05 in rural areas, respectively. On the other hand, it was more predominant in urban areas. It was 54.3 per cent for men and 16.4 per cent for women in urban areas during 2004–05. Moreover, under UPS almost same trend is observed during the same period. The Labour Force Participation Rate was 54.9 per cent (1993–94) for men and 23.7 per cent (2004–05) for women in rural areas, while it was 54.6 per cent (2004–05) for men and 24.9 per cent (2004–05) for women in rural areas, and 53.8 per cent for men (1993–94) and 13.2 per cent (1993–94) women, and 56.6 per cent for men (2004–05) and 14.8 per cent for women during 2004–05 in urban areas.

Changes in the women's employment can be regarded as the outcome of subsidiary status of their employment. Therefore, an increase in women's work participation occurs if the number of subsidiary status of women workers increases and vice versa. Women under subsidiary status are found to be in agriculture which is seasonal and any decision of shift in production affects the demand for women labour (both paid and unpaid). In urban areas (Rustagi, 2007), the increase in women worker in UPSS is greater than that of the subsidiary works while the Principal Status labour force for urban women was 13 per cent in 1999–2000 which increased up to 15 per cent in 2004–05. The subsidiary status labour force moved from 2 per cent to 3 per cent over the same period.

Many studies undertaken by the experts like Chadha (2002 and 2007), Biswajit and Kundu (2002) and others highlight that the process of casualization in employment, both in rural and urban areas, has increased with the opening up of the economy. This process has affected women workers more severely than men. As per NSS data, large number of labourers, both men and women, in farm sector are working as casual contract labour. Jatav (2010) also observes that such a casualization was much higher for women workers who are engaged in farm work, i.e. there are nearly 6,600 female casual wage labourers for every 100 regular labourers. The extent of casualization has also increased in rural non-farm sector where the value of the index of casualization is 110 for all (it is higher in males 115 as compared to females).

Wage Discrimination

It is a well accepted fact that women in India are getting wages lower than men. Not only this, there existed a wide wage differential between men and women workers' wages, both in rural and urban areas and also in informal and formal sectors of the economy. A comparison of the NSS data of 55th round (1999–2000) and 61st round (2004–05) shows that this gap has increased over time. Debi and Das (2010) while taking into consideration the wage rate of the NSS at two points of time (1999–2000 and 2004–05) observed that the percentage share of the wages of women to those of men has declined over the years in both the formal and informal sectors. Despite the increase in the absolute value of the wage rate for men and women workers, the relative wage of women to that of men has declined during the period mentioned above. The difference in wage rate (women's wage as percentage of men's wage) was observed in rural and urban areas respectively. Further, the incidence of women's participation is high in the low paid informal sectors and in backward regions. The wage differential for women has increased manifold during 1993–94 to 2004–05, in terms of regular wages in rural areas, while such differential was almost constant for casual workers in rural areas. It can be observed that average wage rate under regular and casual work has remained in favour of males during the period under reference.

Madheswaran (2010) has corroborated the findings when he mentions that not only do female casual workers receive lower wages but also that the differential is quite high, roughly 39 per cent less in urban areas and 25 per cent less in rural areas for regular workers during 2004–05. He also suggests that the higher wage growth for women workers, particularly for urban regular workers, during the post-liberalization period can be accounted for by three important factors: (i) before the 1990s, women's wages were highly suppressed. During the 1990s, though female wages were lower than those of their male counterparts, the wage growth was higher for women workers.

(ii) During the 1990s, most of the subsidiary status female workers were observed to be withdrawing from the labour markets. This led to increased average wages of women workers as most of the principal status workers may have been better paid as compared to subsidiary status workers, (iii) Increasing participation of women in education, in general, and higher education, in particular, has led to better placement of women workers in the labour markets at least as compared to the situation prevalent during the 1980s and earlier periods. In some sectors, women workers are found to have outperformed men workers, even displacing them, particularly in the organized sector (Rustagi, 2003, 2005). In sum, the above result is an evidence of wage differentials that is still exhibited by gender across regular and causal labour markets in India.

Education and Wage Gap

As per NSS data, education plays an important and determining role in fixing the wages of the labourer. Labourers with higher education level are assumed to face fewer barriers across different segments of the labour market, while those with lower levels of education face strict barriers for entry into different labour markets. Accordingly, workers with higher educational achievements are likely to get higher wages as compared to those who are less educated. This can be lucidly inferred from the data presented in Tables 3 and 4. By comparing both of these Tables one can easily notice that there is a wide variation in the regular wages of workers across educational categories. Both in rural and urban areas, the gap between illiterate and graduate and above category workers was far more than the other levels of education. Even with the same levels of education, the rural-urban divide persists for females. Though no significant effect has been found for illiterate workers in both areas but education has been found to be a significant factor in determining the wage rate in rural and urban areas.

Table 3

Average Daily Wages (in ₹) for Regular Workers; By Levels of Education, 2004–05

Location/Educational Levels	*Male*	*Female*	*Person*
		Rural	
Not literate	72.47	35.74	60.42
Literate up to the primary level	98.59	47.75	91.23
Secondary and higher secondary level	158.04	100.19	148.39
Diploma/Certificate	214.38	200.4	211.13
Graduate and above	270.02	172.7	253.19
		Urban	
Not literate	98.79	48.7	77.34
Literate up to the primary level	111.44	64.79	105.16
Secondary and higher secondary level	182.58	150.41	178.29
Diploma/Certificate	274.87	237.02	267.11
Graduate and above	366.76	269.17	344.14

Source: NSS Reports from different rounds.

Table 4

Average Daily Wage (in ₹) for Casual Workers, By Levels of Education, 2004–05

Location/Educational Levels	*Male*	*Female*	*Person*
		Rural	
Not literate	50.25	34.38	43.21
Literate but below the primary level	55.15	36.88	51.12
Primary level	58.9	36.4	54.6
Middle level	63.34	36.76	59.2
Secondary level	61.67	36.16	58.37
Above the secondary level	61.96	37.59	59.66
		Urban	
Not literate	67.52	43.09	58.37
Literate but below the primary level	75.01	48.42	71.06
Primary level	75.41	43.34	70.09
Middle level	80.85	43.53	76.85
Secondary level	83.28	46.97	81.06
Above the secondary level	83.06	49.91	79.73

Source: NSS Reports from different rounds.

The wage gap by gender across all educational groups indicates that women are in a disadvantaged position. The daily wage earnings of a regular wage/salaried person in the rural areas was, on an average, ₹ 134 and in the urban areas, ₹ 194; nearly one-and-a-half times the wage of his/her counterparts in the rural areas. Secondly, a male regular wage earner earned nearly 1.7 times that of a female regular wage earner in the rural areas, and about 1.3 times in the urban areas.

At present when informal sector is fast expanding and the number of workers in this sector is increasing year by year, the daily wages of casual workers in the informal sector constitute an important factor for determining the standard of living and the extent and magnitude of poverty among casual workers, in general, and urban casual workers, in particular.

Karan and Sakthivel (2007) find that the variation in wages across sectors is more prominent in the case of urban casual workers (especially, female workers) as compared to rural ones; and secondly, in terms of gender, the male average daily wage rates vary across sectors relative to those of female workers. Lastly, an analysis of the wage differential across sectors shows that, in rural areas, the wage gap between male and female workers is highest in community-social-personal services and lowest in financial services. The corresponding sectors for urban areas are financial services and transport, respectively. To recapitulate, the overall results suggest that in the informal labour market, the wages paid to male and female workers tend to be very low. The women workers, in general, and rural women workers, in particular, face huge wage discrimination and are at a disadvantage vis-à-vis their male counterparts.

Many studies have also highlighted that females wage discrimination is prominent in the private sector. In private sector there is no proper record and also it has been observed that women have to work for longer hours. The data computed from the NFHS–3 Report (Tripathi and Mishra, 2010) indicate that women are doubly disadvantaged. Not only are women much less likely than men to be employed but also when employed they are less likely to earn cash. A wide gap can be observed in that women working in rural areas are less likely to get wages in cash. Women enter into labour market just to supplement their meagre family income. About 54 per cent of women get wages in cash as compared to 73 per cent for men; 12 per cent women and 17 per cent men get wages in cash and kind while 10.6 per cent women and 3 per cent men worker get wages in kind only. It is interesting to note that around 22 per cent women are not paid wages as compared to 5.8 per cent men (NFHS–3).

Conclusion

The women's participation is observed to be high in the low paid informal sectors. Despite efforts made at various levels to equalize the wage rate for men and women, there persists differences in the wage rate by gender (This difference is more prominent in backward areas and among illiterate women). On an average, women work for longer hours than men but they are given lower wages than men. The lower wages earned by women may place them in a disadvantageous position in respect of employment and economic independence. However, they suffer not only from a wage disadvantage but also from acute poverty, unemployment and hunger, which, in turn, affect their empowerment and economic independence. This may have a serious effect on the economic development of the country, as about half of the population consists of women. Therefore, government should have a permanent commission on women workers in informal sector in the Planning Commission which could suggest protective measures for women in this sector, including the provision of education, health, nutrition, employment, maternity benefits, sickness allowances and all other benefits as are provided to the regular employees. Every sector of the economy, therefore, should have special provisions to improve the position of women to achieve inclusive growth.

Notes

1. Although it may be noted that the latest thin rounds 62nd and 64th (which are based on a reasonable large sample size) again report a slight decline in the work participation rates for females. This is, however, not taken for trend analysis, as most thin rounds generally report a lower work participation rate for females.
2. In early seventies the concept of informal sector was first used by the International Labour Office with the launch of World Employment Programme and the classical report on employment and poverty in Kenya.
3. Majority of the workforce in the unorganized sector comprised of those who failed and dropped out or did not have access to formal education. Only 5 per cent in the age group of 18–24 had vocational skills, so the remaining could not get decent jobs. The Planning Commission (2001) noted that only 44 per cent of all workers in 1999–2000 were illiterate and another 22.7 per cent had schooling only up to the primary level.

References

Chadha, G.K., 'Education and Quality Gaps in Indian Workforce: What Does Future Demand?', *Punjab University Research Journal (Arts)*, xxxiv: (142): 1–38, 2007.

Chadha, G.K., 'Rural Non-Farm Employment in India: What Does Recent Experience Teach US?', *The Indian Journal of Labour Economics*, Vol. 45, No. 4, pp. 663–94, 2002.

Chatterjee, B. and A. Kundu, 'Rural Non-farm Employment in India and Globalization: A Critical Analysis', *The Indian Journal of Labour Economics*, xlv (4) pp. 71–81.

Committee of Feminist Economists, *Towards Inclusive Growth: The Gender Dimension*, a report submitted to the Planning Commission during the formulation of the Eleventh Five-Year Plan 2007–2012.

Debi, Sailabal and Atal Behari Das, 'Education and Labour Market Discrimination in Gender Perspectives: Empirical Evidence from the KBK Districts of Orissa', *Indian Journal of Labour Economics*, Vol. 53, No. 3, 2010.

Deshpande, Ashwini, 'Recasting Economic Inequality', *Review of Social Economy*, Vol. LVIII, September 2010.

Government of India, *Towards Faster and More Inclusive Growth: An Approach to the 11th Five-Year Plan*, Planning Commission, 2006.

International Labour Office, *Decent Work and the Informal Economy*, Report VI, International Labour Conference, ILO, Geneva, 2002.

Jatav, M., 'Casualization of Workforce in Rural Non-farm Sector of India: A Regional Level Analysis Across Industries', *Indian Journal of Labour Economics*, Vol. 50, No. 4, pp. 612–42.

Karan, A. and Selvaraj Sakthivel, *Trends in Wages and Earnings in India: Increasing Wage Differentials in a Segmented Labour Market*, ILO, New Delhi, 2007.

Kaur, Parminder and Arjinder Kaur, 'Gender Disparities in Rural Workforce Participation in India', paper presented at the ISLE Conference, 2009.

Kundu, Amitabh and Alak N. Sharma (eds), *Informal Sector in India: Perspectives and Policies*, Institute of Human Development and Institute of Applied Manpower Research, New Delhi, 2001.

Kundu, Amitab and Niranjan Sarangi, 'Dynamics of Labour Market under Globalization: Changing Characteristics of Informal Employment in India', *Indian Journal of Labour Economics*, Vol. 50, No. 2, 2007.

Madheswaran, S., 'Labour Market Discrimination in India: Issues in Theory and Methods,' *Indian Journal of Labour Economics*, Vol. 53 No. 3, July–September 2010.

Mazumdar, Dipak and Sandip Sarkar, *Globalization, Labour Markets and Inequality in India*, Routledge, London, 2008.

Narain, Ashish, 'Labour Force Participation Rates, Wages and Their Determinants in India', paper presented in the Conference on 'India: Meeting the Employment Challenge', Institute for Human Development, New Delhi, 27–29 July 2006.

Nath, G.B., 'Globalization and Growth of Precarious Jobs in the Indian Labour Market: Implications for Economic Policy', *Indian Journal of Labour Economics*, Vol. 51, No. 4, 2008.

NCEUS, *Report on Conditions of Work and Promotion of Livelihoods in the Unorganized Sector*, Government of India, New Delhi, 2008.

Ramaswamy, K.V., *Globalization, Employment and Labour Market Flexibility*, India Development Report, Oxford University Press, New Delhi, 2008.

Rangarajan, C. et al., 'Revisiting Employment and Growth', *Money and Finance Bulletin*, September 2007.

Reddy, Narasimha D., 'Challenges of Decent Work in the Globalizing World', *Indian Journal of Labour Economics*, Vol. 48, No. 1, 2005.

Rustagi, Preet, 'Gender Biases and Discrimination Against Women: What Do Different Indicators Say?' CWDS in Collaboration with UNIFEM, South Asia, 2003.

——, 'Understanding Gender Inequalities in Wages and Incomes in India', *Indian Journal of Labour Economics,* Vol. 46, No. 4, pp. 927–39, 2005.

——, 'Women and Poverty: Rural-Urban Dimensions', *Social Change,* Vol. 37, No. 4, December 2007.

——, 'Continuing Gender Stereotypes or Signs of Change: Occupational Pattern of Women Workers', *Indian Journal of Labour Economics,* Vol. 53, No. 3, 2010.

Sakthivel, S. and Pinaki Joddar, 'Unorganized Sector Workforce in India: Trends, Patterns and Social Security Coverage', *Economic and Political Weekly,* 27 May 2006.

Srivastava, N. and Srivastava, R., 'Women, Work and Employment Outcomes in Rural India', *Economic and Political Weekly,* 45(28), 49–63, 2010.

Talwar, Sabanna and B.P. Bulla, 'Labour Market Discriminations: An Analysis of Gender Composition in India', paper presented at the ISLE Conference, 2009.

Tripathi, Tulika and N.K. Mishra, 'Discrimination among the Discriminated: Evidences from National Family Health Survey–3', *Indian Journal of Labour Economics,* Vol. 53, No. 3, 2010.

Unni, Jeemol, 'Women Workers in the New Economy', *Indian Journal of Labour Economics,* Vol. 51, No. 4, 2008.

——, 'Wages and Incomes in Formal and Informal Sectors in India', *Indian Journal of Labour Economics,* Vol. 48, No. 2, 2005.

Unni, Jeemol and Ming Lu, 'Informal Employment in India', *Indian Journal of Labour Economics,* Vol. 50, No. 3, 2007.

CHAPTER 2

Social and Spatial Meanings of Respect

Migration and Identity of Women Domestic Workers in India

NITYA RAO

Accounts of paid domestic work exist across various points in history, countries and contexts. It is not a new occupation, yet its nature and form have changed with particular historical time-space conjunctions. The contemporary interest in paid domestic work is driven by the huge expansion of migrant workers, largely women from poor, undeveloped regions, for the performance of these tasks. Several reasons have been attributed for this shift – women's large-scale entry into the paid workforce in developed countries resulting from a decline in male employment and male wages, increasing flexibility in the labour market as well as higher levels of female education (Standing, 1999; Kabeer, 2007); changes in the demographic profile with declining fertility and an increase in ageing populations alongside the cut in public services (including health,

This article is an earlier version of the Paper titled. 'Respect, Status and Domestic Work: Female Migrants at Home and Work', European Journal of Development Research, 2011, 23 (5): 758–773.

childcare and infrastructure) in most welfare states (Yeates, 2005; Razavi, 2007), as well as the desire for prestige and upward social mobility.

Migrants are preferred as they are cheaper, apparently 'submissive' and easier to control, lacking as they do local social contacts, and their work, conducted within the home, remains largely invisible and undervalued (Anderson, 2000). Despite stories of exploitation, both sending and receiving states generally support such migration due to the remittances received and the services provided (Chin, 1998; Carling, 2005). The migrant workers too make a deliberate choice in consideration of their future well-being. They often earn and save more than what is locally possible, escape oppressive cultures and gain new experiences. The construction of their identities has a spatial dimension, with the definitions of work connected to lives beyond the workplace (Parrenas, 2001; Stenning, 2008), enabling them to negotiate their rights and earn respect from their communities.

This paper focuses on the changing context of domestic work in Delhi, India, with a growing demand for female, ethnic minority, migrant strangers, and the experience of that work by these women, given the shifts in their own rural context. Though identities and status of the domestic workers and their employers are often constructed in opposition to each other (e.g. employers often see workers' claims as diminishing their own standing) (Dickey and Adams, 2000), my focus here is on the interaction between the identities of the migrant domestic workers at the workplace and 'back home' in their village communities as shaping their social position (Moors, 2003). I also explore how education influences women's agency, especially in terms of generating political voice to legitimize and gain recognition and value for domestic work.

The paper is based on field research in Katona village,[1] Simdega district Jharkhand, a major sending area, as well as interviews with a few key informants in Delhi. Katona is a small village with 112 households, and due to the presence of Roman Catholic missionaries since the 1870s, boasts of high levels of literacy. Yet with uncertain, rainfed agriculture, the rate of out-migration is high. A census survey of the village was conducted during October-November 2006 to identify the key occupations, educational and migration profile of all households. Out of a total of 31 domestic workers identified during the survey, in-depth interviews were conducted with eight of them (four with less than 5 years of education and four with different levels of secondary schooling). These interviews were conducted in the village in January 2007, when some of them had come home for Christmas, and others had recently quit their jobs and returned home. As all of them were live-in domestic workers in Delhi, it was not possible to interview them at their workplace. While this may be a limitation of this study in terms of understanding the employer-employee relationship from both sides, it allowed for an exploration of notions of dignity and respect across spatial contexts, in terms set by the women workers themselves. Additional interviews were conducted with the parish priests in the locality, organizers of the domestic workers movement, both locally and in Delhi, and two placement agencies in Delhi.

Methodologically, the use of both quantitative and qualitative methods was important for drawing attention to the key issues involved in the process of migration of ethnic minority women for domestic work in urban metros, and a deeper understanding of the nuances of such movement. The narratives provided insights into the conditions of work and the role of women's agency in changing the nature of both domestic work, and gender relations, with reference to the urban middle classes and the village community. In the next section, I provide a brief review of the gendered ideologies embedded in the arena of domestic work. I then briefly set out the nature and dimensions of the domestic work sector in Delhi, as well as the rural homes and contexts from which the migrant women domestic workers are drawn, before exploring their aspirations, experiences and the contradictions they face in their quest for respect.

Conceptualizing Migration for Domestic Work

In spite of continuing feminist scholarship on the value of domestic labour, both unpaid 'economic' work (e.g. subsistence production) and the unpaid 'care' aspects of social reproduction (the sustenance of human beings throughout their life cycle more broadly, not just servicing male workers),[2] essential for human survival, different forms of reproductive work continue to be marginalized and not included in national accounts (Razavi, 2007). After much lobbying, the System of National Accounts (SNA) was revised in 1993 to include subsistence work and unpaid, home-based or self-employed work (Hirway, 2005), however, the production of services, defined as the preparation of meals, laundry, cleaning, shopping, care of children, the elderly and sick, and volunteer services, continued to be excluded. Perceived to have limited repercussions on the rest of the economy, domestic work is ignored, given a low status, and left out of work-led entitlements such as social insurance, ending up levying what Elson (1995), calls a 'reproductive tax' on women, due to enhanced and unsupported burdens of domestic work.

Despite the theoretical possibility that both productive and reproductive tasks can be undertaken by either sex, biological reproduction has led to reproduction and care tasks being naturalized as part of women's role, while production and breadwinning get coded as masculine. These tasks are then also divided spatially, with reproduction performed within the home and production outside. As Arendt (1958) points out, whether an activity is performed in the private or public sphere is not a matter of indifference, as it changes the value given to the activity, with those performed in the public realm, getting socially recognized and valued. This division of activities and their spatial separation are an essential element of the social construction of gender, with the quite systematic 'non-valorization of women's labour' ultimately leading to their subordination (Edholm et al., 1977: 123).

Apart from the problems of spatial, economic and ideological invisibility, reproductive work also has both material elements (labour) and non-material or affective ones, making it difficult to fit into a straightjacket 'labour' discourse (Uttal and Tuominen, 1999). While the former includes everyday tasks of cleaning, cooking, washing, feeding and so on, the latter relates more to what Hochschild (1983) calls 'emotional labour', which includes emotional bonds and relationships, the desire to give quality time to a child to facilitate its development, and to make life cheerful and pleasant for an elderly person for instance. Apart from variable efforts and techniques, the ability to manage effectively the process of domestic work, requires social skills, has an emotional input and a high degree of stress involved in terms of the fear of failing in one's task, of criticism, of displacement, which all lead to self-exploitation by the worker. The very personal, complex and even ambiguous relations of subordination inherent in domestic work then make it not just undervalued but also servile (Anderson, 2002).

The commodification of domestic work has given it visibility and an economic value, but there remains a strong gender and class-ethnic dimension to the market, with a preference for migrant, female domestic workers, from poorer regions and countries (Cheng, 2004). While this has facilitated a large number of middle-class, urban working women and those with surplus incomes to pass on at least the labour component of their reproductive work responsibilities to domestic workers, yet the preference for women reflects their 'supposed attributes of femininity – docility, deference and empathy' as opposed to the 'street bravado and machismo of young men (which) makes them less attractive as potential employees in the interactive service economy where deferential service with a smile is a key attribute of a successful exchange between consumer and employer' (McDowell, 2007: 278). While ensuring that some women are not overburdened in terms of working a double day, and others gain in terms of securing paid work and an income, it has allowed the existing gendered division of labour to continue unchallenged, with reproductive work continuing to be divided amongst women (Lister, 1997; Ehrenreich, 2002).[3] Associated with femininity, it often ends up denying domestic workers their personhood, and equality in terms of respect and recognition for their work.

As Fraser (1994) points out, there are at least three dimensions of gender equality that need attention. The first is income inequality and the need to value and ensure adequate compensation to women's work, as globally, women's earnings are only 60–70 per cent that of men across sectors. The second refers to leisure-time equality, with women increasingly facing time poverty, having to engage in both productive and reproductive work. A multi-site time use survey conducted by the Government of India in 1998–1999, found that men on an average spent 36 minutes on care work, while women spent five hours a day, and if this were indeed counted as work, women would be performing 55 per cent of total work (Government of India, Report of the Time-use Survey, New Delhi, p. 81, 2000). A third kind of equality pertains to status and respect, and the 'equality of respect requires recognition of women's personhood, alongside women's work' (Fraser, 1994: 598). There are both contradictions and trade-offs between earning incomes and gaining respect socially for their 'domestic' work, yet domestic workers use a host of strategies, often deliberate, to shift the very criteria for understanding respect. The nature of work performed and employer-employee relations are crucial to their experience, yet they speak too of the shifts in broader social and gender relations resulting from particular urban lifestyles, and the experience of a new place and culture, which gives them a sense of identity and personhood.

Domestic workers do exercise individual agency[4] in strategically thinking about their lives and careers, but the spatial location of the work in individual homes, which isolates them alongside invisibilizing the content of their work, restricts the opportunity for social mobility in the urban context. Recognizing the limited scope for the exercise of collective agency vis-à-vis the urban workplace, they place greater emphasis on strategies for gaining respect in their rural homes. They attempt to negotiate identity across spaces and arenas of everyday life, operationalizing respect and responsibility in complex ways in the process of seeking mutuality, rather than automatic deference in view of existing status hierarchies.

Changing Contexts: Moving from the Rural to the Urban

India's modern growth period, 1980–2005, has been characterized as one of 'jobless growth'. Agriculture and the rural sector have stagnated, while there has been a massive expansion in the informal services sector (Rao et al., 2008). Domestic work is an important component of such informal employment, the largest sector for female employment in urban India, with the numbers estimated to have doubled from around 1.25 million women paid, domestic workers, both full-time and part-time, in 1995 (Gopalan, 1995) to over 3 million in 2004–05 (NSS survey data). While elite families and professionals even earlier needed support with domestic work and child-care in big cities like Delhi, the current additional demand is not just to meet the needs of working women with higher levels of education as suggested by Kaur (2004),[5] rather employing 'maids' is seen as a mechanism for asserting upward mobility amongst the new middle classes, through withdrawal from domestic and care work of their own women (Kumar, 2003). The domestic worker affirms the status of the woman of the household as manager rather than labourer, reproducing a particular middle-class status and lifestyle. As Mita, a 16 year old Hindu girl narrated,

> I did all the housework, cleaning the house, washing utensils, cooking food, making tea several times, while madam watched television all day. She didn't go out to work, but never helped at all. Unable to cope with the amount of work, I finally complained to the master. But he got angry and reprimanded me for being lazy.

With the work taking place within the employers' home, there is an effort to create a self-other contrast, not seen as sharply in other work settings (Dickey and Adams, 2000: 2); the discourse of kindness and support to the domestic workers, identified as poor women, helping to sustain hierarchical power relations between the employer and employee (Anderson, 2002).

Alongside its rapid expansion as a sector of employment, in India too, domestic work has become feminized (Rollins, 1985; NIUA, 1991). While Pereira's (1984) study revealed that 78 per cent of domestic helpers in 12 cities were female (1984); and Shramshakti (1988) found 1.6 out of 2.3 million domestic workers to be women (70%); recent studies estimate that women now comprise about 90 per cent of the domestic workforce (Pathare, 2000). This feminization of the domestic work sector is also substantiated by Kaur (2004), in her analysis of two groups of workers, the first consisting of maids and other housekeeping services (childminders, nurse maids, etc.), and the second of all other occupations, based on National Sample Survey (NSS) data from 1983 to 1999. She finds that while the total number of those engaged in Group 1 increased from 1.2 to 2 million during this period, the number of men working as domestic help was stagnant at 0.3 million. Men do undertake cleaning and cooking tasks in public spaces, such as offices, shops and restaurants, or then work as drivers and guards. The growing spatial segregation, the public-private divide, however, further highlights the gendered construction of domestic work, with men, lacking submissive attributes, seen as threats in the private space of the home on one hand, while the conditions of work and personalised services seen as demeaning to their own identities as workers on the other.

Parallel to this process of feminization, there is also a growing recruitment of poor migrant, ethnic minority women as domestic workers, especially those from the tribal areas of eastern India. In Delhi, there are close to 3,00,000 domestic and related workers as per the NSS 2004/05, with some estimates going upto 5,00,000. While it is difficult to estimate exact numbers, Kujur and Jha (2006), in a study of migrant domestic workers in Delhi, calculate that close to a third of them (about 1,00,000) belong to the Scheduled Tribes. Neetha (2004) found in her study of domestic workers in Delhi that a majority of live-out maids and almost all the live-in maids were migrants, with Christian tribal women accounting for 90 per cent of the live-ins (see also Kujur and Jha, 2006: 70–72). There seems to be a preference for young tribal women as live-in domestic workers, given the existing stereotype of tribal women as being simple, honest, obedient and hard-working, all positively valued attributes in domestic service, and hence easier to control than their Hindu counterparts, local women, seen as more irreverent due to their exposure to urban life and the media. Over 50 per cent of such tribal women workers belong to Jharkhand[6] (Neetha, 2004). Census 2001 data confirm the presence of 38,364 female in-migrants from Jharkhand to urban Delhi, more than double the number over the previous decade. This is also clear from data on rural to urban female in-migrants in search of work which reveals that the position of Jharkhand jumped from 11th to 4th over the 1991–2001 decade, and further to 3rd rank in 2001 (Census of India, 2001).

Domestic work, especially live-in work, is one migration stream where trust is very important. The worker lives in the home of the employer, so employers in Delhi prefer going through agencies to ensure some security for themselves. The past six years have seen a huge jump in the number of such agencies bringing girls from the villages and placing them in urban homes. 'There are more than 500 such agencies spread all over New Delhi today and there are tribal girls from Jharkhand in almost every middle and upper-middle class home from South Extension and Defence Colony to Vasant Vihar and Pitampura', says Sister Prachi of Chetanalaya, a domestic workers' support organization. In Katona, several agencies are active. Parents have their visiting cards, but repeated phone calls produce no results in terms of contacting their daughters. Geeta, the daughter of a fisherman, returned this year, but had no news of the four other girls who left with her. She was in Delhi for three years; each year the agency moved her to a different home, in order to earn an additional commission. Her wages too were collected from her employer by the agent each month. They would not let her come home, so she left secretly, in the process losing a large part of her earnings. Interviews with a few placement agencies in Delhi revealed that it was a common practice for the agency to collect the monthly salary from the employer. While supposedly kept in deposit for the domestic worker, a large number of them received only a small fraction of their wage, even less, if like Geeta, they tried to break free of the tied labour relations with the placement agency.

The agencies are run by locals in Delhi. They hire women and sometimes men from these ethnic minority groups as agents (jobbers) in the villages to ensure a steady supply of workers. These jobbers are referred to in kinship terms locally, but this does not necessarily make them sensitive to the interests of the workers. Nina, a young migrant noted,

> Seven of us were taken by an 'aunt' from the locality to Delhi by train and left in a placement agency. We were kept in a tiny room, allowed to come out only when some prospective employer came and wanted to interview us. I was given some clothes and toiletries by the placement agency and for this they deducted the first two months' salary. I worked from dawn to late in the night, cooking for six people, making umpteen cups of tea, cleaning the house, washing clothes and utensils. I slept on the kitchen floor and was threatened with beatings if I complained of fatigue and overwork. I was to be paid ₹ 1,200 per month. I left in three months, as I could not stand it any longer, so got only a month's pay. Even this was taken by my aunt's daughter at the station, so I returned home empty-handed.

Incidences abound of these local 'aunts' becoming prosperous overnight through the supply of domestic workers. As the Coordinator of the Chota Nagpur Working Women's Society (CNWWS) said, 'Within a few months they have a bungalow in Delhi and several mobile phones. They are not concerned about the welfare of the girls'. While agencies do provide information, access to jobs and first residence, in the absence of any regulation, many of them have turned into grossly exploitative institutions. Given the predominance of tribal Christian girls, several denominations of the Church, especially the Catholics, have also set up agencies in Delhi (such as CNWWS mentioned above), to help recruit and train workers, but also ensure them a decent wage and living conditions. A few girls from Katona like Sruti Soreng have secured jobs in Delhi this way – they get regular leave, both to visit home once a year, and on Sundays to go to church, and the agreed wages. While they too take a commission to meet their overheads, the worker directly receives the salary from her employer.

While the world of Delhi is mediated through the plethora of placement agencies, how does this relate to their own village, Katona, 15 kilometres away from the district headquarter? A single-lane district road runs through the village and the settlements (or *tolis*) lie mainly along this road. The population largely (80%) belongs to the Kharia and Oraon Scheduled Tribes, a majority Roman Catholic, though a few continue to follow the animistic Sarna faith. Most of the Roman Catholics are not just literate, but have completed at least 8–10 years of schooling, in the mission-run secondary school in the village.

Agriculture is the main source of livelihood in the region, yet only 12 per cent of the arable land is irrigated. Paddy, maize, groundnut and black-eyed beans are the major crops. The productivity is low, and insufficient to fulfil their needs. In this context, migration has become a key livelihood strategy for both men and women, for as in other tribal-dominated regions, women and men participate almost equally in the workforce, with agriculture followed by wage labour in agriculture, in the brick kilns or public works programmes and a range of household production and forest produce related activities. According to Mili, a school teacher, 'The church and priests are telling people not to go. But what can be done? People are not growing enough in their own fields and getting jobs is tough'. Almost 19 per cent of the population is currently migrant (25% male and 15% female), both for seasonal and more permanent work. While older men either migrate for agricultural work in the Green Revolution belt of North-West India or road construction in the border areas, younger men prefer to look for factory jobs or other private sector jobs such as peons, clerks or security guards in Delhi and other cities. For girls and women, these options hardly exist; rather their hard work in rural areas is seen to prepare them for domestic service in the cities (Radcliffe, 1990).

There is a marked gender difference in the age-profile of migrants. While over 75 per cent of male migrants are over the age of 18, technically adults, a large number of them married, close to half of the female migrants are not yet 18 years old, all of them unmarried (Table 1). This pattern points not just to a preference for young, unmarried women in the market for domestic workers, but also to gender differences in life-cycle patterns and social norms, with women expected to eventually settle down with their own families rather than continuing to migrate for work. Roughly, half the domestic workers are illiterate, or have not completed their primary education, and 35 per cent educated to the secondary level. An analysis of records maintained by the Simdega Parish revealed that 24 per cent of the migrant women had completed primary schooling; while 41 per cent had different levels of secondary education (between grades 6 and 10).

Table 1

Age and Level of Schooling of Domestic Workers

Age	*Illiterate*	*Primary*	*Secondary*	*Total*
12–14	2	0	0	2
15–17	7	3	2	12
18–20	3	0	3	6
21–25	2	1	1	4
26–30	0	0	2	2
Over 31	2	0	3	5
Total	16	4	11	31

Source: Village survey data.

While for men, migration is important for performing their breadwinning roles, for women the reasons are more varied. Some like Priti, took the active step of running away from home to Delhi due to the disappointment on her failure in the secondary school certificate examination and the consequent chiding by her relatives, while others like Dorothy, went to earn money to support their families. Some wished to see the city life before they got married, and others were trying to escape the burdens of reproductive work at home. When asked what motivated her to go, Mita said,

> I had heard about Delhi since several women from the village are working there. When they return home during Christmas, they wear beautiful clothes and bring expensive gifts. The financial situation at home was worsening and I realized that more work was available in Delhi and one could earn a lot of money. I also wanted to see the big city since I had heard so much about it. I had never attended school, but my brothers were in school. I felt bad so left for Delhi without informing them.

Apart from the placement agencies, their migration is also facilitated by migrant women, returning home during Christmas, and actively encouraging their sisters and friends to migrate, to experience a different life and culture, an exposure to new ideas and gadgets.

The Spatial Dimensions of Respect

Working life is often not easy for the domestic workers, yet there are elements they draw from this experience, both material in terms of incomes, skills and familiarity with consumption goods, as well as discursive in terms of cultural representation and recognition, that they use to strengthen their claims for respect at home. In this section, the workplace experience was examined first and then the strategies they adopt vis-à-vis their rural home, to draw out both the spatial and social interconnections between them.

Experiencing Domestic Work in Delhi

Gaining respect at the workplace is perhaps the most contested domain in the life of a domestic worker, with unceasing personal service being the expectation from the employer. While the hard working conditions and long hours of work are almost taken as granted the experience of domestic work is shaped to a large extent by the personality of the employer and the respect they show towards the domestic worker. A 26-year-old, Priti Barla is very fond of her employers; in fact the fear of any criticism from them makes her work very hard.

> I wake up at 7 a.m. then make tea, help the children get ready for school, clean the house, and make breakfast for madam, sir and me. They all leave by 10 a.m. and cleaning and cooking take up the rest of the day. There is another girl who works in the house and we wash clothes in the machine and then iron them. It is past midnight when we go to bed. Sometimes, I feel burdened by the work and begin hating myself for running away to Delhi because I failed in my exams. But everyone is not lucky to get to do what they want. The work is not bad and the lifestyle is good. I have a room of my own, which I share with the other girl, and get good food. I hardly spend any of my earnings on myself, as *didi* (she refers to her employer as sister) gives me clothes and toiletries, all that I need.

Priti's current salary is ₹ 2,500 per month, in addition to free board and lodging. This is more than what some of the teachers in the village Holy Cross School get. Yet she sometimes resents being a domestic worker, perhaps because in the village, her parents and relatives had higher expectations of her. Like Priti, 38-year-old Dorothy Dungdung too has employers who treat her well. She perceives her working experience as largely positive, except for restrictions on her mobility.

> I look after my employers' 9-year-old daughter, though if needed, I do other things as well, including cooking and cleaning. The girl is very sweet, I take her to the club, and she insists I play badminton with her. She also teaches me some

> English. If there is extra work, I do it, I do not think of it as overtime, as it is like working for my family. Yet, there are restrictions on my mobility; I am not allowed to leave the house, except for 3 to 4 hours once a month.

Dorothy is no longer a young girl, yet tribal women domestic workers are in many respects stereotyped as simple and childlike. Their lack of fluency in Hindi, the local language, is used to enhance controls on their physical movement and autonomy, albeit in a discourse of protection. In fact, the use of kinship terms such as 'daughter' or 'younger sister' is a commonly used device to incorporate domestic workers into the private space of the family, while simultaneously defining areas of exclusion. As Parrenas (2001: 170) notes, maternalism can perpetrate non-egalitarian, hierarchical relationships, that facilitate the extraction of unpaid labour, especially emotional labour. The discourse of being a part of the family reinforces their personal loyalty, while allowing minimal external interaction contributes to preventing social recognition and the organization of collective voice. Bourdieu (1977) refers to this phenomenon as 'practical kinship', wherein social ties are created, based on gifts and patronage, which reflect the employers' interests more than that of the workers, as while making the latter feel wanted, they do not dissolve the social boundaries, rather reinforce them in subtle ways.

A majority of domestic workers are unmarried, 77 per cent below the age of 25. In fact, marriage often poses a barrier for continuing with domestic work, as for Prakash's wife, who first started as a domestic worker in Delhi, while her husband worked in a factory. The birth of a child meant giving up paid domestic work, as while responsible for caring for the employers' children, it is considered unacceptable for them to keep their own child with them while working. In the construction of their relationship with the employer, their personal sexual lives and identities as mothers are denied and a childlike dependence and need for protection emphasized. This dependent relationship enables control, for as Shah (2000: 107) notes, recognizing the sexuality of the servant can potentially disrupt the domestic order as adult aspirations are not easy to accommodate and subordinate.

To some extent, Priti and Dorothy had their physical and social needs recognized; the majority experience is more like that of Mita and Nina narrated earlier. Shabnam worked in Delhi for two years, washing, cleaning, cooking, dusting, from 6 a.m. to 10 p.m. Her work was literally non-stop as there were two young girls to look after too. Working with water led to a boil on her leg, and without any treatment, this got infected. She could barely move and was in intense pain. She, however, got scolded for being lazy rather than receiving any medical treatment. At that point, she left the job and returned to the village. Geeta's story is similar. She now prefers working in the brick kilns near the village. While they may have got a bad deal, they did exercise the agency in exiting this oppressive situation, with no support whatsoever.

Domestic workers are all expected to work hard and be completely loyal to their employers, yet many of them get beaten and ill-treated by the employer, get no proper place to sleep and little food. Even when they have some leisure between tasks, they are not allowed to watch TV, a family activity in middle-class homes, nor allowed to go outside the house. The spatial inequality and segregation in terms of food rationing, use of separate utensils, wearing hand-me-down clothing, sleeping arrangements, being prevented from sitting on the couch or watching TV, all signify forms of personalized control and lesser social status of the domestic worker in relation to the employer. While expected to work sincerely, non-stop, like a member of the family, they are however excluded from leisure time activities of family members, thus reinforcing the asymmetrical relationship in existence (Shah, 2000: 88).

Dorothy speaks of playing badminton with her employers' daughter, or learning English from her. The participation in such leisure activities constitutes an important element of their identity as a person, not just a worker. It gives them a sense of self-respect, yet is often the most uncertain element of the work experience. Incomes can in the ultimate analysis be claimed, but it is respect in interpersonal relations, expressed through the granting of personal space, sharing of the same food, or participation in leisure activities, that are often the hardest to negotiate and defend.

Contributions and Representations: Gaining Respect at Home

Dorothy, educated up to class 7, was one of the first women from Katona to move to Delhi in 1986. She has now worked in the city for over two decades. She spoke candidly of her work and working conditions, savings and remittances, the role of obligations and the social valuation of domestic work.

> My father served for 15 years in the army and had six more years of service to go when the death of my grandfather made him opt for early retirement. I was then in class 3. He came home, but we have little land, so while he cultivated some paddy, this was not enough. There was no money in the house, and being the eldest of seven siblings, I decided to move to Delhi after I completed grade 7, so I could earn to support my siblings. This was in 1986. My uncle and aunt moved to work in a garments export house in Okhla (in Delhi) and I went with them. I initially worked in their house, but I was not paid and could not go out anywhere. A friend introduced me to the family of Mr Thakur in Punjabi Bagh. Here I spent 8 years as a domestic maid. They were very nice people who never made me feel out of place. I was able to send some money home to my parents.
>
> A few years later, my father fell ill; first it was diagnosed as asthma and then TB. I brought him to Delhi and spent ₹ 7,000 for his treatment. He stayed for a month and returned to the village fully recovered. He died in 1996. The period after my father's death was a very difficult time. I cannot even begin to explain to you how I managed to live and survive those days. I worked so hard to ensure that my brothers and sisters were taken care of. My mother worked in the fields, yet she could not manage, so I returned to the village to help. I stayed in the village till 2002. We applied for my father's pension from the

> army and after much struggle started receiving this at the State Bank in Simdega. My mother ran the household on this income, but it was not enough. My youngest brother migrated to Punjab to find work there, but he never sent any money home, nor was there any news from him. Two of my brothers in the meantime got married, one moved to his wife's village and only one now lives here. Life was tough for us, so I decided to return to Delhi.

Dorothy's narrative demonstrates the burden of responsibilities, both economic and emotional, she shouldered, and that led to her migration. When her father left the army, he was no longer able to support his family; hence as the eldest child, she decided to migrate to Delhi to earn money. When he died, her remittances were not enough to tide them through; her mother needed emotional support and she had to prioritize this element of her responsibility. It is often assumed that sons will support their widowed mothers, but this is not necessarily the case, and as the eldest, it fell on Dorothy to do so. Taking over the male role of provision and care of her widowed mother, however, strengthened her influence in her village home, vis-à-vis her siblings and enhanced respect in the community. Yet this did not come easily, as while women's work in the village is valued, their work outside is seen as low status, highlighting once again the role of context in shaping identity. As she noted, 'people do comment that female migration to Delhi is a bad trend and look down on girls who leave the village, yet it is these very girls who are often the major financial support for their households, and their families at least, recognize and appreciate this'.

While domestic work in general is looked down upon, constructing the discourse as one of fulfilling responsibilities, leads to respect in the village community. Cultivation is no longer sufficient for subsistence and their remittances become crucial contributors to daily maintenance and quality of life of the rural household, debt repayments and education of the siblings. Their economic contributions entitle them to participate in decision-making at home, like in the education or marriage of their siblings; at the same time, they also provide a more legitimate face to female autonomy and independence.

Working conditions are harsh, so the migrant domestic workers identify other criteria of status. This could include the monetary remuneration they receive for their work, substantially more than what they could earn locally, savings, exposure to urbane lifestyles including dress and personal effects, fluency in a different language and form of speech and familiarity with technology. As Dorothy said,

> I get my salary in cash. Presently it is ₹ 2,700 per month, but it could be increased when I return. I send this to my mother through money orders, once in every three months, and she deposits this into my bank account. In the past, I used my savings to finance my father's health care expenses, manage wedding expenses, school fees and household expenditures for my family. I buy gifts from Delhi for everyone in the family when I come home during Christmas. This time I bought a jacket, sweater, suits and saris and watches for my sister and brother. I thought I would get some utensils, but my mother is scared of the pressure cooker. I am contemplating on getting a solar panel so that our home can be electrified.

Here, respect is linked to markers of class difference as reflected in clothing, consumer goods, having a bank account, understanding technology (as reflected in her reference to the pressure cooker and solar panel), language and mannerisms. As these are privileged signs of class distinction, and cannot fully be claimed as signs of status vis-à-vis the employers (Tolen, 2000), domestic workers shift the site of expression to recreate themselves in their rural homes, constructing their claims to respect on the basis of their new knowledge, skills and practices. At the workplace, they receive gifts from their employers, a sign of their patronage and higher status; at home, the domestic workers are able to reproduce the same patronage ties based on their higher earnings through their gift-giving rituals.

The idea of status itself then needs to be reworked from the perspective of women's agency and their ability to claim a sense of personhood, while negotiating unequal gender relations with their families, employers, community, or the state. Their connection to the home and construction of a respected identity there, is visible in their aspirations for the future. Once again, as evident from Dorothy's narrative,

> I want to build a house now. My brother can give me land and I can use some space to open a shop in the village. If I do anything, it will be for my mother and brothers. What they do for me is up to them. I can only hope that my brothers will see my need and what I have done and give me some property. There have been several offers for marriage in the village, yet I do not think there is any need for me to marry now. My mother is alone and I need to take care of her. Who else does she have? I am her eldest daughter and have to be her support. While I may wear new saris in the city, I feel that I still don't fit in as a Delhi citizen. On occasion, I feel a sense of slavery. In the village there is a strong sense of collective ties, but people in cities do not even talk to people within their own homes.

While for Dorothy and many others, domestic work indeed becomes a career, it is relatively well-paying in relation to other options in their local contexts; they still aspire to ultimately leave domestic work which continues to be perceived as lacking in dignity. It is not seen as a life-long option, even though employers may be kind and as in the case of Dorothy, who was included in their leisure activities. They then consciously work towards this end, adopting a range of strategies to ensure their future security, be it gift-giving or saving money in a bank account. In the past, Dorothy had used her savings for her siblings, but now hopes to use it for constructing a house in the village and setting up a small shop.

Having lived in the city for many years, and been exposed to less oppressive urban cultures (Unnithan-Kumar, 2003), Dorothy's aspirations had changed, and she was not interested in the local proposals, or even in marriage any more. Priti would definitely like to get married and have a family, once her siblings have finished their basic education and her responsibilities towards them are complete. She says, 'There are marriage offers from the village, but now people know that I will refuse till my brothers finish studying. I like the city and would like to live here. I told *Didi* that I want to marry a Christian but there is no one suitable in Delhi so far'. Priti has a strong aspiration of moving on either to a respectable marriage or a higher status job, despite her positive experience of domestic work, as a strategy for acquiring and sustaining respectability.

The urban-rural contrast in gender relations is important in Dorothy's narrative. Even though she speaks of the collective ties in the village, she is uncertain about the treatment from her brothers and whether they would give her a share of the property. She has been giving them gifts and meeting their expenses for two decades, so can only hope for reciprocity, yet the obligations of adult brothers to their sisters are not so clear. In the city, however, she has seen and experienced much greater equality of gender relations, even though her own freedom of movement was restricted. While she did have access to a privileged space in her employer's home, this was not as an equal. The experience of urban culture and lifestyle in an upper middle-class home, however, developed in her a sense of independence and autonomy, of wanting to have a place of her own before she is too old rather than depending on marriage as the only form of social support. Experience such as hers, in terms of the interaction of different worlds, the urban and the rural, the rich and the poor, the material and the social, in shaping elements of identity and agency, is often not given adequate consideration in most discussions of domestic workers.

Representation, Voice and Respect: The Role of Education

Coming back to Fraser's conceptualization of the principle of equality as including income, leisure-time and respect, one finds that while domestic work is able to provide income (some like Dorothy and Priti earning more than teachers in the local high school), it has a poor record in terms of leisure-time (though often, women in the village too work long hours) and most of all in terms of respect at the workplace, which clearly matters to the women domestic workers' sense of identity and personhood. In this section, I explore the ways in which women workers both individually and collectively exercise the agency to secure recognition and respect for their work, while at the same time shifting the terms of discourse to include respect in other domains of life, especially vis-à-vis their rural home.

At the individual level, education can potentially contribute to opening up new opportunities, as teachers, nurses or nuns for girls, but given the competitive market for jobs, education does not necessarily guarantee a job (Chopra, 2005). Mili Dung Dung, 27 years old, completed her post graduation in Hindi. Her friend Suman had studied up to BA with her, but neither of them found proper jobs. She says, 'If people like me and him (Suman) are sitting at home and doing labour work, why would others want to study? People know what kind of education we are getting'. Father Xavier at the local church elaborated upon the point. 'Why will they study? They are poor and if one can earn more in Delhi than in the village, why will anyone stay here and study? It has become tough for educated people to find jobs here. And those in Delhi make more money'. Given their ethnicity, gender and location within the social hierarchy, it is difficult for tribal women to break through segmented labour markets and the power relations therein into new areas of work, which provide respect alongside a fair earning, despite their education.

Education is nevertheless seen to provide cultural capital and is perceived as status-giving, while migration for domestic and other forms of labouring tasks provides income (economic capital), yet is often seen as degrading. While schooling choices are influenced by the economic position of the household, this is never a simple trade-off as the cultural location in terms of status within the community and aspirations for the future also matter equally if not more than incomes. Despite the financial contributions, underlying all the accounts is an ambiguity regarding the low status accorded to domestic work. Marcel, a village leader said, 'While they do earn money, they return with tales of violence and exploitation. Once a girl comes back from Delhi, she has no respect. It is a matter of respect. That is all'. A high school teacher added, 'I have studied till my post-graduation. I did my schooling from the Holy Cross School and the sisters wanted me to teach here. I joined, but after all these years of study, the pay is only ₹ 2,000 a month. Even the domestic workers earn more. Yet I stay at home and am respected by the students'. In the long run, then, women want to move out of employment in domestic service which is endless and exhausting, and engage with other forms of self-employment, even if lower paying, as a strategy for earning respect. 'Respectability is one of the most ubiquitous signifiers of class. It informs how we speak, who we speak to, how we classify others'. It is these ways of defining people in terms of respectability that domestic workers seek to overturn.

Priti was a good student at school, yet failed her matriculation by a single mark. Her parents and relatives chided her, blaming her for not studying hard and wasting their investments in her schooling. She got angry and ran away to Delhi. She was planning to return home to complete her secondary school, but the sudden death of her mother meant that as the eldest she became responsible for supporting her siblings. She says,

> I have to stay in Delhi till my brothers are studying, maybe another three years, as I have to pay for their education. They want to study and these days without studying there is no hope in terms of jobs and money. I took one of my brothers to Delhi and paid for his driving lessons. He now works for my employers in their office.

Like Dorothy, Priti's contribution too is recognized within the village community, she has turned her initial rejection into an acceptance of her contributions. Yet for her, there is a constant tension in terms of status and personal growth on one hand, and earning income to fulfil her responsibility towards her family and satisfy her employers on the other. As she said,

> My employers are very nice. *Didi* asked me to take the matriculation exam from the Open school in Delhi. I thought about it and was worried if I would manage to study alongside the housework, so eventually refused. If I do study, who will take care of the house? But if I study further, I can get a better job.

She realizes that if she completes her secondary education, she could get a more respectable job as a teacher or an office-worker, fulfilling also the expectations of her parents. Despite all the comforts she may have at present, the income and the security, she herself sees domestic work as low status, yet is caught in a vicious cycle from which she cannot escape.

Both Dorothy and Priti had higher aspirations, yet have managed to keep up their dignity and a level of self-respect. They see their domestic work as legitimate labour, a means of earning and supporting their families, and this has led to some respect from their employers as well as recognition from the village community. Many of the illiterate Hindu or Sarna tribal girls like Mita and Shabnam, however, were overworked and underfed, hardly able to negotiate with their employers or contribute substantially to their families. Yet one cannot deny the agency exercised by them in leaving their work, even if it meant giving up their earnings and returning home empty handed, instead of accepting exploitative work conditions for too long. Whether the difference in outcomes and experiences can be attributed wholly to education is not clear, but basic education does seem to provide these women some personal confidence to negotiate both at home and in the workplace.

At a collective level, while convents recruit girls to join their respective orders, they realize that not all can become nuns, a large number of tribal christian girls will move to Delhi for domestic work. The christian religious organizations have hence been trying to organize them, to get them both income security and fair working conditions, as well as political voice and identity.[7] Sruti Soreng dropped out of school early and sought employment as a domestic worker in Delhi through the Convent at Punjabi Bagh. When she first arrived in Delhi, she and other girls were trained for two weeks before being placed in homes. The sisters negotiated wages and work conditions with the employer and also monitored this for irregularities through weekly meetings with the girls.

> I get ₹ 2,000 per month now and they (employers) have increased my wages. Earlier I got ₹ 1,600. The sisters ensure it. We get holiday on sunday between 12 and 5 pm and we go to the sisters for a meeting. There are more than 1,000 girls in that area, and we all meet and talk, so we don't feel lonely.

While tied to attending church and the classes that follow, with little scope for fulfilling their own aspirations or seeing the city, domestic workers like Sruti have nonetheless made several friends, other domestic workers whom they meet each week, with whom they can share news and experiences. Such support networks are, however, virtually restricted to the church-based agencies.

The Jesuits have historically played an activist role in Jharkhand, supporting tribal claims to land and other forms of protest against exploitation, but the organizational effort with domestic workers started in earnest in the early 1990s, with a visible growth in this migration stream (Aaron, 2007). A study on the conditions of domestic workers in Delhi led to the establishment of the Delhi Domestic Working Women's Forum (Indian Social Institute, 1993). The Church later partnered with other NGOs to initiate Chetanalaya – the National Domestic Workers Movement, as it was clear that the activities of the private placement agencies were leading to the exploitation of these workers. The National Domestic Workers Movement currently has 23 branches across India. According to Sister Prachi, one of the main organizers between November 2002 and March 2006, it was during this period that Chetanalaya also started lobbying again for protective legislation for domestic workers. Bills had been introduced in 1959, and then in 1989, but shelved each time. Petitions were filed in the Supreme Court of India for a comprehensive legislation in 2002 and 2003, yet till date this has not happened. While domestic work is one of the fastest growing employment sectors, yet a majority of workers being women, and restricted to the private space of the home, this identity as 'worker' continues to be invisibilised. Recent agitation by activists has led to the creation of the Domestic Workers (Regulation of Employment, conditions of work, social security and welfare) Bill, 2008, perhaps also motivated by the International Labour Organization's (ILO) move to introduce a Convention on Domestic Workers in 2010. Constraints on mobility, however, restrict the participation of women domestic workers themselves in such action, though information on the provisions is provided, at least in the sunday meetings of the church-based placement agencies.

Conclusion

In line with global trends, India too has seen a massive expansion in the domestic work sector in the last decade. While domestic work has a long historical tradition, its performance is now dominated by migrant women from poor backgrounds. There are several motivations behind female migration for domestic work, be it economic need and family responsibility, the desire to see the world, make an alternate livelihood or escape from educational failure or household oppression. While not trying to generalize, this paper has made an attempt to unpack and highlight women's agency as a critical element in their experience of domestic work and its outcomes in terms of dignity and self-respect.

Unlike caste-based groups in India, amongst the tribal communities (Scheduled Tribes), both men and women are recognized as workers and hence equally responsible for household livelihoods. Both also have equal access to education, yet poverty, the need to earn incomes or the failure to secure good results, often lead to dropouts. While men have been migrating for agricultural and construction labour, factory employment, the army and other private sector jobs, a majority of women from the village have migrated for domestic work. While male migrants are usually older and married, female migrants are younger and unmarried. Once they are married and have children, domestic responsibilities in their own home take over and while continuing with wage-work locally, they usually stop migrating. Ironically, once they have children, live-in, paid domestic work is no longer even an option for them, unless they make alternate care arrangements, as they are not allowed to keep their children with them. This would distract them from their personal loyalty and undivided service to the employer and in turn their treatment of domestics virtually as 'children', to be protected and controlled. In fact, it is this element of personal relationship and servility that has led to a decline in male participation in domestic work and a preference for other jobs, often lower paid and more insecure.

The experience of domestic work by migrant women is not straightforward, nor always positive, but rather demonstrates attempts to exercise the agency in a context of constraint, influenced by locally determined hierarchies and power relations, personal interactions of domestic service, as well as the larger socio-economic context within which migrant domestic workers are located. The placement agencies have turned into quick, money-making enterprises for the agents, appropriating virtually the entire salary of the workers, with little concern about her rights or well-being. Regulation of such agencies remains a major challenge. In the best scenarios, they earn reasonable incomes and are treated well by their employers, but given its association with reproduction rather than skills, domestic work continues to be socially and ideologically devalued. Yet the women workers have sought to shift the markers of status, delinking it from the nature of work itself and tying it more closely to elements of consumption, lifestyles, self-dignity and voice at home. Education does contribute to improve workplace negotiation and terms of employment to some extent, yet the real gain seems to be in terms of respect and involvement in decision-making, vis-à-vis their rural households.

Acknowledgements

This paper is based on a research project funded by the Development Research Centre on Globalization, Migration and Poverty at the University of Sussex, UK, entitled 'Gender Differences in Migration Opportunities, Educational Choices and Wellbeing Outcomes'. I would like to thank Shrayana Bhattacharya for research support and Ann Whitehead, Mina Swaminathan and Amit Mitra for detailed comments on an earlier draft. I would also like to thank participants at the University of Warwick conference on Waged Domestic Work, May 2008, for comments on the paper.

Notes

1. All names have been changed in the paper.
2. See for instance the work of Molyneux (1979), Folbre (1994) and other contributors to the domestic labour debate.
3. Kabeer (2007) cites global evidence to confirm this trend. In the US, increasing numbers of women with young children are entering the workforce. While in the 1980s men shared the domestic work burdens, by the 1990s this was absorbed by a reliance on paid domestic workers.
4. Agency is an important dimension of power as it relates to people's 'ability to define their goals and act upon them. It encompasses the meaning, motivation and purpose which people bring to their activity' (Kabeer, 1999: 438). It can take the form of bargaining and negotiation, but equally manipulation and resistance or the more intangible processes of reflection and analysis. It can involve both individual and collective action, depending on the context and the structures of constraint, be they market mechanisms, state policy or social norms that need to be overcome.
5. An analysis of the National Sample Survey (NSS) data by education level shows that while at higher, post-secondary levels of education, women's employment has been stable at about 12–13 per cent in urban areas, there has been a rapid expansion for women with less than primary levels of education in 'low-paid jobs, often in a subsidiary capacity, in the service sector, in schools and hospitals or as domestic help in households' (Unni and Raveendran, 2007: 197). Micro studies on women's employment in Delhi also highlight that work participation rates are lowest amongst the highest income group (Sudarshan and Bhattacharya, 2009).
6. Jharkhand, formerly part of Bihar, was constituted as a separate state in August 2000 on grounds of poverty and marginalization within Bihar. It has a relatively large proportion of tribal population, locally referring to themselves as Adivasis, concentrated in the

south-western and north-eastern parts of the state. The former consists of Simdega, Gumla and Ranchi districts, which not only provide the largest number of domestic workers to Delhi, but also have a strong network of missionary schools and long-standing missionary activity.

7. See also Parrenas' (2005) discussion of the Filipino chaplaincy in Rome advocating for the rights of Filipino domestic workers, providing with spiritual and cultural activities as well as social services.

References

Anderson, B., 'Just Another Job? The Commodification of Domestic Labour', in B. Ehrenreich and A.R. Hochschild (eds), *Global Woman: Nannies, Maids and Sex Workers in the New Economy*, Granta Books, London, 2002: 104–114.

——, *Doing the Dirty Work? The Global Politics of Domestic Labour*, Zed Books, London, 2000.

Aaron, S.J., *Contrarian Lives: Christians and Contemporary Protest in Jharkhand*, London School of Economics and Political Science, London, 2007.

Arendt, H., *The Human Condition*, The University of Chicago Press, Chicago, 1958.

Bourdieu, P., *Outline of a Theory of Practice*, Cambridge University Press, Cambridge, 1977.

Carling, J., 'Gender Dimensions of International Migration', Global Migration Perspectives No. 35, Global Commission on International Migration, Geneva, 2005.

Cheng, S.A., 'Contextual Politics of Difference in Transnational Care: The Rhetoric of Filipina Domestics' Employers in Taiwan', *Feminist Review*, Vol. 77, 2004: 46–64.

Chin, C., *In Service and Servitude: Foreign Domestic Workers and the Malaysian Modernity Project*, Columbia University Press, New York, 1998.

Chopra, R., 'Sisters and Brothers: Schooling, Family and Migration', in R. Chopra and P. Jeffery (eds), *Educational Regimes in Contemporary India*, Sage, New Delhi, 2005: 299–315.

Dickey, S. and K. Adams, 'Introduction: Negotiating Homes, Hegemonies, Identities and Politics', in K. Adams and S. Dickey (eds), *Home and Hegemony: Domestic Service and Identity Politics in South and Southeast Asia*, University of Michigan Press, Ann Arbor, 2000: 1–29.

Edholm, F. et al., 'Conceptualizing Women', *Critique of Anthropology*, Vol. 3, Nos 9 and 10, 1977: 101–130.

Ehrenreich, B., 'Maid to Order', in B. Ehrenreich and A.R. Hochschild (eds.), *Global Woman: Nannies, Maids and Sex Workers in the New Economy*, Granta Books, London, 2002: 85–103.

Elson, D., 'Gender Awareness in Modelling Structural Adjustment', *World Development*, Vol. 23, No. 11, 1995: 1851–1868.

Folbre, N., *Who Pays for the Kids? Gender and Structures of Constraint*, Routledge, London, 1994.

Fraser, N., 'After the Family Wage: Gender Equity and the Welfare State', *Political Theory*, Vol. 22, No. 4, 1994: 591–618.

Gopalan, S., *Women and Employment in India*, Har-Anand Publications, New Delhi, 1995.

Hirway, I., *Unpaid Work and the Economy: Gender, Poverty and the Millennium Development Goals*, United Nations and Levy Economics Institute of Bard College, Annandale-on-Hudson, New York, 2005.

Hochschild, A.R., *The Managed Heart: The Commercialization of Human Feeling*, University of California Press, Berkeley, 1983.

ISI, *The Tribal Domestic Worker at the Crossroads: A Report on the Status of Tribal Delhi Domestic Working Women*, Indian Social Institute, New Delhi, 1993.

Kabeer, N., *Marriage, Motherhood and Masculinity in the Global Economy: Reconfigurations of Personal and Economic Life*, Institute of Development Studies at the University of Sussex, Brighton, 2007.

——, 'Resources, Agency, Achievements: Reflections on the Measurement of Women's Empowerment', *Development and Change*, Vol. 30, No. 3, 1999: 435–464.

Kaur, R. 'Empowerment and the City: The Case of Female Migrants in Domestic Work', *Harvard Asia Quarterly*, Vol. 8, No. 3, 2004.

Kujur, J. and V. Jha, *Women Tribal Domestic Workers in Delhi: A Study of Deprivation and Migration*, Indian Social Institute, New Delhi, 2006: 200.

Kumar, N., *Working Conditions of Female Domestic Workers in Delhi*, Deshkal Publications, Delhi, 2003.

Lister, R., *Citizenship: Feminist Perspectives*, Palgrave Macmillan, Basingstoke and New York, 1997.

McDowell, L., 'Respect, Deference, Respectability and Place: What is the Problem with/for Working Class Boys?', *Geoforum*, Vol. 38, 2007: 276–286.

Moors, A., 'Migrant Domestic Workers: Debating Transnationalism, Identity Politics and Family Relations: A Review Essay', *Society for*

Comparative Study of Society and History, Vol. 45, No. 2, 2003: 386–394.

Molyneux, M., 'Beyond the Domestic Labour Debate', *New Left Review*, Vol. 1, No. 116, 1979: 3–27.

Neetha N., 'Making of Female Bread Winners: Migration and Social Networking of Women Domestics in Delhi', *Economic and Political Weekly*, April 24, pp. 1681–88.

NIUA, *Women in the Urban Informal Sector*, National Institute of Urban Affairs, New Delhi, 1991.

Parrenas, R.S., *Servants of Globalization: Women, Migration and Domestic Work*, Stanford University Press, Stanford, 2001.

Pathare, S., 'Domestic Workers in Delhi: An Overview', *Contemporary Social Work*, Vol. 17, 2000: 63–71.

Pereira, O., *Domestic Workers Struggle for Life*, CBCI Centre, New Delhi, 1984.

Radcliffe, S.A., 'Ethnicity, Patriarchy and Incorporation into the Nation: Female Migrants as Domestic Servants in Peru', *Environment and Planning D: Society and Space*, Vol. 8, 1990: 379–393.

Rao, N., A. Verschoor, A. Deshpande and A. Dubey, *Gender, Caste and Growth Assessment – India*, Report submitted to the Department for International Development, UK, DEV/ODG, Norwich, 2008.

Razavi, S., *The Political and Social Economy of Care in a Development Context*, UNRISD, Geneva, 2007.

Rollins, J., *Between Women: Domestics and Their Employers*, Temple University Press, Philadelphia, 1985.

Shah, S., 'Service or Servitude: The Domestication of Household Labour in Nepal', in K. Adams and S. Dickey (eds), *Home and Hegemony: Domestic Service and Identity Politics in South and Southeast Asia*, University of Michigan Press, Ann Arbor, 2000: 87–117.

Shramshakti, 'Report on the National Commission on Self Employed Women and Women in the Informal Sector', New Delhi, 1988.

Standing, G., 'Global Feminization Through Flexible Labour: A Theme Revisited', *World Development*, Vol. 27, No. 3, 1999: 583–602.

Stenning, A., 'Geography and the New Working Class Studies', *Antipode*, Vol. 40, 2008: 9–14.

Sudarshan, R.M. and S. Bhattacharya, 'Through the Magnifying Glass: Women's Work and Labour Force Participation in Urban Delhi', *Economic and Political Weekly*, Vol. 44, No. 48, 2009: 59–66.

Tolen, R., 'Transfers of Knowledge and Privileged Spheres of Practice: Servants and Employers in a Madras Railway Colony', in K. Adams and S. Dickey (eds.), *Home and Hegemony: Domestic Service and Identity Politics in South and Southeast Asia*, University of Michigan Press, Ann Arbor, 2000: 63–86.

Unni, J. and G. Raveendran, 'Growth of Employment (1993–94 to 2004–05): Illusion of Inclusiveness', *Economic and Political Weekly*, Vol. 42, No. 3, 2007: 196–199.

Uttal, L. and M. Tuominen, 'Tenuous Relationships: Exploitation, Emotion and Racial Ethnic Significance in Paid Child Care Work', *Gender and Society*, Vol. 13, No. 6, 1999: 758–780.

Yeates, N., 'Global Care Chains: A Critical Introduction', Global Migration Perspectives No. 44, Global Commission for International Migration, Geneva, 2005.

CHAPTER 3

The Emerging Market of Care Work

Issues and Challenges

VINITA SINGH AND KALINATH JHA

A girl minding her younger siblings, a woman caring for her elderly husband, a man assisting his disabled brother to do daily tasks such as bathing and dressing, a nurse caring for an ill patient in a hospital, clinic or the person's home, a migrant domestic worker cooking and cleaning in her own home for her family are all forms of care.

Care involves both the direct care of persons – such as feeding and bathing a young child – and the domestic tasks that are a precondition to care giving, such as preparing meals, cleaning utensils and clothes, purchasing food or collecting water or fuel. Those with intense care needs include young children; frail elderly people and people with various illnesses and disabilities, but able-bodied adults also require and receive care. Care can be unpaid, being performed for one's family, friends or community without any monetary reward. It may also be paid being performed by nannies, domestic workers, nurses and carers in homes for elderly people.

Women continue to provide a larger amount of care than men across all societies, especially in respect of unpaid care

(UNDP, 1995, 2007; Budlender, 2007a, b, c, d and forthcoming). More striking still is that these inequalities persist in spite of marked increases in female participation in the labour force in almost every region of the world (Elson, 1999, 2005; Kabeer, 2007, 2008; Molyneux, 2007; Pearson, 2007; Cornwall et al., 2007). Further variations in this organization of care exist across different contexts and over individual life cycles, while also reflecting diverse family arrangements and household forms. But, for the most part men have been unwilling to assume a larger share of unpaid care work and domestic work – even in the face of women's willingness to share men's 'breadwinning' responsibilities (Kabeer, 2007). At the same time, there has been barely any improvement in the provision of state subsidized care services in the majority of countries.

Care Work as Women's Work: The Justification

The patriarchal character of the sexual division of labour, manifests itself in women's work in a number of interrelated ways. Sexual division of labour is a complex analytical concept. Biologistic explanation treats sexual division of labour as a natural division rooted in reproductive functions. This results in women's labour being undermined in the family and in the wage sector, because both are characterized by sex specific tasks and job allocation. Thus, tasks are labelled specifically 'feminine' and 'masculine' by direct reference to biology or making analogies between biologically determined activities.

The concept of 'nature' has been used to explain social inequalities as 'natural' or inborn and hence beyond the scope of social change. The dominance of this concept has led to the dominance of the human being – male over female (nature). Thus, a woman's work is giving birth and raising children as well as domestic work (which includes care work) does not appear as work or labour. Women are generally defined as housewives, as non-workers.

Sexual division of labour can be seen as being socially determined too. This can be done by studying the notion of patriarchy.

Patriarchy can be defined as an autonomous system of social relations between men and women in which men are structurally dominant. Patriarchy designates male-female relations as social relations which, among other things, organize biological reproduction rather than being themselves determined by biology. Patriarchy as an analytical category inscribes the sexual division of labour as a social division and not a natural one. Thus, the unequal, hierarchical and exploitative relationships between men and women are due to social and not biological factors. The sexual division of labour is also an ideological representation of work distribution in society. It extends patriarchal relations into the non-familial labour process.

The sexual division of labour offers another view of 'women and work'. The patriarchal exploitation of women by men is located within the family. When women get married they exchange their labour power for their upkeep. The value of this upkeep is less than the value of the goods and services she produces. Moreover, the goods and services she produces are use values rather than exchange values which belong to the husband. It is argued that marriage contract is a labour contract by which men appropriate women's labour power. The marital relations constitute the relations of domestic production and hence structure the 'domestic mode of production'. The domestic mode of production depends on the transfer of ownership and control over the wife's labour power to the husband. In the domestic mode production, the wife's upkeep is a function of her class, position and income. The implication of this mode of work and task allocation lies in its emphasis on sex differences rather than on human similarities and this provides a legitimation for hierarchical differences between men and women (Hearn, 1989).

According to Maria Mies, men use their hands and heads and through instruments dominate nature, whereas women experience their entire bodies in the production of life which concludes in reproduction and 'subsistence' production and men become in-charge of 'commodity', production which was considered superior (Pringle, 1988).

Thus, the sexual division of labour identifies all women as a separate category of workers. It divides all work processes into male and female tasks. It subordinates tasks defined as female (secretarial work, nursing, care giving, low paid work, formal and informal sector work) to those defined as male. The sexual division of labour designates jobs as being sex specific. It extends patriarchal relations into non-familial labour powers. The 'housewifization' of women is a result of, this process.

Unpaid Care Work

A parent looking after their baby is providing care. When adults attend to the physical and emotional needs of their frail elderly parents or disabled members of their household, it is going to represent care. Members of the household who are not normally dependent may also require intensive care for brief periods. They may be ill and need care at home or to be taken to health services. At times, care may be required over extended periods. Along with direct physical care, carers often provide 'passive care' or supervision when they must remain near to the person been cared for in case they should require assistance. Passive care can be carried out at the same time as other activities, but these activities must be able to be interrupted at short notice and be performed near to the person being supervised.

Care encompasses more than activities such and feeding and bathing – the direct care of persons. The food needs to be cooked, the utensils cleaned and the clothes washed. In order for the food to be cooked and the clothes washed, fuel and water must also be collected. Domestic tasks which are not done directly to or with the person being cared for, constitute another essential aspect of care.

Care is not only about looking after the very young, elderly, ill or disabled. When the same tasks are performed for the benefit of more independent household members – it is caretaking.

Care may also be carried out for people who are not members of a person's own household. Unpaid care beyond the household refers to the unpaid assistance individuals provide to family and friends when they are ill, elderly or disabled or when their children need care.

Paid Care Work

In spite of the fact that care work falls within the 'female' notion of work yet there is a decreasing availability and willingness of women and girls to do unpaid care work, thus creating a 'care crises'. The need for care is escalating. The net population in need of care is going on increasing day by day. The aged, the sick, the children, the household are in need of 'care'. As the health sector reforms are exacerbating, these already fragile situations are leading to greater commercialization of health care and a heavier reliance on private payment and user fees. As a result, institutional health care has become unaffordable for many, shifting responsibility for care to the household. While affluent households may have the option of paying for care, in poorer households, intense care needs are often at increasing cost to women's and girls' physical and emotional well-being.

Many women work longer hours to cope with the dual responsibilities of providing care and earning an income – sacrificing their time for rest and leisure. It is in this context that the need for 'paying' or for 'buying' care emerges. Paid care may be done within the home by nannies or domestic workers. It may extend beyond the home, for example, in orphanages, old-age homes or homes for disabled people. Paid care beyond the home can also be argued to include some of the work done by nurses, cleaners and teachers of young children.

Some of this care is provided by the state in the form of public health and social welfare services. In the state sector, care providers will almost always be paid. At other times, paid care is provided through a commercial service – paid for either directly by the care recipient and their family or through insurance contributions. Market provision includes a corporate sector made up of big companies who invest to make profits. For example, a high proportion of elderly care in high income countries is provided by large corporate companies. In low, middle income countries, on the other hand, paid care service tend to be provided at the informal end of the market by nannies and domestic workers.

The Market of Care Work

Paid care services are making up a growing sector of the economy, particularly in middle and high income countries. The reasons for this are as follows: first of all, rising female education levels and aspirations, and resulting increases in women's participation in the paid labour force – reduces the availability and willingness of women to provide unpaid care. They include greater geographical mobility, which means that many women no longer live near their families who used to provide unpaid care. They also include the growing demand for care in many middle and high income countries – a consequence of ageing populations. While poor working women generally turn to family, kin and neighbours for help, more affluent women turn to the market (Kabeer, 2007).

In low and middle income countries, commercial services providing quality care tend to be underdeveloped and are too expensive for most households (Razavi, 2007). Instead, it is mostly at the informal end of the market that care is provided – namely through the employment of domestic workers in middle-class homes. Domestic workers perform for remuneration the many tasks that housewives and others perform unpaid such as cleaning, cooking and caring for dependents. While many countries have a long history of women migrating from rural areas to take up domestic service in urban areas, this work is increasingly being performed by women migrating across states, national and international borders.

This phenomenon has been described as 'global care chain' (Ehrenreich and Hochschild, 2003) of women leaving dependents in the care of extended family members and migrating to wealthier countries or cities where they relieve more wealthy women of care responsibilities. Rather than creating conditions that might enable existing ways of organizing and valuing care to shift, importing care workers displaces the problem, leaving inequitable gender division of labour intact (Zimmerman et al., 2006). At the same time it does little to encourage better state provision of care services, or improvised social protection measures for care providers.

These trends are not simply a reflection of the fact that wealthier women need care services and poorer women need employment (Ehrenreich and Hochschild, 2003; Kabeer, 2007). More fundamentally, they are about the politics of unpaid care work and the reluctance of men on the whole to take up a larger share of care and domestic work in spite of women's increasing financial contribution (Kabeer, 2007). They also reflect the reluctance of governments to provide affordable and accessible public care services. The result is that global inequalities among women of different ethnicities, races and classes are increasing.

All paid care work is poorly paid and lacks social status. But the care work that takes place inside the domestic homes is of particular concern because of the invisible nature of such work – especially, for the vast majority of domestic workers, who live with their employers. There is much variation in the ways in which domestic workers are remunerated. Some receive money wages only, some receive only in kind payment and some receive a mixture of the two. Receiving no payment beyond board and lodging is particularly common in respect of children typically from the rural areas, whom the employer may refer to as 'relatives' for whom they are providing care in return for domestic services.

Whatever the form of payment, domestic workers tend to be among the lowest paid workers in the economy. Indications abound in abuses against domestic workers and violation of their labour rights – in terms of physical, psychological and sexual abuses; non-payment of wages; excessively long hours; no rest days and forced confinement in the work place (HRW, 2006).

Migrant domestic workers may experience additional vulnerabilities as a result of their legal status and social isolation (ILO, 2003). Commonly reported experiences include exceptionally low wages, non-payment of wages, no day off and no meal breaks. The fact that they work in private homes isolated from co-workers makes it difficult for them to organize themselves into unions and stand up for rights to decent pay and working conditions.

Role of Migration and Placement Agencies

Recent trends in migration have been a witness to increased incidents of autonomous migration of tribal women to the cities. Tribal women are equal partners in the traditional tribal economy. They are labourious and docile. They are easily manipulated. Hence, the fear of exploitation by middle men who lure them on the pretext of fetching jobs in the cities. Most often, these women are illiterate, unconscious of their rights and privileges, and hence vulnerable. Because of these factors there is a clear cut preference for tribal women in certain occupations such as domestic work. Yet another noticeable trend in migration is the exodus of semi-literate and even matriculate girls and women. Most of these women who migrate are single and unmarried. They try to help their parents, save for dowries, and contribute towards education of their brothers and sisters back home. At times, it is sheer economic need (like freeing of mortgaged land) that is responsible for migration. At other times, it is the desire to explore the world on their own. At still other times, it is the breakdown in family relations that induces migration. Obviously, the 'push and pull' factors contribute towards autonomous migration of women from Jharkhand (Jha and Singh, 2006).

Due to globalization, that is, emerging of new markets and the revolution in communication media, lure for modern lifestyle has made these women realize the importance of economic independence; this enables the woman to gain independent social status, because now she is doing 'work' other than her own household chores – the work which is always, in all societies and in all social strata, unpaid, unrecognized and, therefore, not valued. In addition to the desire of establishing her own identity, a woman today earns to contribute towards the family income or to utilize her leisure time in her own interest. It is very significant that working in the city for young girls is an escape route from the exploitation they face at home. A tribal girl has a heavy burden of domestic responsibilities and no rights. If she goes to the cities to work, she does not have to work in the fields or fetch water and firewood. There is a great 'demand' for Jharkhand's young tribal women because of their characteristics of honesty, discipline and submissiveness.

Placement agencies are spread all over New Delhi. There are tribal girls from Jharkhand in almost every middle- and upper-class homes. Placement agencies in the capital, recruit local agents across Jharkhand's villages. These agents scour their constituencies for women who wish to work in Delhi (or those who can be persuaded to). The agent also carries out a reference check, gets the women to sign a contract with the placement firm and puts them on a train to Delhi. Apart from the agents working exclusively for them, most agencies resort to freelance 'guarantors' who serve as an informal employment exchange (apart from vouching for the women on their roster). Placement agencies pay guarantors half a month's salary of the women referred to by them.

Majority of Jharkhand's women in Delhi and in other cities prefer to carry the cash in person when they return home for Christmas. Predictably, they receive a heroine's welcome with some families organizing villagewide feasts for their selfless daughters. However, a woman who spends sometime in Delhi is also hackled for being a 'Dilli rahti hai', a pejorative with associations that range from 'sexual deviance' to undesirable modernity.

Today, a significant proportion of the state's tribals are Christians. Every village boasts of its own parish. Attendance at Sunday mass and assorted 'moral values' lectures is mandatory. The Catholic nuns and priests who run missions teach parishioners practical lessons related to personal hygiene. The church also serves as a support system, keeping an eye on elderly parents and young children of the women who work in Delhi.

The result of this is an army of women with great ethics. Many institutions, organizations and NGOs are conscious about the situation, trying their best for the upliftment of these tribal domestics and organize them for their cause.

The Cost of Care Giving

The number of working women aged fifty-five and more is projected to increase by 52 per cent between 2000 and 2010, from 6.4 million to 10.1 million (National Alliance for Care Giving, 1998). As workforce participation increases, care giving could pose even greater financial challenges for many women workers, due mostly to lost wages from reduced work hours, time out of the workforce, family leave or early retirement.

The time out of the workforce for care giving may compound the impact of earlier leave taken to care for a child. Further, care giving is expensive in itself. Studies have indicated that women care givers have suffered financial hardship as a result of their care giving responsibilities (Dethinger and Clarkberg, 2002). While the costs of providing care are high, the demands on care giver's time are also substantial. Estimates indicate that 25 per cent of the entire American workforce provided informal care during 1996 (Pavalko and Artis, 1997).

One national study on women and care giving, highlighted the conflicting demands of work and elder care. The study found that 33 per cent of working women decreased work hours, 29 per cent passed up a job promotion, training or assignment, 22 per cent took a leave of absence, 20 per cent switched from full time to part time employment, 16 per cent quit their jobs and 13 per cent opted for early retirement. Researchers have cited that women who reduced their work hours while care giving did not increase work hours once care giving had stopped.

Care giving also has a substantial impact on business. Absenteeism and replacing employees who quit, can have serious financial consequences to employers for providing care and other care giving activities. The cost to businesses to replace women care givers who quit their jobs because of their care giving responsibilities has been estimated at 3.3 billion dollars. Absenteeism among women care givers due to care giving responsibilities costs businesses almost 270 million dollars. The cost to businesses because of partial absenteeism (e.g. extended lunch breaks, leaving work early or arriving late) due to women's care giving has been estimated at 327 million dollars.

Care giving also implies health consequences for women. Higher levels of depression, anxiety and other mental health challenges are common. Studies find that men respond to care giving responsibilities in a fundamentally different way. Women tend to stay home to provide time consuming care to one or more ill or disabled friends or family members while men respond to loved one's needs for support by delaying retirement, in part to shoulder the financial burden associated with long term care. Other health impacts include elevated blood pressure and increased risk of developing hypertension; lower perceived health status; poorer immune function, slower wound healing and an increased risk of mortality.

Making Care Work More Valuable: Providing Protection for Domestic Workers under National Labour Laws

Many governments regard care work as being beyond the scope of regulation, so denying the domestic workers of labour protection as extended to other workers – rights to decent working conditions and minimum wages, to basic benefits and protections such as health insurance and to freedom of association (HRW, 2006). Combined with the freedom to form associations and trade unions, domestic workers in these countries have greater awareness of their rights, and ability to negotiate better working conditions and are trying to access legal avenues for reporting labour exploitation (HRW, website).

Supporting Domestic Workers to Organize for their Rights

Organizing is one of the most important ways for workers to take action to challenge discrimination and to advance and defend their rights and interests. Organizing can enable them with few assets to pool their resources, thereby increasing their economic power, it can help them to access services and social protection provisions; and it can facilitate their representation in local, national and international policy making forums. However, the fact remains that care workers often work in private homes isolated from co-workers, makes it more difficult for them to organize themselves into unions and stand up for their rights. Unlike those who work in larger work places, each worker faces a separate employer, so there is not the same strength in unity when negotiating. Long and tedious working hours can also reduce the time available for social and political activities. In addition, the personalized nature of employer – employee relations in case of domestic worker makes it more difficult for workers to state their demands firmly. Further difficulties result out of the uncertain legal status of workers as after all – they are migrants and in foreign land and culture (Singh, 2007).

Thus, the organization of the domestic and other care workers needs to have multiple foci, including informing care workers of the rights they already have – fighting for increased rights and targeting both the governments and employers.

References

Budlender, D., *Political and Social Economy of Care*, Research Report 1 on South Africa, United Nations Research Institute for Social Development, Geneva, 2007a.

——, *Political and Social Economy of Care*, Research Report 2 on South Africa, United Nations Research Institute for Social Development, Geneva, 2007b.

——, *Analysis of Time Use Data on Work/Care Regimes and Macro Data on the Care Diamond*, South Africa Research Report 2, United Nations Research Institute for Social Development, Geneva, 2007c.

——, 'A Critical Review of Selected Time Use Surveys', Gender and Development Programme Paper No. 2, United Nations Research Institute for Social Development, Geneva, 2007d.

——, *The Statistical Evidence on Care and Non-Care Work across Six Countries*, United Nations Research Institute for Social Development, Geneva, forthcoming.

Cornwall, A., E. Harrison and A. Whitehead (eds.), *Feminisms in Development: Contradictions, Contestations and Challenges*, Zed Books, New York and London, 2007.

Dethinger, E. and M. Clarkberg, 'Informal Care Giving and Retirement Timing among Men and Women: Gender and Care Giving Relationship in Late Mid Life', *Journal of Family Issues*, Vol. 23, No. 7, 2002.

Elson, D., *Gender-Neutral, Gender-Blind or Gender-Sensitive Budgets? Changing the Conceptual Framework to Include Women's Empowerment and the Economy of Car*, Commonwealth Secretariat, London, 1999.

——, 'Unpaid Work, the Millennium Development Goals and Capital Accumulation', Notes for a Presentation at the Conference on 'Unpaid Work and the Economy: Gender, Poverty and the MDGS', United Nations Research Institute for Social Development, 1–3 October 2005.

Ehrenreich, B. and A.R. Hochschild (eds), *Global Women: Nannies, Maids and Sex Workers in the New Economy*, Granta Books, London, 2003.

Hearn, Jeff, Deborah L. Sheppard, Peta Tancred-Sheriff and Gibson Burrell (eds.), *The Sexuality of Organization*, Sage, London, 1989.

Human Rights Watch, *Swept under the Rug: Abuses against Domestic Workers around the World*, New York, 2006, http//:hrw.org/reports/2007/guinea 0606/

——, http//: www.hrw.org/wr2k7/essays/globalization/index.htm

International Labour Organization, *Preventive Discrimination, Exploitation and Abuse of Women Migrant Workers: An Information Guide*, Geneva Promotion Programme, Geneva, 2003.

Jha, Kali Nath and Vinita Singh, 'Globalization and the Migrating Tribal Women', in Sakarama Somayaji and Ganesha Somayaji (eds.), *Sociology of Globalization*, Rawat Publications, Jaipur and New Delhi, 2006.

Kabeer, N., 'Marriage, Motherhood and Masculinity in the Global Economy: Reconfigurations of Personal and Economic Life', IDS Working Paper 290, Institute of Development Studies, Brighton, 2007.

——, *Mainstreaming Gender in Social Protection for the Informal Economy*, Commonwealth Secretariat, London, 2008.

Molyneux, M., 'The Chimera of Success: Gender Ennui and the Changed International Policy Environment', in A. Cornwall, E. Harrison and A. Whitehead (eds.), *Feminisms in Development: Contradictions, Contestations and Challenges*, Zed Books, New York and London, 2007.

National Alliance for Care Giving, *The Care Giving Boom: Baby Boomer Giving Care*, Washington, DC, 1998.

Pavalko, E.K. and J.E. Artis, 'Women's Care Giving and Paid Work: Causal Relationships in Late Mid Life', *Journal of Gerontology: Social Sciences*, Vol. 52B, No. 4, 1997.

Pearson, R. 'Reassessing Paid Work and Women's Empowerment: Lessons from the Global Economy', in A. Cornwall, E. Harrison and A. Whitehead (eds.), *Feminisms in Development: Contradictions, Contestations and Challenges*, Zed Books, New York and London, 2007.

Pringle, Rosemary, *Secretaries Talk: Sexuality, Power and Work*, Allen and Unwin, Sydney, 1988.

Razavi, S., *The Political and Social Economy of Care in a Development Context: Contextual Issues, Research Questions and Policy Options*, United Nations Research Institute for Social Development, Geneva, 2007.

Singh, Vinita, *Women Domestics: Workers within Households*, Rawat Publications, Jaipur and New Delhi, 2007.

United Nations Development Programme, *Human Development Report*, Oxford University Press, New York, http//: hdr.undp.org/en/reports/global/hdr1999 and http//: hdr.undp.org/en/reports/global/hdr2007–2008.

Zimmerman, M.K., J.S. Litt and C.E. Bose (eds), *Global Dimensions of Gender and Care Work*, Stanford University Press, Stanford, 2006.

CHAPTER 4

Feminine Representation and Identity as the Vulnerable Workforce in the Indian Cinema Industry

NIRMALA M.N.

The stereotypical imagery, or of the relationship between women's subjectivity and objectivity in the Indian cinema; the feminine identity on and off screen in the industry, the largest producer of cinema, is still elusive.

The other proposition is signaled in the key term marginalization. Quite to the contrary it is maintained that women have never been allowed to make their full and proper contribution to the society. They are not visible because, expressly or by default, they have been excluded from certain domains of activity, notably the political, and relatively speaking confined to domestic space.

Indeed, the social order of capitalism is especially implicated as one in which the objectification and commoditization of women has reached, an unprecedented height.

Governed by paradox – actresses are expected to represent globalized images of the liberated female sexuality, but are still circumscribed by shifting, yet narrow definitions of 'Indian' femininity. The global flows of media products and the existing media ecology set the stage where an archetype such as Sita or Draupadi, is rehearsed for the contemporary era through global idioms.

Since the liberalization of national economy, the media scene has witnessed a proliferation of outlets; however, this enlarged media space has not expanded subject positions available to actresses as one would predict, especially with respect to their sexuality. Rather, even as contemporary actresses actively negotiate their public personas using global media archetypes for female sexual agency, media representational practices repeatedly fetishes these women as feminized bodies, subjecting them to a voyeuristic male gaze – their sexual and gendered selves continued to be circumscribed. Caught between these competing subject positions, contemporary Indian actresses have very little room for manoeuvering. And, although their star status hinges on their sexualized persona, this public display of sexuality also binds their career within the 'Item girl' roles. Strategies for resistance or subverting hegemonic norms of Indian womanhood through the media, consequently, are very limited.

Sandra Bartky's analysis of power offers a gendered view, one that contends that women in patriarchal societies internalize disciplinary procedures and self-regulate their bodies and sexuality. And, in patriarchal societies there is no need for external surveillance mechanisms to control women. Actresses' presentations on-screen are either altered to match their personalities off-screen, or vice versa, but both of these strategies are ultimately reproductive of the same patriarchy that disciplines and regulates women's sexuality.

Redefining the Identity On- and Off-Screen

In general, rumour, gossip and scandal, as modes of circulating knowledge about celebrities, were attached to low art forms and tended to be gendered as female.

The prevalence of photographs and fiction, together with the dearth of personal information on actresses, denied them agency and suggests, rather, their primary status as objects of spectacle and speculation.

Devika Rani was the 'first lady of the Indian screen'. If one looks at film journalism both then and now, even the most acerbic writings on her, such as *Film-India* on her role as producer, remain silent on any aspect of her private life other than the most public and respectable events, such as the death of her husband and her marriage to the Russian painter Svetoslav Roerich. She is mostly celebrated as the pre-eminent female Indian star, the one who represented the best of Indian cinema in pre-independence times. Not until 1950, in a work on Indian stars by Saadat Hasan Manto, written after he had left Bombay and in a self-consciously provocative style, we get a glimpse into what oral gossip around her might have been like.

Privacy is the commodity that sells magazines, through its promise of revelation of secrets. Scandals concentrating on actresses' behaviour during the productions and her numerous affairs to show her off-screen persona, while coinciding with modern women in sensationalism.

Ideologies of individualism and authenticity were to be found in the articles promising truth about the star, even if the truth inevitably disappointed, because the titles of the articles were far more extravagant than the actual truth revealed. Nevertheless, in all these pieces there was a general emphasis on private information and 'inner' identity of the star.

In the Indian public sphere, actresses have to locate themselves strategically within a limited rubric of sexual identities – the vamp, the virgin, or some blurring of the two.

Bollywood actress Priyanka Chopra who started her career by starring in sexualized roles later, to avoid being typecast as sex symbol, used new vehicles of celebrity construction to build her star image. In April 2005, Filmfare awarded Chopra 'best performance in a villainous role' for 'Aitraaz'. In her acceptance speech the actress stressed that the role played by her as absolute antithesis of what she stood for, stating that she is an emotional person and least aggressive.

While actresses redefine their identity by constantly distinguishing self from the role, the supporting or character actresses have no such choice and are usually, once they are typecast in a particular role, continue to be identified only in those frames.

Hierarchy, Class and Caste Conflict

The 'star system', as defined in the specific context of Indian cinema, emphasizes the inherently ephemeral nature of stardom, especially for female stars, producing a structure of intensive capitalization of what is understood to be a fast-depleting resource. In this context, one cannot overestimate the structural importance of enduring careers of figures that might not ordinarily be considered stars, like Helen, who had a long career playing the westernized cabaret girl, from her first credited roles in the early 1950s to 1980s.

The heterogeneous affiliations of the Nadia/stunt film inter text complicate their low-brow status in the precise hierarchies of class, ethnicity, national, culture, and performance expertise of the time.

Though in the contemporary discourse, 'fearless Nadia' had no star persona outside her identification with the stunt genre – Apart from the occasional reviews or news items about the studio or its latest productions, there were no articles, star profiles, or interviews devoted exclusively to Nadia as there were for more 'reputable' actresses.

Sulochana and fearless Nadia occupied extremes in the hierarchy of 1930s Indian star discourse, while Sulochana, by the early 1930s, was the most popular Indian star of the silent era. Nadia equally popular but due to her identification with the low-brow stunt genre did not qualify her for the designation of a star.

The class composition of the actresses associated with the cinema became the single and most important issue for redefining the moral status of cinema, with the greatest emphasis on education and well-known families. One sign by which the social respectability of female stars was prominently announced was to attached degrees (BA, MA) after the names of the educated stars.

For instance an advertisement in *Filmindia*, July 1943, read like this:

> Wanted Cultured Ladies Only!! For a Leading Role in 'Bhai-Bahen'. If you dream of shining in the film firmament as a star and wish to see your dream come true, apply. (with photographs)

Popular actress Durga Khote, initially her public image was constituted by too frequently publicized details that she was the first middle-class, educated, upper-caste woman of good family to dare to become an actress.

The rhetoric of improvement, through its valorization of cultured women completely rejected the democratic aspiration underlying Hollywood star ideology as in India; cinema itself aspired to class mobility.

The discussions of female stars implicitly extended the argument of the link between class and moral status of women to criteria for evaluating acting ability. For Dhiren Ganguly, cinema's problem was not the moral danger to respectable ladies in the studios, but rather the harmful effects on film texts of the presence of lower-class women as actresses 'their unfitness lies neither in their birth nor in their downfall; it lies in their mode of base living, in their vicious environment, in their want of culture and their difference to education'.

By reiterating the need for educated classes to send their daughters to this profession, many articles in early 1930s reinforced the assumption that all other female performers who were uneducated or from low-class families were justifiably identified by the public as little other than prostitutes (Majumdar, 2010: 50–90)

If in the early decades of cinema in India, social and 'cultured' status were most coveted qualities in film stars, this has now been replaced by star genealogy.

This analysis of the star system as inherently dynastic in contemporary Hindi cinema is sharply implicit in the 2007 blockbuster homage to Bollywood's, 'Om Shanti Om' (dir. Farah Khan), whose hero, Om, starts out as a minor actor in the 1970s. The film hyperbolically demonstrates the impossibility of the dream of rising from humble beginnings to fame, by having Om lack any means to realize his dreams of stardom except through death and reincarnation as the son of the top Bollywood star. Occasionally, the industry mocks at itself by narrating the real life struggle and hardship faced by small-town girls aspiring to be part of cinema, like in 2003 film 'Mein Madhuri Dixit Banna Chahiti Hoon' (dir. Chandan Arora).

Kapoors, Rai, Kaif and Chopra with star genealogy or pageant/modelling canvas, overseas actress with Indian ancestry dominate the industry. Aspiring female artist from lower strata of society find Bollywood a distant dream and the gap has further increased with industry focusing on catering to diasporic audience.

The junior artists, who do dancing in most of the India's myriad films, occupy the lowest rank in the hierarchy of the Indian cinema industry. With the promises of better emoluments and working conditions mostly remaining unimplemented, the plight of extras is pathetic. Though most of them work for years under the same banner or studio, the unorganized industry neither provides legally enforceable minimum wages nor any social security benefits such as provident fund, gratuity, medical allowance, etc.

The most vulnerable workforce are the junior artists and the industry prefers to address this vital workforce as EXTRAS, a strategy to keep them submissive by depriving them of a dignified identity and pride of being associated with the industry.

Most exploited are the female junior artists, most often they are victims of sexual abuse and exploitations. With no fixed working hours nor regular job security, delay in minimum wages and absence of security at workplace continues to affect the female workforce in the industry.

In recent past with Indian movies made glossier to reach to the global audience, the junior artists are replaced by college students and aspiring models. And, every time this newer glamorous urban artists/models are hired, a family of ten junior artists are done out of week's ration, forcing the female junior artist into becoming a commercial sex worker.

The above situation in Indian film industry is in total contrast to the situation that exists in USA or Europe. For instance, in US, most major film and television production fall under the jurisdiction of Screen Actors Guild (SAG) and these junior actors are protected and guaranteed the same working conditions as actors with speaking roles. And, producers are allowed to hire non-union extras only after a certain number of SAG performers have been cast and the non-union extras are paid the minimum wages.

Unfortunately, the need to create an Indian cinematic identity still continues to be seen in terms of the absence of, or the need to redefine, Indian stars.

Marginalization and Hegemony

Women marginalized by caste and gender, continue to search for identity in the almost century old cinema industry. The classic portrait of female subjectivity and gender exploitation in a patriarchal society was evident in Shyam Benegel's 'Bhumika' a fiery women's quest for autonomy.

Bhumika, the first Indian film based on woman's autobiography, is about Hansa Wadkar, a Maharashtrian film actress. Pulled out of school to become the sole earner in a poor family, she started an acting career at the age of 11 and went on to become one of the most sought after actresses. Victim of patriarchal hegemony – alcoholic and broken in health, she died at the age of fifty.

In 1970s, Amitab Bachchan's vigilante films valorized violence and marginalized female characters to stereotypes as the archetypal mother or glamour object. Films like 'Bhumika' portrayed the off-screen image of the on-screen actresses.

Indian films dominated by dance and songs sequences, dance becomes more than a spectacle. Here, Madhava Prasad's analysis of dancers in films as sites of 'Temporary permission' is particularly compelling. Distinguished between the private and the public and what is acceptable in Hindi films, Prasad proposes ways in which dance sequences provide glimpses of the otherwise hidden private sphere. Though his analysis focuses on representation of sexuality in the context of strict censorship, the discussion nevertheless points out that dance performs the important function of creating a temporary permissive, even transgressive expressive realm.

Though women have been playing a vital role behind the camera as directors, editors or cinematographers they are rarely recognized by film historians and media. Today, the most sought after editors in the industry are women such as Deepa Bhatia ('Hazaar Chaurasi Ki Maa', 'Taare Zameen Par') and Aarti Bajaj ('Black Friday', 'Dev D'). But still, women's struggle for identity continues in the cinema industry.

Conclusion

With the patriarchal conspiracy preventing women's contribution from receiving its due recognition, the effort is made to locate women's voices within the patriarchal discourse, to 'retrieve' women's history to bear witness to their contemporary productivity, and ensure that their labour is both recognized and properly rewarded.

Effort to redefine the representation and identity of women on screen is being made by directors like Aparna Sen and Deepa Mehta. But, political foray of actress in real life has not contributed much to improve the reel nor real life of female workforce in the Indian film industry.

References

Barnouw, Erik and S. Krishnaswamy, *Indian Film*, Columbia University Press, New York, 1963.

Bartky, Sandra Lee, 'Foucault, Feminity and the Modernization of the Patriarchal Power', in I. Diamond and L. Quinby (eds.), *Feminism and Foucault: Reflections on Resistance*, Northeastern University Press, Boston, 1988: 61–86.

Bharucha, Rustom, *The Politics of Cultural Practice*, Oxford University Press, New Delhi, 2009.

Datta, Sangeeta, *Shyam Benegal*, British Film Institute, London, 2002.

Foucault, M., 'Schizo-Culture: Infantile Sexuality', in S. Lotringer (ed.), *Foucault Live: Interviews 1961–1984*, Semiotext(e), New York, 1978: 154–167.

Govindan, Padma P. and Bisakha Dutta, 'From Villain to Traditional Housewife', in Anandam P. Kavoori and Aswin Punathambar (eds), *Global Bollywood*, Oxford University Press, New Delhi, 2008: 180–195.

Kavoori, Anandam P. and Aswin Punathambekar, *Global Bollywood*, Oxford University Press, New Delhi, 2008.

Majumdar, Neepa, *Wanted Cultured Ladies Only*, Oxford University Press, New Delhi, 2010.

Manto, Saadat Hasan, *Stars from Another Sky*, Penguin Books, New Delhi, 1998.

Prasad, Madhava, *Ideology of the Hindi Film: A Historical Construction*, Oxford University Press, New Delhi, 1998.

Vasudevan, Ravi S., *Making Meaning in Indian Cinema*, Oxford University Press, New Delhi, 2008.

SECTION II

Market Economy of Marriage

CHAPTER 5

Ghataks, Marriage Bureaus, Astrologers

Studying Intermediaries in the Kolkata Marriage Market

MADHURIMA MUKHOPADHYAYA

Marriage system in India, perceived often as an alliance between families rather than merely a conjugal union between two individuals, has always depended on intermediation, both formal and informal. In India, marriage remains firmly heterosexual, and its importance lies in its self-conscious agenda to reproduce the social order through caste and class endogamy. Blood line and its purity are the two main targets of caste-endogamous arranged marriages. Descent is always patrilineal and blood is inherited through the male-line by the intermediation of the female. 'A child inherits whatever purity is contained in the parental blood. Line preserving liaisons occur-between persons from the same caste group or *jati*'.[1] Therefore, the notion of a marriage being arranged by family is very common even today. Marriage alliance is very crucial in an arranged marriage. Informal forms of marriage alliance being pursued through relatives, friends and neighbours are quite common. This paper intends to study a few of the formal agents of marriage that is visible in the marriage market of Kolkata – the ghataks (matchmakers), marriage bureaus and astrologers with respect to their Hindu Bengali clientele. In contemporary urban Kolkata, besides the 'never married',[2] who are prospective brides and grooms, the 'late marriers'[3] and 'divorcees'[4] also seek suitable match availing the services of these intermediaries. It was also significant to observe that astrologers though not directly in the traditional match-making business, also in certain cases act as match-makers now. The parents having children of marriageable age rely on their choice more, since they offer double service of finding a match as well as paying heed to the fact that the match is astrologically perfect. Gender, class and marital status segregation exists very strongly in the choice of the agents by the clients and vice versa. In the volatile market of marriage, the matrimonial websites are a comparatively new entry. The traditional forms face competition from these 'new' agents in the market and modify their functioning accordingly.

The 'never married' are the majority of the clients in the marriage market. They are the most preferred clients of the intermediaries. Besides them, the 'divorcees' and the 'late marriers' also seek soul mates. In Hindu society, marriage was seen as a sacrament and, therefore, indissoluble. Men were allowed polygamy without any divorce, but women were allowed to marry only once. Among the higher castes, they were forbidden to marry a second time even if their husband died, until the legislation of the Widow Remarriage Act in 1856. A hundred years later, in 1955–56, a series of legislations were passed in Independent India, which while acknowledging the sacral nature of Hindu marriage, also introduced some of the advantages of a 'contract'. Divorce became legal – for men and women. Age of marriage has been an area of contestation in history and though an age has been fixed as the legal age for marriage, there still remains much ado regarding it in the marriage market. Child marriage has been one of India's persistent social problems. An oft-quoted medieval legal/prescriptive text recommends eight as the ideal age for a girl's marriage. Even in the 1950s, the bulk of India's girls were married by 11 years of age. Today, the scenario has changed but age of marriage for girls' remains low.

The Census data of 2001 give us the mean age of marriage for females married in the last five years as 19.6 years. In the case of males, the mean age is 23.5 years.[5] The data on West Bengal from NFHS–3 show the median age at first marriage to be 17 years among women aged 20–49 and 24 years among men aged 25–49. On an average, men get married almost 7 years later than women. More than one-half (54%) women aged 20–24 years get married before the legal minimum age of 18 and 27 per cent of men aged 25–29 years married before the legal minimum age of 21.[6] Mean age for marriage of girls according to the District Level Household and Facility Survey 3 – Fact Sheet, West Bengal (2007–08) is 21.0.[7] It is a 0.2 per cent rise from the DLHS – 2 data of 2002–04, where it was 20.8. This general data must be considered in relation to *class, caste, regional* and rural-urban disparities. In some elite social groups, however, marriage is considerably delayed (for women and men) due to increased opportunities of education and employment.

This paper studies how these intermediaries differentiate between a prospective male and female client in three categories of 'never married', 'late marriers' and 'divorcees' and in this differentiation of the three categories how these intermediaries produce and reproduce the stereotypical structures of patriarchal subjugation. It also seeks to investigate further the negotiations between these intermediaries as they coexist in the 'marriage market' facing competition from global intermediaries like the matrimonial websites and how they modify their functioning, in keeping with the 'modern' needs of the clients, while retaining traditional practices and norms.

Methodology

The data used in this paper has been the findings of a study done on marriage by the School of Women's Studies, Jadavpur University, between 2007 and 2009. There were in-depth interviews conducted with the intermediaries and prospective brides and grooms from working and middle classes. To elucidate the points, data from the statistical survey conducted in the 141 municipal wards of Kolkata and 23 wards of Bidhannagar, a comparatively newer township, adjacent to Kolkata, has also been referred. The survey had a sample of 6,000 as a part of the project mentioned above. For the purpose of categorizing class; Monthly Household Income (MHI) was taken as a control factor. Respondents having an MHI less than or equal to ₹ 10,000 constituted the 'working class' and above ₹ 10,000 were considered to belong to 'middle class'. The same definition of class has been maintained for the quantitative and qualitative surveys to allow both complementary and comparative analysis. Interviews were conducted with ghataks, astrologers and marriage bureaus in the municipal wards of Kolkata and Bidhannagar. In the first round of interviews, we found that more than thirty per cent of a bureau's clients were divorcees. There are also a substantial number of clients who have crossed the usual age of marriage and can be included in category of 'late marriers'. This prompted another round of enquiry with the marriage bureaus, to study available data on divorcees and people who are marrying late and to explore the function of the bureau as agents or intermediaries in such marriages. Names of respondents and organizations (marriage bureaus) have been changed to ensure privacy of their comments and opinions.

Profile of the Respondents

Intermediaries

Ghataks in Kolkata are difficult to locate now. Most of the ghataks interviewed are engaged in *ghatkali* (Bengali term for process of match-making) as part-timers while having a different full-time remunerative occupation. Their usual charges are around ₹ 301 to ₹ 501 for approaching the parties interested in entering an alliance. After the final match has been fixed, ₹ 3,000 is charged from the grooms family and ₹ 6,000 from the bride's family. The categories of astrologers as respondents included a heterogeneous group of palmists, numerologists, *Vaastu* specialists, *Samudrik Vidya, Tantra* experts, etc. Most of the astrologers interviewed have been in this profession for years, ranging from 10 to 37. Palmistry, numerology and study of horoscopes are practices common to all. The fee charged by such astrologers range from ₹ 100 to ₹ 1,000 per session. Twenty-two proprietors and owners of marriage bureaus in the municipal wards under Kolkata Corporation and Bidhannagar Municipality were interviewed. The oldest bureau in our survey was established in 1968 and has been in this business for more than forty years now. It is now dealing with NRIs as well as local clients. The rates for registering with bureaus differ from ₹ 300 to ₹ 1,000 for 2–6 months of service. Fees vary according to the tenure of availing services of internet matching, marriage counselling and other allied facilities. Many bureaus also charge a lump-sum amount post-settlement of marriage. In contemporary Kolkata, these bureaus have emerged as one of the primary forms of intermediation. Their clientele consisted mainly of Bengali Hindu men and women. Within this group, there is a high proportion of young boys and girls of marriageable age, who approach these bureaus directly.

Individual Respondents: Interviews have been conducted with males and females in the two categories of 'going to be married' and 'married'[8] from middle and working class families living in the municipal wards of Kolkata and Bidhannagar.

The Findings

Choice of Agents by Clients and vice versa: The statistical survey[9] conducted by the School of Women's Studies, Jadavpur University found 1,805 singles in the total sample size of 5,939. Out of them, there are 1,331 males and 474 females. Out of 1,331 single males, 912 want to get married in the near future. Out of 474 single females, 420 want to get married in the near future. Therefore, in total 1,332 out of 1,805 singles want to get married in the near future. Out of the 912 single males who want to get married, 395 males want to go for arranged marriage. Out of 420 single females who want to get married in the near future, 336 females want to go for arranged marriage. In total, 731 persons want to go for arranged marriage, i.e. 55 per cent of single respondents who plan to get married in the near future want to go for arranged marriage.

So arranged marriage is the choice of quite a significant number of the sample (see Figure 5.1).

Figure 5.1

Marriage Preference of Single Respondents

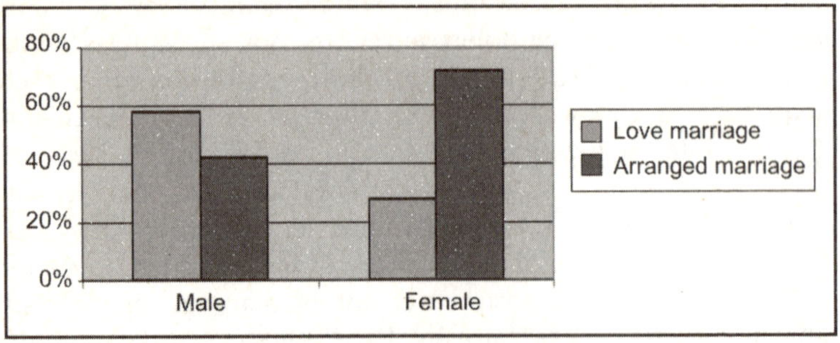

Source: Quantitative Survey on Marriage undertaken by School of Women's Studies, Jadavpur University 2007–09.

In colonial Calcutta with the rise of the *bhadralok,* the ghatak cult slowly lost its popularity. Initially, the ghataks functioned within the community as the main agent for establishing marriage alliances. Their main function was selection of appropriate matches, as they functioned as genealogists who determined caste ranks and catalogued the position of people and families within the caste hierarchy. It was up to them to maintain caste 'purity'. As genealogists and not as marriage contractors did they earn the title of *kulacharya* and were highly revered in society. Larger formal institutions replaced free agents in marriage negotiations and this suited the changing nature of Calcutta as it grew in size and in social composition. This history becomes very important for us to understand the growing popularity of newspaper advertisements even now, and also get an idea about how marriage bureaus started functioning as an important intermediary in the matrimonial market. Matrimonial columns and marriage bureaus served the function of match-making as well as centres for matching horoscopes. This was better suited to the urban householder. The marked changes in the nature of caste during the second half of the nineteenth century was a major cause of the decline of the ghataks whose main function was that of guarding the caste principles.[10]

Even today ghataks exist and 'ghatkali' is an accepted form of marriage alliance. The ghataks it was found cater mainly to the working classes. The data analysed across gender and class brings out the general differences. Maximum numbers of working class males had opted for 'reference by relatives' and ghatkali, while maximum numbers of working class females had opted for 'parent's decision' and 'reference by relatives'. Maximum percentages of middle class males had opted for 'reference by relatives' and ghatkali, while for females it was 'newspaper' and 'parent's decision'. When working class parents were asked regarding their choice of intermediation for their children, in maximum cases it was ghatkali. The middle class parents on the contrary chose 'newspapers' and 'reference by relatives', 'friends' and 'personal contacts'. Astrologers as mediating agents were mentioned by some middle-class parents too. This data formed a basis for the study of different intermediating agents in marriage in Kolkata. These graphs in Figures 5.2 and 5.3 reflect the views of the singles 'wanting to get married in near future', which helps in forming a general idea regarding the choices.

Figure 5.2

Options for Forming Marriage Alliances

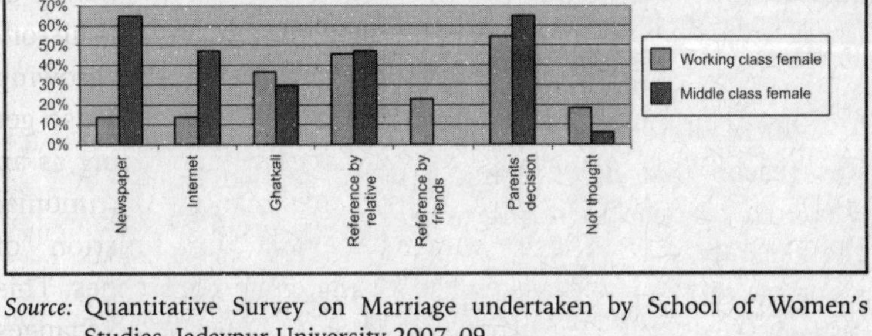

Source: Quantitative Survey on Marriage undertaken by School of Women's Studies, Jadavpur University 2007–09.

Figure 5.3

Options for Forming Marriage Alliances

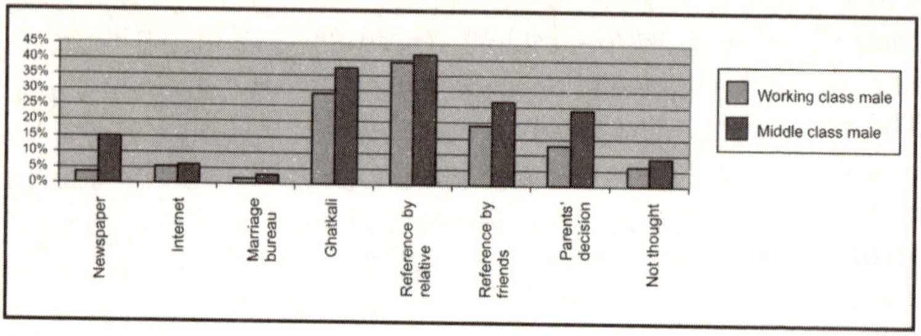

Source: Quantitative Survey on Marriage undertaken by School of Women's Studies, Jadavpur University 2007–09.

A very clear class differentiation exists in the choice of the agents by the clients. When the agents were questioned regarding the choice of the clients, a similar standpoint was raised. Never married males and females are the ghatak's preferred clients. Ghataks do not find divorcees and late-marriers suitable for finding a match. One of the ghataks commented: firstly, it is difficult to find someone among the working-classes who had gone through the formal legal process of a divorce; secondly, they believe, it is difficult to find a match when a person is a divorcee or late marrier, especially for female candidates. Though the rate for fixing the marriage alliance differed amongst the ghataks, the amount charged for fixing the alliance was always more for the bride's family than for the groom's family. When asked, Mr Majumdar, one of the ghataks answered,

> The father is burdened with the daughter of a marriageable age, because I free him from his burden, I charge an extra sum ...[11]

Mr Majumdar, like all his fellow ghataks, feels that it is for this reason that he is doing a social service. Such kinds of gendered practice in terms of fees were common among the ghataks only.

Very clearly, marriage bureaus were the choice of the middle class and above. The amount of fees charged by them and the kinds of services provided by them was more akin to the demands of the middle classes. The bureaus also informed that their clients were mostly middle classes mentioning professions like teachers, engineers, doctors, lawyers, government officials. The marriage bureaus in urban Kolkata have a fixed charge when it comes to registering and finding match for a prospective bride or groom, there was no discrimination in terms of fees. It varied according to the tenure of service. However, what was mandatory for women was the photograph which was to be submitted while registering at the bureau. This was optional for men. A North Kolkata based bureau informed,

> Looks still remain very important in choosing a bride. It is for this reason we need to maintain a database of photographs of our female clients, to show it to the groom's family. She may be qualified and earning in thousands but a woman who is not good looking has no value in the marriage market.[12]

What was worth noticing was the underlying tone of social service that all the intermediaries linked with their work. The three different groups of intermediaries felt strongly that though they charge an amount as service fee, actually they are doing a great service to society by arranging marriages for the *kanyadaygrasta pita*[13] (a father who is burdened with a daughter of marriageable age) as well as for the divorcees and late-marriers since marriage is seen as a 'sacred tie' or as an 'an ever-lasting bond'.

The proprietor of 'Life Partner', a North Kolkata based Bureau, said,

> Marriage is a divine bond. It cannot be mediated as it is pre-fixed, so our role of connecting those pre-established links between people is invaluable.[14]

Netai Chakraborty, an astrologer, mentioned,

> ... Jyotish means *Jyoti* + *Ish*. *Jyoti* means Light and *Ish* is *Ishwar* or God. If we take the words together it means, 'the light of

God' which is over us forever. That is why we always try and render service to mankind.[15]

Besides the ghataks who maintain a strict preference for fixing alliance of 'never married' people, astrologers and marriage bureaus admitted to having a mixed clientele – both in terms of class and marital status. However, in terms of class it is mostly the middle class and upper-middle class who are their regular clients. Two bureaus do not receive applications from divorcees because, in their experience, such marriages encounter a lot of 'problems'. In most cases, divorcees are not happy with the kind of match they get. Their demands are high and intermediaries fail to negotiate that kind of demand. In south Kolkata a bureau which caters specifically to 'divorcees' and 'late marriers' have a clientele of people above the age of forty, having crossed the usual age of being in the 'never married' category. For divorcees, having legal documents of previous divorce is a must since marriage registration has been made compulsory.[16]

There was unanimity among the intermediaries regarding the ideal age of marriage for women and men. It ranged from 21 to 30 years for women and 28 to 35 years for men. Regarding late age of marriage, most of them mentioned that above 30 years for women and above the age of 40 years for men would be considered late. New prospects of education and employment as an effect of globalization, of course for the middle classes, were a cause of discomfort for the intermediaries which had led to a rise in age of marriage. Almost all the bureaus agreed that the average age of marriage has risen but not all of them were happy with such a trend. Too much delay in marriage – especially in the case of women – was not approved. It was not clear whether this was a reflection of social prejudice or a calculation of business interest. A number of concerns were voiced, especially with regard to social and parental discomfort with postponing child-bearing.

The age-gap between men and women considered ideal was also justified in terms of reproduction, though the grounds for such an argument remain unclear. Since there is absolutely no biological justification, social prejudice must rule here too. None of these arguments take into account the extension of women's reproductive age or the much enhanced longevity of the population. The proprietor of 'Marriage Mate' stated,

> If a man would not take the responsibility of child rearing at this age he would become old when he would finally become a father and hence the filial duties would remain neglected by him.[17]

Regarding late age of marriage, certain bureaus commented that since women were in the best of their looks, and at the peak of their reproductive capabilities in their twenties, delaying of marriage further was undesirable. The denial of marriage is simply unthinkable. In keeping with the opinion of the bureaus and ghataks, Haradhan Pal, an astrologer mentioned,[18]

> Marriage within the age of 30 could be accepted but later than that marriage could neither be accepted nor questioned because marriage is a part of our tradition.

Certain bureaus also pointed out that mental adjustment in marriage could be a major problem for couples married at a later age so it is always preferable for women to marry within 30 years and men within 35 years of age.

Hegemonising Demands – Setting Standards for Ideal Brides and Grooms: For prospective bride and groom preference, the stereotypes dominate. Among the working classes, a prospective bride should be 'good-looking', somewhat similar to the middle-class demand of 'tall, fair and slim'. The only demand in a prospective groom is a stable income. Many working class families, the ghataks informed, are ready to pay dowry of rupees fifty thousand or above for getting a suitable match for their daughter, a groom with a stable government job. According to the marriage bureaus, which cater mainly to the middle classes, 'tall, fair and slim' still continue to be the catch line for desired prospective brides. Stable job with a high annual income is the most desired quality of a groom for the 'never married'. It is in keeping with these stereotypical demands that both ghataks and bureaus make it compulsory for their women clients to submit photographs. Working women are preferred by some families but in non-hazardous professions like teaching.[19] Ironically, the quality most desired in brides after beauty is 'homely'. Homely is an adjective defined by the Webster Dictionary as 'ugly', 'unattractive', or 'unappealing'. In Indian English, however, homely means home loving or domesticated. It is a word that recurs in a huge majority of matrimonial advertisements, especially in newspapers. For most Indians being homely is an essential attribute in a prospective bride. Even a working woman must be homely – willing to shoulder the entire burden of household duties. The stereotypical picture of the man revered as master and provider seems to still hold sway over the imagination. Thus, men are valued for providing financial security and stability, while women start as beautiful brides to go on to be housewives and mothers. These gender roles presumed to be entrenched in 'nature' and the needs of reproduction are resistant to change even though social and technological development have outstripped their utility.

Divorcee women still appear to be low in the wish list while for a divorcee male the prospective bride best preferred is 'never married'. In many cases for a divorcee male with a high annual income, demand is met by supply. Until very recently, however, divorce was a stigma and a last resort. Only in the last few years have the younger generation opened up to divorce as a means of exiting unhappy marriages. The rates of divorce have increased considerably. This is certainly the perception of the heads of marriage bureaus and popular matrimonial websites. The CEO of secondshaadi.com reported in *The Telegraph*, 'Do it again':[20] 'The number of people looking for online matrimonial alliances is increasing at the rate of 30 to 50 per cent per year in India. A big chunk of these are divorcees looking for remarriage. Launched in June 2007, secondshaadi.com already has 30,000 members. One of the survey respondents, Mr Ghosh of Happy Life, a central Kolkata based bureau reported:

> I now have a database of divorcee clients of around twenty-five to thirty per cent. Divorce rates have increased radically over the years. I had established this bureau in 1970 and I have noticed this steep rise in percentage of divorce over the years.

With regard to demand for 'working' or 'non-working' women, responses were mixed, the proprietor of a bureau aptly summed up saying,

> People who have experienced divorce learn from their previous experience. If in the previous marriage, the wife was working, they want a homely bride for their second marriage because most of the people are afraid that working women can have extra-marital affairs in office, so they would prefer someone who stays at home. People who have had a divorce-experience with a wife who stayed at home prefer a working bride for their second marriage, so there is demand for both kinds.[21]

In case of women, 'good looks' are always in demand. Divorced women with children were not preferred as compared to divorced women without children who have a comparative advantage in the marriage market. Age was also an important factor for spouse selection especially for divorced men. They preferred 'never-married' younger women or a woman who 'looked young' even if she was a little older. For divorced women, the primary criteria for spouse selection were 'income' and 'stability'. The looks of the groom were not taken into consideration. The proprietor of a bureau in north Kolkata said,

> Looks don't matter for selection of men as for women. In very few instances we get a female candidate who demands a good-looking groom, all the others state that a presentable groom would do. Any sensible person now would vote for a man with high income and proper establishment than good looks.[22]

Few of the bureaus mentioned that for divorced women who have experienced trauma in their first marriage, elements of 'mental adjustment', 'care', 'sharing' and 'bonding' with partner seem more important than financial stability and income.

Late-marrying women are concerned with income, assets and stability. 'Education' and 'family background' are two other important coordinates. Nuclear families are preferred to joint families. Generally, 'never-married' men who are marrying late are the first priority followed by divorced men without children in the list of preference.

Marriage Negotiation Process and the '.com' Companies

Regarding the process of negotiation it was found that all the three intermediaries mixed traditional methods with modern ways. The standard of the modern ways is set by the matrimonial websites that has posed a serious competition to these intermediaries. The indigenous intermediaries modify their practices accordingly.

The ghataks mentioned that after they approach the two-families, i.e. of the prospective bride and groom, and the two parties agree to meet, they also ensure a third meeting of the boy and the girl. They termed this process as 'dating' where according to them; the boy and the girl would meet each other in a neutral place like a shopping mall, restaurant or park and try to gauge their compatibility by interacting with each other. Most of the ghataks expressed their anxiety regarding easily 'failing marriage nowadays' so this dating practice was a must-step in their negotiation process.

Most of the marriage bureaus especially the new ones, which have entered the market within a span of five years, informed, that they also administer a website where their entire database is updated. Their clients can log in with a username and password and check for themselves the type of alliance they want. This website is in certain cases, specially designed so that the search criterion filters the search according to the requirement of the individual. The bureaus also arrange a meeting between the two families wanting to enter into a marriage alliance. This meeting is termed as 'sitting' by the bureaus and most of the proprietors added that 'marriage was after all a family affair'. Therefore, the bureaus monitor websites ensuring that parents of both sides meet and have mutual consent to the match.

Astrologers have a number of clients visiting them for marriage-related problems where mismatch of the *kusti* or *kundli* is seen to be a major problem. The *kusti* of the bride and groom is said to be ideally matching when the 36 *gunas* are judged and according to that the match is fixed. When there is a match of 29 *gunas* and above it is called *Rajjotak*. A marriage can be fixed with 18 *gunas* matching but the greater the number of match the more perfect the adjustment between the couple will be. These *vicharas* are also done by the astrologers and they suggest and offer on-line counselling on these issues and horoscope matching over the net. Stones are suggested as long-time remedies. A few astrologers, also doubling as *vaastu* experts advises *vaastu* remedies.

Conclusion

It can be stated without a speck of doubt that marriage as an institution thrives quite well and so does intermediation. The gendered practices in terms of equating the daughter with a liability for the father still continue to dominate the functioning of the ghataks even today. It is no wonder that the girl child sex ratio from the decadal Census of 2011 records 914 among children aged 0–6 years. The ratio has declined from 976 females (for every 1,000 males) in 1961 to 914 in 2011. Preliminary data from the 2011 Census have recorded many districts with as less as 850.[23] The prevalent patriarchal framework places an ideological bar on any practice which seeks to achieve gender justice. The hegemonic norms of an 'ideal bride' as beautiful, 'tall, fair and slim', 'within 30 years of age', 'working' and such clauses are justified and projected by these intermediaries as the standard to which the 'never married' women have to live up to. The stereotypes across ages are produced and reproduced through such set demands of these intermediaries, where it is expected more from women than men to maintain the standards. The crucial factor is that women have to follow the standards which dominate the marriage market. Such standards are set by tradition and also packaged in a new garb by capitalist commodification and cultures of consumption.

Besides gender bias and hegemonizing patriarchal practices, what is notable is the inevitability and importance of marriage among Indian societies and communities. People with varied marital status continually explore situations and factors of compatibility. Generally speaking, the 'never married' wants to get married, so do the late marriers and the divorcees, quite often, want to re-marry. Being married is considered the ideal position in our societies, as evident from emerging research done on the intermediaries in Kolkata.

Notes

1. Lindsay Harlan and Paul B. Courtright (eds.), *From the Margins of Hindu Marriage: Essays on Gender, Religion and Culture*, Introduction: On Hindu Marriage and Its Margins, Oxford University Press, New York, 1995, p. 6.
2. Men and women who are in the desired age of marriage, i.e. from early 20s to late 20s for women and late 20s to early 30s for men.
3. People who have crossed the usual age of marriage, and are around the age of 40, but are not divorcees.
4. About 0.3 per cent in India according to the Census data of 2001. According to the statistical survey conducted by SWS, JU, it was 0.1 per cent male and 0.4 per cent female divorcees in the sample in urban Kolkata (total males 3,035 and total females 2,904).
5. 'Age Structure and Marital Status', *Census and You: Basic Results from Census 2001 Catalogue and Services*, p. 22.
6. NFHS–3-West-Bengal-state-report.pdf (p. 21) from hetv.org/india/nfhs/index.html, accessed on 4 January 2011.
7. http://www.rchiips.org/pdf/rch3/state/WBengal.pdf, accessed on 4 January 2011.
8. Under the married category, men and women married for a period ranging from a few months to over a year were interviewed.
9. Statistical Survey was conducted in 164 municipal wards of Kolkata and Bidhannagar in 2007–2009 as a part of the project

'Re-Negotiating Gender Relations in Marriage: Family, Class and Community in Kolkata in an Era of Globalization' funded by the Rosa Luxemburg Foundation, Berlin. The total number of respondents in this survey has been 5,939. For details on this project see the report *Re-Negotiating Gender Relations in Marriage: Family, Class and Community in Kolkata in an Era of Globalization*, School of Women's Studies, Jadavpur University, Kolkata, December 2009.

10. Rochona Majumdar, 'Looking for Brides and Grooms: Ghataks, Matrimonial and Marriage Market in Colonial Calcutta, circa 1875–1940', *Journal of Asian Studies*, Vol. 63, No. 4, November 2004, pp. 911–935.
11. Jadav Majumdar, Ghatak, personal interview, 3 August 2009, translated by the author.
12. Proprietor, Match-Fix, personal interview, 9 September 2009, translated by the author.
13. This is termed in Bengali as *Kanyadaygrasta Pita* (*Kanya* is the daughter, *Dayagrasta* means burdened and *Pita* is the father). In literal rendering the word means a father who is burdened with a daughter of marriageable age until and unless she is married to a person who can take charge of her.
14. Proprietor, 'Life Partner', personal interview, 6 September 2009, translated by the author.
15. Netai Chakraborty, astrologer, personal interview, 16 September 2009, translated by the author.
16. Registration of marriages had become mandatory in West Bengal from 4 February 2008; see *Times of India*, 1 February 2008.
17. Proprietor, 'Marriage Mate', personal interview, 9 November 2009, translated by the author.
18. Haradhan Pal, astrologer, personal interview, 19 September 2009, translated by the author.
19. Fixed working hours would allow the wife to give total attention to the housework after pursuing a profession.
20. 'Do it Again', *The Telegraph*, Wednesday, 27 February 2008.
21. Proprietor, Life Partner, personal interview, 6 September 2009, translated by the author.
22. Proprietor, Marriage Bazaar, personal interview, 6 September 2009, translated by the author.
23. 'Sex Ratio, Patriarchy and Ethics', *The Hindu*, Editorial, Sunday, 1 May 2011, p. 8.

Further Readings

Bhadra, M., 'Changing Age at Marriage of Girls in India', *International Journal of Anthropology*, Vol. 15, Nos 1 and 2, 2000: 33–50.

Donner, Henrike, *Domestic Goddesses: Maternity, Globalization and Middle-Class Identity in Contemporary India*, Ashgate Publishing, Farnham, 2008.

Harlan, Lindsay and Paul B. Courtright (eds.), *From the Margins of Hindu Marriage: Essays on Gender, Religion and Culture*, Introduction: On Hindu Marriage and Its Margins, Oxford University Press, New York, 1995.

Majumdar, Rochona, *Marriage and Modernity: Family Values in Colonial Bengal*, Oxford University Press, New Delhi, 2009.

Misra, Kamal K. and Janet Huber Lowry (eds), *Recent Studies on Indian Women: Empirical Work of Social Scientists*, Rawat Publications, Jaipur and New Delhi, 2007.

Modi, Perveez, 'Love-Marriage and the Law in Delhi', *Modern Asian Studies*, Vol. 36, No. 1, 2002: 223–256.

Re-Negotiating Gender Relations in Marriage: Family, Class and Community in Kolkata in an Era of Globalization, School of Women's Studies, Jadavpur University, Kolkata, December 2009.

Scrase, Tim, 'The New Middle Class in India', paper presented to the 16th Biennial Conference of the Asian Studies Association of Australia in Wollongong, 26–29 June 2006, http://coombs.anu.edu.au/SpecialProj/ASAA/biennial-conference/2006/Scrase-Tim-ASAA2006.pdf, accessed on 14 February 2010.

Uberoi, Patricia, *Freedom and Destiny: Gender, Family and Popular Culture in India*, Oxford University Press, New Delhi, 2006.

CHAPTER 6

Internet Arranged Marriages

Passions of the Indian Eve

NAMRATHA MOGARAL

Even though the *Hindu Shastras* advocate at least seven different types of marriage, the custom of arranged marriage has dominated from time immemorial. In the past, this custom may have been practised in other parts of the world but only in India has it prevailed so much, so that today India, is identified by its 'unique' culture. The practice is so strongly prevalent that even communities other than Hindu have adopted it. Advocates of arranged marriage today hold it as the most civilized form of mate selection as opposed to a natural one based on biological affinity. They also argue that this method of mate selection is most rational and realistic. Both of these qualities are a must for enduring marriage, since permanence in sexual relations is viewed as important for a well-ordered society.

Characterizing Arranged Marriage in India

Several distinct features of the custom of arranged marriage may be listed here. First of all, mate selection and fixing of marriage is carried out by a third party, a 'match fixer' who may be a total outsider in terms of kinship of the marrying individuals. There may be several criteria for selection; social, such as caste and community, *kula and gothra* (i.e. ancestors), economic, such as ownership of property and profession or in today's lingo, class. But the most important of them is the criteria of matching horoscopes drawn on the basis of the accurate time of birth.

We can make the following observations: humans' sexual relation is primarily governed by social and economic rather than biological norms, and is long term rather than seasonal. Marriage is, therefore, never a matter between two individuals but involves whole family and more often the community also. A third observation is that there is a preference for wider and wider selection rather than limiting it to the immediate community.

Arranged Marriages Today

The tradition of arranged marriage in India has taken a new fillip with the advent of online matchmaking sites. If the number of such websites that have cropped up in the last decade and the estimate of membership on them are to be considered, then this culture has especially caught the wannabe middle-class marriage market, which in India today is an ever-burgeoning stratum. The diversity of websites that have emerged in the last six to ten years, which one can access either individually or via an agent for no great cost, stand testimony to this. Under the umbrella label of matchmaking for marriages these websites offer a range of services centred around sex-gender related institutions and practices ranging from family to housing, beauty to vacationing. The more adventurous of them offer daring short-term liaisons from purely platonic dating to hot one-night affairs. Others offer fully fledged relationships described conventionally. Most of these websites claim to cater to individualized needs and choices. For instance, a woman wanting to upload her biodata with a view to locating a suitable match is at liberty to express her needs including the traditional categories like caste, class and horoscope or she may forgo all these and project herself as a liberal free individual.

Several prominent factors explain the rise of internet arranged marriages. First among them is clear that the phenomenon is mainly the outcome of the growth of the new media and their general availability to everyone. The invention of the user-friendly graphical multi-user domain has lead to unprecedented use of the internet, globally. The other important factor is the increasing global migration away from local communities. The internet marriage sites seem to organize a virtual community which compensates for the loss of location.

There is a good point in comparing internet matchmaking sites to the traditional *dalali* translated as broker or graft. Customarily the dalali or the matchmaker is a key person in the practice of arranged marriage. The dalali functions as a go-between the two parties for a commission. In a traditional society the *dalali* was an informal profession usually performed by the *jyothish* (the horoscope reader) as a spin-off. But the dalali could be anyone and also of either sex, who had a high mobility among the various interrelated castes and communities, was seldom related to the persons wanting to marry and often adopted specific castes or community to work on. In the twentieth century many institutions developed, which play the role of the *dalali* or aid them in matchmaking. These institutions are greatly brought about by urbanization and migration from village to cities and by the growth of the mass media. Some of these are the marriage bureaus or centres, alongwith newspapers and other media-driven matrimonial columns.

Characterizing Online Marriage Websites

Online matchmaking websites are basically electronic databases of eligible men and women desiring to marry. The database may be accessed by either logging on to the website via the internet by taking an individual membership or via another person acting on behalf. Membership is usually free but if one opts for the full range of services offered by the sites then, in order to get the best, it is better to opt for the paid membership. Taking a membership whether free or paid allows one to publish one's profile and expectations online and add to the database but only paid member may view freely all the profiles registered with the sites. Paid membership can range for duration of three months to six months, which may be extended until one finds a suitable match.

But it is insufficient to describe these websites as merely databases. They can be better defined as web induced social networking for the purpose of mate selecting. This becomes clearer when we observe that these websites are a digital simulation of our real world which is structured by the meta stratification factors of our age such as nationality, community, class and region. The technology used in constructing the website is specially designed to segregate the data according to several criteria relating to them.

In addition to this it must be emphasized that the websites are oriented towards the market. As in the case of other media such as TV, companies looking to do businesses advertise on the network and function as sponsors. Therefore, undertaking a liaison with the help of these websites is a package affair that ties up with a range of other goods being sold on these same websites, such as fashion, food, entertainment (like partying at a restaurant or a short holiday during courtship, or a beauty pageant for a group of prospective couples) and housing goods. The package may even include small time jobs and the news media. A marriage so contracted may cover, if one is willing to shell out the money, counselling for modes of courtship, beauty tips for the couple involved, with follow up on family planning and setting up house. Themes are offered for the actual marriage ceremony with ready-made venues and honeymoon spots.

Thus, while characterizing online matchmaking we must make the important observation that they are not just a database but a *virtual community* shaped, one by technology; two by the market forces, and three by sociocultural forces such as caste, religion, and region. It is on this account that the new phenomenon differs from both the traditional *dalali* or even newspaper matrimonial and the marriage bureau. Online matchmaking is of a different species on many accounts.

It is in this view that paper is a study of the cultural dynamics of web induced matchmaking. It is an attempt to answer the questions such as: What is the nature of the cultural space created by online matchmaking? What are the factors that shape it and how in turn it impacts on our existing spaces? How are the normative categories of gender, caste, class and religion addressed by these matchmaking sites. Most importantly, what does it mean for our sexuality?

Methodology, Scope and Limitations of this Paper

The scope of my paper is limited to the study of mainly four websites, the most visible and prolific among them, namely *jeevansaathi.com, shaadi.com, bharatmatrimony.com* and *lava.com*. Even though all the four sites give online matchmaking services they have differences. *Jeevansaathi.com,* the oldest of the websites boasts of a million of profiles, is an offshoot of naukri.com and is still affiliated to the parent site. In addition it also collaborates with other sister services like investment banking. It further networks with offline marriage counselling centres named Match point Centres located in almost all the major cities all over India and in the US and UK. *Shaadi.com* has some of these features. It further networks with Shaadi Dish TV. Bharatmatrimony on the other hand grew as an offshoot of newspaper matrimonial advertising and still runs the column. This online database networks with the newspaper column ads and marriage centres located in all the major cities of India. The last of these websites *Lava.com* is the more adventurous of them, in that it offers in addition to marriage matchmaking, possibility for dating and finding friends (not necessarily leading to marriage) and other kinds of short-term liaisons.

In addition to the above four matchmaking sites two more sites need to be described here namely *CommunityMatrimony. com* and *GreatMatrimony.com* (or *Indianmatrimony.com*). The specialty of these sites is that they advertise specifically on caste based matchmaking. For instance, Communitymatrimony.com which is a network of 350 websites, each dedicated to specific castes has the following text inscribed under their trademark: 'An exclusive matrimony service catering to every community'.

'In India it is still believed that marriage within the community is healthy, happy and strengthens the bond within the community. *CommunityMatrimony.com* is a union of over 350 community matrimony sites catering to the unique needs of various communities. Start your community search now!'

Membership on this marriage site is only for persons seeking a match either of Indian nationality or of Indian origin and Indian heritage. This is also the case with *Great Matrimony.com,* even though it 'offers matrimonial solutions to our customers worldwide' and has networking in India and Dubai. While *CommunityMatrimony.com* has even wider network covering US, Malaysia and Australia.

On an average, charges for membership on any of these websites can range from ₹ 3,000 for a 3-month membership to ₹ 5,000 for a 6-month membership. The cost could further mount if one opts for higher-end technology driven modes like e-mail, chatting, and video conferencing. Features like dish TV showcasing (as one website estimates, reaches up to 3.5 million subscribers) further add to the cost. There is no doubt that mate selection is treated seriously and provided with such a massive choice!

Before I launch into my findings, a word about the method I pursued. I had to take a free membership of one of the marriage websites in order to browse it. Even though this yielded to me a mine of information, I must confess that it can be said to be only a preliminary research since I haven't delved into the site all the way leading to a real marriage. In addition, meeting the counsellors especially at the offline centres with which the website is coordinated is an excellent idea but which I have not undertaken here.

The newsletter published by the website was an important source of information and has personal accounts of successfully married couples. I also received e-mails offering information on types of membership, modes of contacting possible suitors such as chatting, and voice mailing. I regularly also received offers for other services ranging from showcase in a TV matrimonial programme to investment and finance information. Browsing FAQs of the websites was of great help. My paper also draws from personal accounts of real people who married with the help of one of the websites.

Theories of Virtuality and Role of Technology

Cultural experts and optimists have characterized the new media as a free and liberal space not bound by traditional biases, prejudices, oppressions and inequalities (Levy, 2001). The internet is supposedly a plastic space of freedom, in which one can shape one's identity and future as one wants. In a country like India stymied in the hegemonic discourses of caste, religion and communal divides, the new media is often posed as providing a new space to get away from the existing social, economic and other constraints. In a direction that is contradicting and which invites scrutiny, looking at the growing popularity of internet arranged marriages today, we can see that it has given a new twist to the custom of arranged marriage in India. As I said earlier, there may be other factors such as increased migration which have boosted online matchmaking but it is clear that the tie-up between the new media and dominant discourses of traditional customs has made arranged marriages even more attractive. Arranged marriage has become almost a symbol of liberal and political correctness in India today. And these websites have begun emerging as a virtual India, albeit a hyper real one.

In the recent years much research has gone into theorizing the nature of virtuality. Let me review some of them in order to understand the nature of online matchmaking social networking. Terms like 'digital simulation' have labelled the virtual world created by cyber technology. The concept of simulation (Turkle, 1999) is often understood as opposing to representation. A simulated world is not the depiction or reflection of any real world or picture but a world in itself. Only, this world is not made of real objects or people but electronic signals. But the simulated nature of the cyber world is concealed by its 'mimicry' of the real by the use of navigation tools and icons that parallel those of the real. Mimicry always differs from the mimicked object by virtue of being a mime or a parody. But in the virtual world the mimicry serves to close the distance between the real world and the simulated and creates a sense of reassurance of the absent world to be close at hand. Thus, the user is made to feel as if they are navigating the real world of people and things (Stallabrass, 1999). Further it has also been argued that virtual culture tends to 'suppress the complexities' (Robins and Webster, 1999) of the real world. This is in order to avoid confronting with conflict and indeterminacy. It won't do business for these websites to cast a doubt at the normative visions of our society. Profit is in avoiding conflict and confrontation; in avoiding indeterminacy.

Another label developed to understand the virtual reality and online social networking is 'translocalization' (Kupenian, 2004). This approximately means creating communities across or beyond specific geographical locations. Most translocated communities do not owe allegiance to any fixed location or geography. A person navigating such a translocal space may be called as 'virtual self'(s) (Negroponte, 1996). The virtual self can be an extension of the self but not its representative or its voice. It is more apt to view this virtual self as another version of the self. There is always a distance and tension between the real self and the virtual, if not outright conflict.

Online marriage sites are no doubt digital simulations of our real world on the basis of mimicry of the real world. This mimicry is the technological rationalization of the real world serving to legitimize the hegemonic stratification factors. Moreover, they serve as spaces of socialization that enforce these divisions even more strictly than in the real. They demonstrate to us how technology can be used to create preprogrammed social cultural space.

While registering a profile ready-made software provides a pre-list of castes and religions for one to choose from. The list is so exhaustive and labels such a large number of castes that it overwhelms. Anyone who fails to choose out of the list is liable to leave his or her profile incomplete. The database, thus, is finely sorted out under several criteria such as religion, caste, profession, region and city, mother tongue and community. Searching the database for a possible choice of spouse is guided by the same software mainly by these criteria.

The software is also ideologically pre-structured in such a way that it is mainly oriented towards the middle classes. This class is further bifurcated in terms of money (or rather buying potential) and property – as rich, affluent, upper and middle class and outlook such as orthodox, conservative, moderate and liberal. This successfully bars the poor from entering into the fray. Similarly, there is also a reorientation to the urban by the limitation of choice of professions and vocations to middle class, white-collared – Government PSU, Private, Self-employed, Defense and Business – even though concession for 'agriculture' as an option is presented in one of the sites.

The orientation towards the urban is further highlighted by another list providing a choice of possible cities of origin choosing from which is mandatory even if one's hometown does not match by any stretch of imagination and one ends up feeling a little guilty for stretching it. For an exception one of them Communitymatrimonial.com does address diversity as <graminmatrimony.com> <40plusmatrimony.com> and <divorceematrimony.com> It also has an <intercastematrimony.com> (or Anycastematrimony.com) site '... for people who look beyond the caste system and are willing to marry from any caste. Lakhs of people from totally different castes and lifestyles come together in their particular search on this site ...' But, of course, the search criterion here again is caste.

In addition, in the virtual world created by these websites the identity of individuals is dominated by family and communal factors. Personal yardsticks that relate to the sexual identity such as looks, colour, height, interests and aspiration take a back seat even though they come next to the community and social factors. Profiles are sifted by software by colour, height and physical disability also but only secondarily. Even though marriage is related to the sexual choice of two individuals and is an intensely intimate business, the new form of online arranged marriage belies this. Individual's sexual choice is thus successfully subordinated to communal and other social factors. An internet arranged marriage is the first marriage between families and communities and only secondarily between two rational individuals.

One can only conclude that online social networks such as these are unashamedly affirmative of all the divisiveness of our real world and do not keep any of the promises that the new media is supposedly to have for the coming generations. As one of the sites claims 'Our vision is to make the search for life partner so easy as your dream partner knocks your door to marry with you'. Who would have thought that this dream partner has the labels of caste, class, region and employment fixed on him or her! These websites thus function to complete the socialization of individuals into the idea of a socio-cultural world as normatively structured by these labels; in doing so, they legitimize the prevailing world-view of our times.

Market as Shaping Force

We come to the other aspect and equally primary of online matchmaking, that is, the role and impact of the market. As I said earlier online matchmaking is different from the traditional *dalali* (go between) arrangement because the websites are promoted by other businesses that sell a diversity of goods which are using the matchmaking social networks as hub. Not only people using the sites are potential customers for a range of goods such as banking and finances, property and jobs, household appliances furnishing, food health, beauty and entertainment but they are also potential market carriers and indirect sellers. In fact, anyone logging on to these websites is the target of new goods and services being tested in the market.

One can only say that online marriage sites serve to create a nexus of sexual needs of humans, commodity and exhibitionist visual media with its reality shows and game shows. It is redefining human sexual identity in a hybrid between traditional categories of family and marriage and the market categories of commodity, consumer and market mover. A case in point is the growing entertainment or better called 'pleasure' industry. This is a new market reaching the larger section of our society via the internet such as spas, dance joints, sex, drugs, food, game parks picnic themes and so on.

The question is, of course, how women are located in this market economy. The emphasis on traditional categories of caste community and family over individual qualifiers that is found in conjunction with the tie-up with the market only intensifies the role of women as consumers and market movers. The primacy given to community and family serves to affirm the traditional sexual roles in the family over the individual to suit the economic interests of investors in the internet hypermarket.

Here, it is useful to relate how women are positioned by the phenomenon of online matchmaking to a theory of consumption that Mary Douglas proposes in her book *World of Goods* (1979). She theorizes consumption in the following manner: consumption does not just involve merely the using up of purchased goods but the participation of the user in a process of structuring of our social reality. This is done by 'marking' of consumers on the basis of their consumption patterns. Ultimately, consumption enables the classification of people on the basis of their consumption. The types of consumption rituals that persons can participate in, determine their position in society. Women of course are key participants in the ritual of consumption in tradition bound societies owing to their roles within the private sphere in, which the actual rituals of consumption is carried out.

From this view it is clear that if the technological rationalization, underlying the digitally simulated virtual space, legitimizes the hegemonic stratification factors that inform our real society, the websites relation to the market parallels and intensifies this relation by legitimizing gender roles and traditional family norms. These social networking spaces provide systems of intelligibility for enacting and legitimizing gendered social relations, and identities that are divisive and enslaved to market, as if they are the inevitable reflection of our real society.

Conclusion

To conclude, online matchmaking may be called as a neophyte socio-economic practice by which the dominant discourses as traditional family and community norms are being yoked to the public sphere of trade and commerce. The technology-driven websites are not merely databases but digital simulations of the real world which legitimize and enforce dominant views of it. This enterprise can only intensify class and gender struggles and requires vigilance.

References

Douglas, M., *The World of Goods*, Basic Books, New York, 1979.

Kupenian, J., 'Internet, Translocalization and Cultural Brokerage in the Pacific', in Jari Kupenian et al. (eds.), *Cultural Identity in Transition*, Atlantic Publishers, New Delhi, 2002.

Levy, P., *Cyberculture*, R. Bononno (trans.), University of Minnesota Press, Minneapolis, 2001.

Maffesoli, M., *The Time of the Tribes: The Decline of Individualism in Mass Society*, Sage, London, 1996.

Negroponte, N., *Being Digital*, Alfred A. Knopf, New York, 1996.

Robins, K. and E. Webster, *Times of the Technocultures: From the Information Society to Virtual Life*, Routledge, London, 1999.

Stallabrass, J., 'The Ideal City and the Virtual Hive: Modernism and Emergent Order in Computer Culture', in J. Downey and J. McGriegun (eds.), *Technocities*, Sage, London, 1999.

Turkle, S., 'Identity in the Age of Internet', in T. Mackay and T.O. Sullivan (eds.), *The Media Reader Continuity and Transformation*, Sage, London, 1999.

CHAPTER 7

Caste-Based Prostitution

Caste, Marriage and Prostitution

ANWESHA GHOSH

> 'Here why can every fifth man
> Only speak in the language of my body,
> How I wish
> Someone should say
> You're such a hard worker, Sugiya
> And so innocent and honest.
> If only someone would say that!'[1]
>
> —Sugiya, by Nirmala Putul
> ('Sex Determination', *Little Magazine*, p. 103)

There are a whopping 6,88,751 'registered' sex workers in the country. The reply by the Ministry of Health and Family Welfare to a response to a Right to Information (RTI) filed by Ved Pal also reveals that the southern states have the largest number of sex workers in the country, at least on government records. Andhra Pradesh leads the list with more than one lakh registered female women in prostitution while Karnataka has 79,000 (Interestingly, there is not a single sex worker as per government records in Dadra and Nagar Haveli as well as Daman and Diu). Jammu and Kashmir has the least number of registered sex workers – 259). Among the metros, Delhi leads the list. Though the capital has only one known red-light area, GB Road, there are

37,900 sex workers – more than those in India's financial capital, Mumbai. Experts say a large number of sex workers in the country go undetected in government records. National Aids Control Organization (NACO) estimates the total number of sex workers in India to be 12.63 lakh.[2]

Hence, from the above one can conclude that prostitution is a raving trade and whether one wants to hide away from it – it is here to stay. Indian feminists have been divided into two groups over the issue of prostitution. The first group is driven by the motive of 'rehabilitation' of women in prostitution, which has a strong support from the policy makers. The second group is driven by the motive of 'unionizing' of women in prostitution, who believe that prostitution is considered as any other work and hence the stigmatization be stopped. The rationale being that women in prostitution are in a way social workers (Gangoli, 2008). Though it is heartening to know that both these groups are against under-age women in prostitution (child sexual abuse), nonetheless it is unfortunate that there has been very few advocators who have questioned the actual root of prostitution – caste, class and patriarchy. Many NGOs are actively involved in working with brothel as well as non-brothel type of prostitution. There's no dearth of local as well as international funding for programmes and activities focused on women in prostitution, especially after the AIDS scare that began in early 1990s. Yet, the number of women in prostitution continues to be on the rise with each year and United Nations Office on Drugs and Crime (UNODC) now claims trafficking for the purpose of prostitution is the most profitable venture, even higher than drugs (UNODC, 2001). Women, willingly or unwillingly, across the world, legitimately or illegally, continue to sell their bodies in large numbers,

Women in prostitution are no doubt at the margins of the society. However, there is one such group within this already marginalized group which is further vulnerable owing to its nature and structure – caste-based or community-based prostitution. The voice of this form of prostitution has largely been silent. Some of the international bodies like Human Rights Watch have also acknowledged prostitution as form of oppressive caste-based labour, along with scavenging and bondage. In this form of prostitution, prostitution becomes the primary caste occupation of the entire community, thereby lending it social legitimacy and sanction. Women belonging to *Nat, Rajnat, Bedia,* and *Kanjar* communities of Rajasthan, Haryana and Madhya Pradesh have been practicing commercial sex for a long time (Swarankar, 2008). Historically, women of these communities were mainly '*nautch* girls' (professional Indian dancing girls) who performed during fairs and festivals. They would get gifts and money in return for their performances. They were part of the *Jajmani* system[3] and had relationship of *Jajaman-Jachak* (patron and performer) in the traditional social structure.

This dissertation primarily focuses on the women of the Perna community, which is also involved in community-based prostitution. What makes this community different from the others of its likes – the *Nats, Bedias,* etc. – is that unlike the others, amongst the Perna, women join the sex trade after their marriage. As such, it offers a fascinating insight in a society that puts marriage, economics, social sanction and family, as we know it on its head. The entire social structure is defined by economics of the sex trade while the community has its own social rules and moral codes to be able to exist as a community.

Literature on prostitution has been mostly descriptive about prostitution in colonial times and more recently on the rights of the women in prostitution. Across the world, women in prostitution have begun to unite and are demanding worker's rights and status. There are debates on whether prostitution be considered as 'work' and not 'exploitation'; can women in prostitution be considered as 'victims' at all times, should prostitution be legalized? Interestingly, all of these debates and issues become irrelevant when it is put in the context of caste-based prostitution. Prostitution in case of the Perna is ritually sanctioned by the community; prostitution is the caste occupation and women in prostitution here are neither 'victim' nor 'chooser', they are by virtue of their birth destined to be women in prostitution. However, there's not enough literature on this parallel universe of community-based prostitution, especially in the academic circles, though many NGOs have been working with pockets of such communities. This paucity of literature on community-based prostitution along with my brief encounter with the Perna community five years back, has led me to take on this topic for my MPhil dissertation. For the purpose of this dissertation, I have undertaken the study of Perna community at Dharampura, (Najafgarh) in New Delhi.

Introduction to the Pernas

History of Origin

Pernas were nomadic shepherds and are known to be originally from North-West Frontier Province (NWFP), Pakistan. Pernas were initially a moving nomadic tribe and they would put up temporary *jhuggis* (slum dwellings) wherever they wished. The community settled down around mid–1975 when the Pradhan of a village called Rewla Khanpur, who incidentally had relations with a Perna woman, offered them the village land. The Pernas were mainly nomadic shepherds who would beg in fairs and temple complexes while the women were '*nautch* girls' in community fairs who also indulged in prostitution during fairs and festivals. Today, they still rear cattle and continue their primary caste occupation of prostitution.

Social Structure

From being nomadic tribes during the 19th century (Rose, 1997: 164), the Pernas have been conferred Other Backward Class (OBC) status in independent India. They now reside in various pockets in and around Rewadi, Bulandshahr, Delhi, Rohtak and other parts of Haryana. They live in small exclusive hamlets and are endogamous in nature; e.g. in a particular case, it was found that the eldest sister was the mother-in-law of the youngest sibling. Children are married between the age of 10–12 years and the *gauna* (ceremony associated with consummation of marriage) happens within a year of the girl gaining puberty. The community practices polygamy; in most cases for economic reasons, although that is not always the case. There is a strong presence of son-preference as it is the daughters-in-law who gets into prostitution. The gender relationship is patriarchal in nature and in most cases though there is recognition of the woman being the main bread earner, her social status is lower than the man of the family.

Community Structure

The community at Dharampura, near Najafgarh in Delhi, consists of 40 households. They live in *pucca* houses (concrete houses with roof) with no water supply from the government or in-built toilets owing to a non-existent drainage system, though most of them have government documents like ration cards or electoral cards. However, they all have high-end televisions, cars or motorcycles, refrigerators, air-coolers, etc. which are more of status symbols, and they lack the affordability of buying petrol for their vehicles. In spite of such consumption patterns and material comforts, the families live in very squalid and unhygienic conditions with low nutritional levels. Their sheep and goats live within the same premises with them.

The community has first-generation learners owing to the efforts of the YWCA Rural Development programme (though most of the children irrespective of sex, drop out by class 8th). Girls from the community also have been learning newer skills at this centre. Institutional birthing is still low, antenatal and post-natal care is negligible and vaccination levels (except polio) are very low. Though, there has been rise in the level of condom-usage but the average number of children per household continues to be around 5. The community as a whole is very hostile to the idea of HIV testing as it considers it as a threat to its caste occupation of prostitution.

Modus Operandi/Economic Structure

Once the girl gives birth to her first child, she is sent into the profession. In earlier times, 'the first child was given as a gift to the grandmother as a compensation for the loss of the mother's gains as a prostitute' (ibid.). However, the custom has long been forgotten. At present, the husband and the sons operate as pimps. Younger, more 'desirable' girls are sent to the farmhouses dotting the peripheries of Delhi, mainly catering to middle-class and upper-middle clients, earning up to ₹ 5,000 a night. The number of clients varies. Those who operate on the streets, which is the case with Dharampura women, the rates vary between ₹ 50 to ₹ 200 per client. The older women have a client portfolio of truckers and bus-drivers, operating on the Delhi-Jaipur highway at Dhaula Kuan sometimes for as little as ₹ 35. The oldest women accompany the other younger women as guardians and 'managers' for them and get a commission in return. The positive point that has come to be seen amongst the women in this particular community is that they all insist on the clients using the condoms and have also known to refuse clients who do not wish to use condoms. These women work from 5 am to 9 am and unlike the women in Rewla Khanpur, have to take the buses to their areas of solicitations. Violence on part of the clients is not unknown. These women have sometimes been abducted by a group of unruly men and gang-raped. Unfortunately, there are no safeguards against such high-handedness.

Women are active in prostitution till the age of 55 years or till her health permits. In recent times, other than prostitution and sheep rearing, the elders of the community have taken to begging and the teenage boys assist the *ghodi-wala* (horse holder) during wedding season. Men of the community are mostly seasonal workers. They are known to be part of the entourage surrounding the *baraat* (bridegrooms wedding procession) during the marriage season. Other than that, they either work in meat shops as assistants or are involved in other petty jobs. Prostitution is the primary source of income. The Pernas consider their women as primary workers but are not free from their primary responsibilities of domestic drudgery and child rearing.

Research Methodology

I have used both primary and secondary data using qualitative method in this study. As secondary data – interviews of NGOs involved with the community – YWCA[4] and MRYDO[5] (Najafgarh, Delhi) as well as literature, directly and distantly related to the objective of the study mentioned above were reviewed. Owing to the nature of the research, purposive sampling method has been used. Primary data of qualitative nature were collected through personal interviews and focus group discussions from the *Dharampura* community.

Literature Review

According to Indian sociologist Dube[6], jatis (castes) are endogamous units, which are hierarchically graded, having a jati-linked occupation. Considerations of purity and pollution determine the interaction between different units and the members of a jati generally share a common culture – the way of life, which is transmitted from one generation to the next by learning and not by biological inheritance. Jatis also have intra-village and inter-village mechanisms of social control and conflict resolution. However, as communities migrate from villages to urban settings, there is greater scope for social mobility. So, while owing to compulsions and temptations outside their little societies, many communities have adjusted the jati rules of commensality; caste rules have not relaxed to the same extent (Stern, 2003). Even in the case of the Pernas though they are an endogamous group, their caste and occupational identity is not open to change, but their lifestyle is strongly influenced by consumerist aspirations. The presence of television in the daily lives, as Rajagopal points out, blurs the boundaries between public and private, and the satellite and cable television becomes an almost tangible intrusion of the outside (the urban lifestyle based on consumerism) into the domain of the most private, sacred, and vulnerable space – the home. So, while a community may have kept their 'private' domains closed to prodding eyes of strangers, the public-private distinction is not distinct in the culturally global world.

The end of the 19th century gave rise to a new, trans-local identity among 'lower castes' collectively as a people with the consciousness of being 'oppressed' by the traditional system of hierarchy. The established categories of the ritual hierarchy was confronted with new categories called the 'depressed castes' and the 'oppressed classes'. The discourse on caste in post-independent India remained bogged down in the dichotomous debate on 'tradition' versus 'modernity' and 'caste' versus 'class' (Sheth, 2009: 2503–2504). In this case, Sheth discusses what he calls 'classization' of caste through the process of de-ritualization and politicization of caste. Caste consciousness is now articulated as political consciousness of groups staking claims to power and to new places in the changed opportunity of structure. It is a different kind of collective consciousness from that of belonging to a 'high' or 'low' ritual status-group. 'This disintegrating system of traditional statuses is now thickly overlaid by the new power system created by elections, political parties and, above all, by social policies such as 'affirmative action of the state'.

Interestingly, the Pernas are an OBC category with some settlements situated in Haryana that has a strong political presence of OBCs. Their caste identity, in spite of politicization, has not yielded any benefits and they continue to live in peripheries of the urban centres with no drinking water or sanitary facilities. Affirmative action has led to no real change in their circumstance. Sheth says, 'Fundamental changes have occurred in the occupational structure of the society ... the traditional ritualistic idea of cleanliness ... of the occupation one follows is unimportant; crucial consideration is what brings a good income to the individual'. In case of the Pernas, the caste occupation rather than the politicization of caste identity is what maintains the community. They are marginalized owing to their 'traditional' occupation and thus, have been situated on the peripheries of the city. According to Leela Fernandes (2004), the production of middle class identity is linked to 'spatial purifications' that centres on middle class claims over public spaces and a corresponding movement to cleanse such spaces of the poor, which she terms as the political project of forgetting subordinated social groups.

There has been very little literature or research done on caste-based 'prostitution'. Prostitution is considered as sex outside those relationships where sex is usually permitted. In prostitution, we often have the man forcing his wife into prostitution and in the case of the Pernas; the entire community legitimizes a married woman's participation in prostitution. This case is different from other communities like the *Nat, Rajnat, Kanjar* and *Bedias,* where female sex workers (FSWs) do not marry into other communities and only unmarried women are allowed to practice, usually to earn bride price for their brothers; in case of the Pernas, only married women are allowed to enter the sex trade after giving birth to their first child. This social truth provides a range of analysis and cannot fit into existing theories and assumptions related to prostitution. The perception and value systems about sex and attitude towards sexuality and sexual relations of such communities/castes are different from the normative pattern of high caste Hindus and requires rigorous research (Swarankar, 2008: 118). This paper makes a humble beginning in this domain.

Analysis

Common caste practices continue in spite of change in 'lifestyle'. For the Pernas, being shepherds and prostitutioners are a part of their caste identity and even though they are no more nomadic tribes, they continue to keep sheep and goats at home as well as carry on the profession of sex-work. They live in squalid surroundings, a characteristic found among lower castes in India (the idea of purity and pollution gains some currency here). As such, it has been observed in Dharampura that in spite of *pucca* houses and consumer goods, the Perna community here continues to live in unhygienic and squalid environs, which is found to be typical with the lower castes in rural and semi-urban belts. The debate of purity and pollution can be cited in this case. Higher the jati the more complex and elaborate are the rules regarding the maintenance of 'purity and avoidance' of 'pollution' (Dube, 1990: 55).

The Perna woman continues to play traditional feminine roles in the household; she continues to be the wife of the house and takes care of all domestic and child-rearing work. It has been observed, that women often agree to their husband's multiple marriages as this gives them some respite from the drudgery of household work. Simply put, marriage norms, roles and structures are followed according to caste and societal scriptures; the thing that changes is the control of sexuality and mobility of women. In case of the Pernas, the sexuality of a married woman becomes a caste property in the form of caste occupation. Unlike *jati* Hindus, the man does not control the wife's sexuality as part of family honour, here a married woman's sexuality is controlled for material gains.

As in most castes in India, the Perna men continue to dominate women even though it is the latter's bodies that help them earn. Women are oppressed and dependent on the men. Disagreement to join the profession can lead to violent outbursts. Even if the woman keeps the money in her name, it is usually paid towards buying a common property. As such, agency of women vis-à-vis their participation in the occupation is curtailed either by socialization or by violence; and the agency to choose clients are not in their hands as the husbands and sons act as pimps and managers. The men take all major household decisions. Polygamy is tolerated in the disguise of economic gain but it often leads to the desertion of the first wife by the husband. This woman then has to look for other male relatives who might get her clients and thereby earn something for her children.

Owing to the fact that daughters-in-law are the main income earners, male children are of utmost importance. The sons marry within the community and bring in the primary earner. Yet the irony of it lies in the fact that while women are recognized as the source of livelihood it is only through their relationship with men. Men being pimps and managers control the entire trade. The woman's body is commodified and put up for sale. As such, the Perna women have no say in the negotiations or the kind of work they would like to take up. Only recently, there have been instances where some girls refuse to enter prostitution but they are under constant pressure to join. Since there is a requisite that women enter the trade only after their first child is born, these girls are postponing their first pregnancies by taking pills or inserting intrauterine devices (IUDs) without the knowledge of their families. Domestic violence – both verbal and physical – is quite common amongst the Pernas. Informal separation is not rare but since women lack the managerial role, they have to be dependent on their male relatives. It is only the present generation of teenage girls who are willing to find alternative work.

Conclusion

This paper is only an initial attempt to understand caste, marriage and economics of prostitution and exploitation of women in communities engaged in caste-based prostitution. The Pernas as a case study offer a completely new perspective even within known structures of caste-based prostitution and hence give a unique opportunity to analyse a new distinctive community and how the agencies of patriarchy function in this community.

Various sociologists, anthropologists and other scholars for a long time now, have done the analysis of caste and marriage. The institution of marriage has been considered the bedrock of any society. Caste identities are manifested and strengthened with marriage. As a result, marriage and caste identity are intrinsically linked. However, for long, marriage within caste has been looked upon as a control over a woman's sexuality that in turn, has led to low status of women in family as well as the community. However, in case of caste-based prostitution, the entire idea of marriage, as we know it is put on its head. A woman's sexuality in case of a community like the Perna is not considered a family honour. The control on a woman's sexuality is in the form of coercion to join the caste occupation of prostitution – the control has a material basis. Marriage, here, has a pure economic basis. Domestic violence is tolerated in spite of the women being the primary earners in the community. The consciousness of being a 'victim' or a 'chooser' never arises as the community sanction leads to the fact that prostitution is a 'way of life'. Hence, Perna women consider themselves to be 'destined' by virtue of birth as being prostitutes. Materialism in today's world has only fuelled more desire for luxurious goods within the community, thereby making it more difficult for any intervention to take root. As one of the women who have resisted entering the trade rued, 'I have only two walls in my share of the room. I need to have the flooring and the other two walls done of my home. It is a necessity as my house has been burgled thrice already. (Pauses) I am the poorest of all my nine siblings. There are days when I contemplate joining the trade ... I pray to God to give me strength never to doubt my decision of not being part of the trade.'

Notes

1. Quoted from Rohini Sahni et al. (eds.), *Prostitution and Beyond*, Sage, New Delhi, 2008.
2. A report in the Delhi subscription of *The Times of India*, 21 July 2010.
3. Jajmani system is the recognized form of interaction between different caste, sub-caste groups that underlies the functioning of a typical Indian village.
4. For more detail on work of YWCA, Najafgarh centre, please visit http://www.ywcaofdelhi.org/?page=projects
5. For more detail on MRYDO, please visit http://www.delhi.gov.in/wps/wcm/connect/lib_dcw/DCW/Home/Partner+NGOs/
6. For detailed discussion on *Jati*, please refer to S.C. Dube, *Indian Society*, 5th edition, National Book Trust, New Delhi, 1990.

References

Beteille, Andre, 'The Reproduction of Inequality: Occupation, Caste and Family', *Contributions to Indian Sociology*, Vol. 25, No. 1, 1991: 3–28.

Dube, S.C., *Indian Society*, 5th edition, National Book Trust, New Delhi, 1990.

Fernandes, Leela, 'The Politics of Forgetting: Class Politics, State Power and Restructuring of Urban Space in India', *Urban Studies*, Vol. 41, No. 12, 2004: 2415–2430.

Gangoli, Geetanjali, 'Immorality, Hurt or Choice: Indian Feminists and Prostitution', in Rohini Sahni et al. (eds.), *Prostitution and Beyond*, Sage, New Delhi, 2008.

Giddens, A., *The Consequences of Modernity*, Polity Press, Cambridge, 1990.

Rose, H.A., *A Glossary of the Tribes and Castes of the Punjab and North-West Frontier Province*, Nirmal Publishers and Distributors, Kolkata, 1997.

Sheth, D.L., 'Secularization of Caste and Making of New Middle Class', *Economic and Political Weekly*, 21–28 August 2009: 2502–2510.

Stern, 'Bourgeois Revolution on the Subcontinent' Cambridge University Press, 2003.

Swarnakar, 'Ethnographic Study of Community Based Sex-work among Nats.' In Rohini Sahni et al. (ed.) Prostitution and Beyond: An Analysis of Sex work in India, Sage, New Delhi, 2008.

United Nations Office on Drugs & Crime (UNDOC) World Drug Report, 2001.

CHAPTER 8

Mysore Kalyanam

An Event Where Violation of Women's Rights are Legitimized

MOLY KURUVILLA AND DILSHAD VALASSERI

> Woman's chief discontent is not with her political, but with her social and particularly her marital bondage.
>
> (Laura Bullard, 1870)

Marriage and family are considered as the two main spheres of women's lives, historically. Even today *wifehood and motherhood are considered as the be all and end all of women's lives* in several patriarchal societies, whereby parents try to make the lives of their daughters safe and secure through marriage. Without having enough education and economic independence there should be someone to protect and maintain them, which makes the institution of marriage overrated in women's lives. The prominence of such a goal has far-reaching impacts on women's lives. Not only are they denied of their due share of opportunities in education, employment and public life but also get confined within the homes for wifehood and mothering. The patriarchal ideology bestows on men the power and authority over women's lives and their bodies. Very often women have no choice in deciding whether to marry or not, when to marry and whom to marry.

The over significance of marriage channelizes women's lives from an independent life with dignity to that of a passive one of mere obedience and subjectivity. The girl children are being socialized from the early childhood to be good wives and mothers. The same socialization is occurring in boy children's life but in an extreme opposite manner, that is to be independent winners in life.

Due to the social notion that men are the breadwinners, parents give more priority for the education of boys than girls. The boy may be sent to private schools with higher fees, whereas the girl will be sent to the nearby government school with no fees. Again when it comes to higher education, majority of parents send their sons to professional education, whereas their daughters will be sent to traditional courses in Arts and Science colleges. When it comes to jobs, the professionally educated boys will get prestigious jobs when compared to girls who have completed the traditional courses. Recently, there is a progressive trend with more and more girls joining technical and professional courses and that provides a ray of hope. But this change happens only when the parents are educated and aware of the value of professional/technical education. Majority of the population, in rural areas and in certain specific communities and regions, still value marriage as a better option for ensuring the future safety of their daughters rather than sending them for higher education and employment.

Having a high level of literacy, low infant and maternal mortality rates, favourable overall sex ratio, high average age of marriage, increased life expectancy along with easy access to health and educational services, has not changed the focus of women's lives in Kerala. According to Kuruvilla and Aanand (2009), the high literacy rate and education standards in Kerala have not made corresponding changes in the mindsets of its people. The institutionalization of marriage leads to the commercialization of marriage with high dowry demands as its inevitable component. The 'Status Study of Women in Kerala' by Sakhi Women's Resource Centre (2006) reveals that with increase in education, dowry is also escalating. Even though the demand of dowry has increased beyond limits, it could not be turned down by the ordinary people because of the stringent societal norms regarding marriage as the life goal of women. So as to avoid social ridicule, a girl and her family are ready to go to any length. That is what is happening in certain specific regions of Kerala where interstate marriages such as Mysore marriages are quite rampant.

Mysore *Kalyanam* (marriage) is a specific type of interstate marriage in which the brides from poor socio-economic background and belonging to rural remote areas of Wayanad and Malappuram districts of Kerala are married to residents of Mysore (Karnataka State) who ask for unusually low dowry. A study conducted in this area by Kuruvilla and Valasseri (2010) using case study method, revealed shocking facts related to the issue. Fifteen case studies were made, during a period of six months time, in the Nilambur Panchayat of Malappuram district. The study was an eye-opener to the grave situation of rural women in certain pockets of the glorified state. There are other types of interstate marriages like Mali, Mangalore and Haryana marriages occurring in different places of Kerala that share similar characteristics with regard to their causes, gender issues and the impacts on women's lives. The characteristic features of Mysore marriage, socio-economic background leading to such marriage and the gender issues involved are highlighted here along with their impacts on the women, their children, the families and the society at large.

Top priority is given to marriages of daughters in rural Malappuram, the district with the lowest marriage age in the state. With home deliveries even now, the high prominence of adolescent marriages, low higher education facilities and still high population growth rate, the district now catches the attention because of the interstate marriages in its specific regions. The study of Kerala Mahila Samakhya Society (2008–09) on 'Status of Women in Nilambur Grama Panchayath' of Malappuram District, highlights the issue of dowry as a major cause for interstate marriages (Mysore Kalyanam) and the subsequent desertion of women by their husbands. Because of the over importance of marriage and the stereotypical roles assigned to women, the human rights violations behind the closed doors are overlooked socially and politically.

Once a girl reaches the age of 20, she is considered as over-age for marriage which in turn leads to higher dowry demands for an alliance within the state of Kerala. Hence, the parents are compelled to take the painful decision to marry their daughters to bridegrooms from the neighbouring state of Karnataka where the dowry demands are comparatively lesser, thus, sending them to a totally strange and far-off place. Women in interstate marriages have to face serious problems like the unfamiliar language, culture, poor life situations, economic dependence, domestic violence, etc. Even after experiencing these painful life situations, the married girls never get any security from their husbands or in-laws. Most of them are treated brutally with violence, negligence, poverty, starvation and finally by desertion. They are not able to react in an assertive manner, because of the lack of awareness about their rights, as human beings and as women. Some of them are living with their husbands, fighting for a decent life in a strange place with strange language and strange customs. Many of them have been deserted and are back in their parental homes; they are neither legally divorced nor getting any support from their husbands for their survival. At the same time, most of them do not expect or wish a rejoining with the husbands. In spite of all these, the occurrences of Mysore marriages are still rampant in the backward regions of Kerala, highlighting the helplessness of rural women in the face of compulsory marriage. In several instances, parents justify their acts on the grounds that their daughter is having a legitimate child to take care of her, whereby the human rights violations involved get legitimized.

Case Studies

The fifteen instances of Mysore Kalyanam subjected to in-depth study and subsequent experiential analysis revealed much in common with regard to their socio-cultural background and the impacts created upon the women and their families. Interviews ranging from two to three hours were conducted with each one of them, sometimes in a single session and in some cases repeated visits had to be made. For maintaining confidentiality, the names of the women are changed without altering the information revealed by them. Three of the cases are presented here.

Case 1

Hafsath is 28 years old, now living in her native house at Nilambur. She was married to Mysore before 3 years. Now she has a male baby aged 6 months. In her relatives' enquiry about the husband's family, he had father, mother, sister and her children. She was given 5 gold sovereigns and ₹ 80,000 as dowry. Her father is a farmer with small earnings. Her elder sister is divorced and living in the native house. There was no other way before him to see her daughter as a 'married woman'.

In Mysore, the house was very small, compared to her house. Without having enough food, her life was going bad. Husband and his family were speaking Urdu, a totally strange language to her and hence she couldn't express her feelings with them. Within a few days she could sense something wrong in the interaction of her husband with his sister. Slowly, she happened to know from the neighbours, that it was not his sister but his first wife. The so-called father and mother were his in-laws. It was a shocking experience, but she was helpless to question anybody.

Thinking of the starving family and her helpless father Hafsath was unable to inform this to her parents. Her husband was a driver who earned enough to take care of a family. His first wife had 3 children; not his children, but her first husband's. Husband spent money only for his needs. When he comes home, he brought vegetables and other food items just sufficient to make his food only. The remaining food was shared by others. The first wife's condition was also the same. Hafsath was not given even a single rupee. There was no calendar or newspaper in the house. She could know the date when someone called from Nilambur. There was no other way to contact with the outer world.

This was going on for the long two and a half years. At the time, when she was 2 months pregnant, husband told her that he was going for a long trip so that she can go to her house. He gave her some money also. After 2 days he called her and asked to go to her house and take rest. After a few days they came to know that he had gone with a woman in the neighbourhood. In this situation Hafsath had no other option but to inform her parents. They came to Mysore and brought her back to Nilambur. Only after this incident, the parents came to know about the realities that their daughter experienced in Mysore.

Now, Hafsath is living with her parents. Her elder sister is doing tailoring and the younger sister works in a shop. They are trying to share a part in the survival of the family, with their father. Her brother has gone to Saudi Arabia in search of a job. She is the third member of the family.

There is no information of her husband for the last one year. She gave birth to a baby boy who is 6 months now. There is no one to make an enquiry or to file a case. Hafsath is not ready to live with her husband, any more. She is not aware of the government projects, and doesn't know about the procedures of women's commission or *Jagratha Samithi* to get legal assistance.

Case 2

30-year-old Sulaikha is now living with her mother and 7-year-old son in Nilambur. She was married to Mysore 8 years before at the age of 22. Her husband was 28 then. Her mother is a divorcee and working as a house maid. She was not provided anything by her father who has a second wife and children, living near Sulaikha's house. Her mother was divorced when she was one year old. He was then working as a wood cutter in a wood mill. Mother is working hard even now in her fifties as a house maid and getting something for their survival. Sulaikha was given 5 cents of land as share of family property where she made a house with the help of panchayath housing scheme.

Sulaikha's mother could not earn anything more than the requirement for their day-to-day life. The alliance came through one of Sulaikha's uncles. When they went to Mysore for further enquiry, everything seemed perfect. Husband had father, mother, six sisters and one brother. He was working as a mechanic in an automobile workshop and earned enough to live. Seven gold sovereigns and ₹ 70,000 were given as dowry. Most of the expenses were met by the contributions of relatives and well-wishers. Her neighbours and relatives asked her father to take the responsibility of the marriage of his daughter and he gave ₹ 30,000, the only help she had ever got from the father.

In the early days of marriage, there was no means to communicate with each other. He was speaking in Urdu and a few words in Malayalam. She could not understand what the other members were speaking. Mother-in-law disliked her talking with husband. She became pregnant in the 5th month of marriage. In-laws behaved indifferently with her. She was not given enough food. There was only one meal per day. All household chores were to be done by her. She cooked the food, washed everyone's clothes, as Sulaikha says, any type of dirty clothes. She could not convey these abuses to her husband. On one side, there was no communicable language and on the other side, in-laws never allowed her to interact with her husband.

She delivered her son at Nilambur. No one from husband's family visited the mother and child. Husband came to see his son after three months of delivery and took them to Mysore. The circumstances were getting worse. All of the members abused her with bad words. Mother-in-law used to say that the Keralite women are 'second grade'. She said they only know to 'seduce men' and to 'make children'. She abused Sulaikha's mother also with bad words.

Any favour done by the husband towards Sulaikha or son provoked his people. If he brought something to her or his son, even a packet of biscuit was enough reason for a big quarrel. Under these circumstances the husband decided to shift their residence to a rented house. Only a few months they could stay there. Father-in-law came often and scolded her. He said that being in a separate house, his son's life expenses have become high, and she is the reason for it. One day, he came to their residence and slapped her on the face. After a few months they went back to the family home.

Sufficient food and clothing were denied to Sulaikha and her small child. She was not allowed to talk with the Malayali neighbours, in Malayalam. Though they could not follow the language, the husband's people suspected that Sulaikha was talking about them and the problems occurring in their house. One day, when she refused to give her one and only good dress to the sister-in-law, in-laws poured kerosene over her. She ran out, and thus escaped from a murder attempt.

This made her life in Mysore fearful. Husband did not give her any support and that was unbearable for her. When her son was four years old, one day, father-in-law gave her some money and asked her to go to Nilambur. She was happy because it was six months since she had left her house. She asked her husband to come with her but he didn't. Then only she knew that it was a conspiracy to avoid her. All of the family asked her to get out of the house and go to her house. She had no good dresses, not even slippers or a bag. There was a Malayali neighbour who gave her some money and a chappal to wear. It was the first time she was travelling alone.

After this incident, her husband contacted Sulaikha over phone six months later. It was a formal talk. Mother and relatives compelled Sulaikha to go back, but she was not ready to go. She knew what was awaiting her. In spite of all, her husband was becoming a drunkard. His only interests were playing cards and consuming liquor. She had nothing to expect from her husband, other than his physical abuses.

Now Sulaikha lives in her home with mother and her 7-year-old son. He is studying in first standard. Mother works as a housemaid for daily wages. She provides everything for their living. The school Parent-Teacher Association (PTA) meetings are being attended by Sulaikha. Her son asks about father and is sad about his absence. She is getting ready to file a case through women's commission.

Case 3

Sunitha aged 35, was married to Mysore, when she was 24. She has mother, 4 sisters and 2 brothers. Her father died 17 years ago. She stopped studies when she failed in 10th standard. She was an active Kabadi player in school and has represented the school team in district games. She is the fourth member of the family. After the death of the father, the family was in severe crisis to survive. Brothers were too small to get a job. Her sisters worked hard as housemaids, and did other small jobs. There were marriage alliances, but her family was not able to meet the expenses of heavy dowry demands. Then this alliance from Mysore was brought by a family friend. She was not ready to get married off to a faraway place, but kept silent, when she thought about the sufferings of the family and their ambition to see her as a 'married woman'. When she objected with helpless words, her relatives and neighbours consoled her, 'even if there wouldn't be a happy married life, she could have a child legally to take care of her later on'.

Her family enquired about the groom who was a driver. He has mother, four sisters, two brothers and no father. He was the second one. When he came to see her, he talked of nothing, they were unable to communicate in each others' language. There was no marriage function in his house, his relatives came to her house, and took part in the function.

She was given 15 gold sovereigns and ₹ 66,000 as dowry. It was a smaller amount when compared to other marriages in the neighbourhood. On the fifth day, mother-in-law asked her to give the gold ornaments to a relative for a while which she promised to give back within a week. Only a portion of it was given back to her after one month.

The circumstances in the spousal family were not fair. Mother-in-law used to scold her for small reasons. She could not share it with the husband, due to language barrier. The house was very small, she slept with the sister-in-laws on several nights. Mother did not allow her to sleep with the husband, even though they had a small room in the house.

When she became pregnant, she was given a pain killer tablet by the sister-in-law for the severe back pain she got due to hard work like grinding and washing. She had severe bleeding. Her husband was not there at the time. After a day and night they took her to a hospital. The doctor was a Malayalee, and helped Sunitha to inform her relatives. After D&C she returned to husband's home, and even in that condition, the mother-in-law asked her to wash the heavy clothes. The elder sister-in-law was a little kind to her and let her take rest. Next week she came to Nilambur with her relatives, and without being accompanied by her husband. She could not talk to him as she wished. After spending six months in her house, she returned to Mysore. Husband was no longer very caring about her. He always compelled her to wear Purdah. He did not like her to talk to other men, even with his friends. Within a year she became pregnant again. She came to Nilmabur and delivered a girl child. There was no financial assistance from the husband.

When the daughter was eight months old, she returned to Mysore. Husband and his family compelled her to demand for a new house from her family. Sunitha, by knowing the financial sufferings of the family was helpless. The abuses continued and the two families were parted by great distance. When her daughter was one and a half year old, the visit of her relatives to Mysore became an explosive event. Neighbours and relatives called police and the husband was not at home. As per the instruction of police officers in Mysore, she returned to her home in Nilambur. She filed a case and now she is legally divorced. Around ₹ 90,000 of compensation was passed, but she got only ₹ 30,000. The husband was imprisoned for several months.

Now, with no information about her husband, Sunitha is living in her native house, with her mother, brothers and sisters. Her daughter is 8 years old studying in third standard. She has some goats and a small attempt of vegetable cultivation. She is not willing to go to Mysore and to live with the husband. She has applied for a house loan in Panchayath housing scheme. Now her only ambition is to provide good education to her daughter.

Features of Mysore Kalyanam

The important features of Mysore Kalyanam that makes it distinct from other marriages include the following:

Comparatively lesser dowry demands: Dowry is given in all Mysore marriages. But it is comparatively lesser than what is persisting in the specific region. Four to 15 gold sovereigns and ₹ 25,000 to ₹ 1,00,000 are given as dowry in Mysore Kalyanam, whereas the lowest dowry rates in the region amount to more than three lakhs in the case of within the state alliances. When the families involved are too poor to meet such high expenses, the marriages of the girls are held with the help of neighbours and relatives who are ready to help in making their lives secure. The dowry demanded by the groom's family in Mysore Kalyanam is thus manageable for the poor families of the brides, all of whom struggle for a survival.

Late marriage age of the bride: Except a few, brides in Mysore Kalyanam are usually in the age group of 22 to 34. Early marriages from the age of 14 are common in this region. The poor condition of families to provide enough dowry and to meet the expenses of the marriage lead to late marriage of the girls which in turn pressurises the girls to make compromises even when the girl or the family do not like the alliance. So girls enter into the interstate marriage with no choices at all.

Barrier of communication: From the first stage of marriage alliance, the difference in languages stand as a barrier to communicate with each other. The relatives, who go to Mysore for an enquiry of the whereabouts of the groom are often misled and the information gathered regarding the groom's job, income, assets and even the marital status will be found incorrect after the marriage.

The problem is more serious when it affects the intimacy of relationship between the husband and wife since the bride and groom cannot share even their love properly. In a far-off place, without having a medium to communicate, the bride faces severe alienation. In an entirely different social and cultural situation, she has no way to share her feelings with her husband. She cannot inform him the different kinds of abuses she experiences inside the house from his family members. At times, when the life situation becomes problematic and dangerous, the women have no way to seek help from neighbours due to the barrier of language.

Interstate transfer of residence: After the marriage, the bride will have to leave her native village and state and get transferred to Mysore of Karnataka state where the groom resides. Transfer of the bride to the groom's residence happens in most of the Indian marriages which are patrilocal. But in Mysore Kalyanam the transfer of residence is not only a change of residing place, but a complete change of social and cultural situations also.

Unpleasant experiences in spousal family: The brides in Mysore Kalyanam often will have to go through bitter experiences like starvation, negligence, lack of basic amenities, verbal and emotional abuses, lack of mobility, economic dependence, control over maintaining the relationship with parental family, further economic demands made on parents and worst of all, physical violence from the spouse and family. The experiences become traumatic when the women lack language skills to share it with anyone.

Return of the wife to the parental home: Because of the problematic conditions in spousal home, most women are compelled to return to parental homes. Majority of them are not aware of the legal steps to get justice and, hence, are not legally divorced. Though inquisitive of seeking compensation, they dare not go for it due to the fear of losing the custodianship of children while going for legal actions.

Socio-economic Background Leading to Mysore Kalyanam

The major factors that lead to the occurrence of such interstate marriages include low level of education of the bride and her family, low level of income of the bride and her family, backwardness of the specific community of the bride and the societal notion leading to overrating of marriage in a woman's life. Low educational status and low family income are found to be the common status of all the women who are victimized in Mysore Kalyanam. Except for a few, the brides in such marriages would not have completed their school education. Lack of finances to meet the educational expenses pressurize the girls to drop out. They also lack vocational skill training to earn a living. Parents of the brides in Mysore Kalyanam are illiterate and belonging to below poverty line (BPL) families. Usually, there will be only one earning member each in every family and that too with a nominal income. In families where women are the main earning members, majority are housemaids. Other than these small jobs, they do not have any profitable assets. The families are compelled to go for interstate marriages because of their poor condition to meet high dowry demands in the alliances within the state.

All the brides in Mysore Kalyanam belong to the Muslim community. Their social and economic backwardness pull them back from the reach of good education and job opportunities. Malappuram lacks higher education facilities when compared to other districts in Kerala. Polygamy perpetuates in the community even today. Because of high dowry demands and the poor life situations of families, most often, the marriage age of girls exceeds the norms and this in turn leads to the occurrence of interstate marriages characterized by a comparatively lower demand of dowry.

The saddest part of the affair is the fact that the bride and her family are fully aware about the consequences of Mysore Kalyanam but are often helpless to reject the marriage, since being a spinster is no more encouraged in the community. Women themselves are pressurized to agree with the interstate marriage to get the social sanction for existence in the society where a woman on her own is not considered as a complete individual. The over importance of marriage in women's lives is accepted socially and culturally. Thus, the lack of resources to combat with the social backwardness holds a crucial role in this issue.

Impacts of Mysore Kalyanam

The impacts of Mysore Kalyanam on the women, the family and the society vary in the nature, extent and gravity, the details of which are given below:

Impact on Women

Women who return to their native homes become more dependent on their families. They have children with them, having no ways to meet their expenses regarding food, clothes, medicine and education. The poor situation of their native homes cannot afford these additional expenses. The social stigma on deserted women controls their lives which prevent them from going out for work and earning anything. In the school PTA meetings the children and their mothers feel humiliated in the absence of fathers. With a few exceptions, majority of them seem to have lost their self-esteem and self-confidence but live a life for the sake of children. All of them realize the value of education for a decent living and are determined to give good education to their children.

Impact on the Family

The families have compromised many things to get the daughters married and see them live a happy life. Several of the families have arranged the dowry for the marriage of the daughters by selling off whatever little they had and taking loans and seeking help from well-wishers, relatives and neighbours, which they are unable to repay. But with the return of the daughter, all the expectations are shattered. Amidst the poor life situations, they have to take care of the daughter and her children also.

The parents cannot offer anything more and hence they console themselves that they could somehow get their daughter married and her legal children would take care of the daughter in her old age.

Impact on the Society

In spite of realizing the traumatic experiences of the victims of Mysore Kalyanam, such marriages are being repeated. Very few of them are surviving without separation. Because of the lesser dowry demands, more and more families are encouraged to go for interstate marriages. Society does not consider this type of marriages as unfair, since to get a woman married is of utmost importance. The society, in general, is ready to adapt with the consequences and while hoping for a better life for the girl, apprehension regarding the unfair experiences and final return of the girl accompanies every marriage celebration. Society does not attach any stigma on such marriages or on the girl who has come back from the spousal family.

But quite recently, after the women's status study conducted in Nilambur panchayath (2008–09), the society has become more conscious about the experiences of the brides in Mysore Kalyanam, their poor life situations and the increasing number of desertions. This realization has led to the commencement of 'Dowry free village campaign', a combined effort of Nilambur grama panchayath and Mahila Samakhya Society in Nilambur to nip the evil of dowry in the bud.

Gender Issues Involved in Mysore Kalyanam

The various gender issues to be discussed in this context are summarized below:

Concept about Woman as a Sex Object

The over importance of marriage in a woman's life is both a reason and an impact of the patriarchal notion to view woman as a sex object. Her feelings and interests are not counted seriously since a woman married in Mysore Kalyanam has no right to express her opinion as to whether she likes it or not, she has to simply obey what the parents and elders direct her to do. She does not get the dignity that a man gets in the family and in intimate relationships. She is not considered as a human being by the spouse or his family. The societal mentality about marriage treats woman only as a physical body that can be claimed by man. Before the marriage, the control is with her parents and at the time of marriage is transferred to the spouse and his family.

Woman Considered as a Liability in Parental Home

A family, with a girl child, holds the cross about her marriage from her birth itself. It is talked about and discussed often, but not so is her education. Parents of daughters are in a dilemma on how to meet the expenses related with the daughter's marriage including the demand of dowry. According to them, they would be freed from the responsibility of a girl child, only after getting her married. There is no consideration given to her education or employment which in turn could boost up her self-esteem and economic independence and it is quite difficult to convince the parents about how good education and employment can make the future of daughters secure and safe.

Reinforcement of Gender Stereotypes

By giving no importance to women's education, employment, feelings and interests, and by giving undue importance to marriage the stereotypical roles of women are being emphasized through Mysore Kalyanam. The stereotypical roles of wife, mother and the house wife are being reinforced. As per these ascriptions women should be married in time, should be obeying and adjustable wives, caring and affectionate mothers and responsible housewives. Women are never given the space to be assertive, active and independent as human beings.

Perception about Woman as Someone to be Protected

The stereotypic women's role considers woman as someone to be protected. Girl children are being protected in the beginning by the parental family and after their marriage, by the spouse and his family. This perception underlines the thought that in all stages of life a woman cannot lead a life of her own but only with the assistance and guardianship/protection of a man or family.

There are parents who explicitly state that they have married their daughters to Mysore, though being fully aware that their daughter would return from the husband's family sooner or later with the hope that she would beget a legal child from the marriage which in turn would ensure her future safety and security. This notion of getting someone to protect the daughters in their later years pressurizes the parents to get their daughters married somehow, taking any risk. Thus, the inter-state marriages are justified socially.

Lack of Decision-making Power

The brides in Mysore Kalyanam are not at all satisfied with the marriage alliances. All of them long to study more, but cannot achieve it because of the low economic conditions of the families. Along with the economic incapability, the mindset on women's stereotype roles make them pull them back from pursuing studies. In the marital relationship, they get only a secondary status throughout their life. On returning from the spousal families, they wish to go for a job and earn something, but they are not able to do so because of familial restrictions. Women are compelled to get married, even if it is to a far-off place. Parents cannot take a stand to reject these alliances as they are not aware of other possibilities and do not have sufficient resources. Before marriage, women do not have any decision-making power to choose between their studies and marriage. And after marriage, they have no voice on any matter in their spousal family. At a do-or-die stage, they take the final decision to return to the parental home without waiting for anybody's permission.

Subjectivity of Women to Domestic Violence

Women wedded in Mysore Kalyanam will have to go through several types of violence and abuses. It includes verbal, emotional, physical and sexual atrocities. The women themselves perceive that they are obligated to undergo these experiences and their husbands have the right to do these atrocities against them. This mindset grows into silent suffering. Many of them do not inform the parents about these cruel experiences and in cases where they do they are advised that the wife should obey and adjust with the husband. This has developed a feeling among the women to subject themselves to fate and give up their independence totally.

Conclusion

The specific features of Mysore Kalyanam make it a strange but unique event happening in the state of Kerala which ironically is famous for its women development indices. The traumatic experiences faced by the women in a strange place with strange customs and traditions along with a strange language are violations of basic human rights. Just to fulfil the societal expectations, women are being victimized through Mysore Kalyanam.

In the present Indian scenario, almost all marriages face the issues of dowry, domestic violence and emotional problems. But, with the barrier of language, different and unfamiliar social conditions, absence of friends and relatives – the effect of such problems become very severe in the case of Mysore Kalyanam.

Historical backwardness of Malappuram district is reflected in every aspect of Mysore Kalyanam. There are no higher education facilities even now; the residents largely depend on neighbouring districts for higher education. The sociological backwardness of the specific community also plays a crucial role in the issue. The lowest marriage age coupled with the over importance of marriage in a girl's life pave the way to this unfavourable social practice. From the very birth of a girl child, the family begins to gather money to get her married. Girls are not given enough education, any kind of skill or vocational training even if they wished for it. Marriage is reckoned as the be-all and end-all of a woman's life and the husband is supposed to protect and take care of her. Husband is the protector, he may provide for the wife while the wife has to obey him in return. He is the earner, and the family naturally, would be under his mastery.

The impacts of these marriages are the consequence of the mentality that a woman is to be protected. The societal norm of 'protector' (husband) and the protected (wife) legitimizes the violence against girls and women. The marriages being patrilocal, the spousal family has a superior role; the wife and her family is compelled to adjust with them. The deserted woman, her children and family, pass through traumatic experiences, while the husband and his family is freed of any responsibilities. In many cases, the victims do not know how to get legal assistance and file a case for compensation or divorce. The deserted woman and her children live with the parental family. Despite all these sufferings, the parents have the satisfaction that they could get their daughters married, and now she has children to take care of her. There is no chance for an employment or economic independence which could lead her to an autonomous life. Women find the restrictions with regard to their mobility as the major reason behind this. In spite of being motivated, the women seem to be helpless in taking any pertinent decision in their life, to become economically productive. This implies the deeper internalization of patriarchal values that a woman is to be protected and must be dependent on men.

The patriarchal construction of womanhood closes the doors of possibilities of self-expression. There is no chance for an independent, self-esteemed life. A woman has no decision-making power, even in the matters related to one's own life. In the parental family, she is considered as a liability while in married life, only as a sex object. The gender role stereotypes again and again reducing a woman's space. The commercialization and institutionalization of marriage has its adverse effect doubly on women. The globally sanctioned sexual rights are not considered as women's human rights within the ideology of patriarchy.

Women's existence in the patriarchal societies is shaped by prejudices and biases. Within these, women live a life of the 'other'. She has no ways of self-expression, other than acting the role which patriarchy has imposed on her. Holding the intense longing for education within herself, she gives it up. Withholding her dream of a profession to survive, she confines herself into the four walls of wifehood, domestic violence, negligence and finally to desertion and alienation. Gender-based violence and the insecurity of women's lives is thus being legitimized in Mysore Kalyanam and the event gets repeated. If this is what is happening in the lives of women in Kerala, the state famous for its women development indices, there might be still more miserable lives lived by women in other pockets of the country that remain unnoticed behind closed doors. The notion of compulsory marriage in women's lives is something that remains as a black spot in our cultural tradition.

The institutionalization and commercialization of marriages should be resisted through people's participation. Local self-governments, activist groups and religious interventions can sharpen the campaign both theoretically and practically. Since 100 per cent of the aggrieved women in Mysore Kalyanam belong to the Muslim community, the social backwardness of the specific community should be addressed politically. A massive campaign is to be evolved to eliminate the notions regarding compulsory marriage in the lives of women and to correct the misconception that marriage is the life goal of women. Wifehood and motherhood should be equated with 'husbandhood' and fatherhood whereby girls and women could be freed from the clutches of compulsory marriage and subsequent life of worthlessness, hopelessness and helplessness.

References

Bullard, Laura, *The Revolution, Suffrage Journal*, United States, 1870.

Kerala Mahila Samakhya Society, 'Status Study of Women in Nilambur Grama Panchayath', 2008–09.

Kuruvilla, Moly and Dilshad Valasseri, 'An Investigation into the Sociocultural Background and Impacts of Mysore Kalyanam', Unpublished Dissertation, Centre for Women's Studies, University of Calicut, Kerala, 2010.

Kuruvilla, Moly and Layana Aanand, 'An Investigation into the Power Relations between Husband and Wife within Marriages', *Osmania Journal of Women's Studies*, Vol. 2, March 2009.

Rao, Mohan (ed.), *The Unheard Scream*, Zubaan, New Delhi, 2004.

Sakhi Women's Resource Centre, 'Status Study of Women in Kerala', Thiruvananthpuram, 2006.

SECTION III

Market Economy of Gender and Health

CHAPTER 9

New Market Economy and Problems of Women's Health in India

HEENA K. BIJLI

India has an impressive record of economic performance since the 1990s, but there has been slow progress in the advancement of its health status. A major recommendation at the Programme of Action (POA), International Conference on Population and Development (ICPD), Cairo (1994), was that population programmes should provide comprehensive Reproductive Health (RH) services that are integrated and coordinated with each other and with other health services. Yet, the underlying conditions in India determining women's health and childbearing are only deteriorating. Population averages of child health and maternal mortality indicators remain unacceptably high compared with countries in the South and East Asian region that have similar income levels, and rates of economic growth. Commercialization increased during the period of liberalization and structural adjustment, through the health sector reform initiatives during the 1990s. These reforms introduced market principles in public health services in order to improve the efficiency and quality of care. Many of these initiatives were introduced as a part of the Structural Adjustment Programme of the World Bank during the 1990s (Baru et al., 2010).

Challenges Facing Women's Health

Women tend to be more economically disadvantaged than men, as they suffer from poor access to food, clean water, sanitation, decent housing, livelihoods, quality education and a healthy working and living environment. Saroj Pachauri of Population Council had recently expressed that while there has been progress in recent years to improve the health of girls and women in India, too many still die of causes that are almost entirely preventable. Every year, 68,000 women in India die from pregnancy-related issues, more than in any other country in the world. An additional 74,118 women die from cervical cancer, the leading cause of cancer-related deaths in India. A large proportion of maternal deaths in India, is attributable not to lack of contraception, or even to little or no access to quality health services, but under nutrition, anaemia and communicable diseases stemming from lack of food, poverty and inequity. Recent discussions of women's health policy in India argue that over time, such policies and the programmes associated with them have grown less narrow in focus; that they are today more inclusive and sensitive to the articulated and apparent needs of the women concerned than they earlier were (Vaidyanathan, 2006; Sen and Iyer, 2002).

Studies at the national level reveal that more than men, women bear the overall burden of disease and disability, which is largely related to their Reproductive Health (RH). As per the National Family Health Survey (NFHS)–3 (2005–06), in India, early marriage prevails at 44.5 per cent overall (52.5% in rural areas). In rural areas 60–70 per cent of the women are married by 18 years of age, particularly in states like Bihar, Jharkhand, Rajasthan, Uttar Pradesh and Madhya Pradesh. On the other hand, the percentages are as low as 20 per cent among rural girls of Kerala and Himachal Pradesh where girls continue to study and get married at a later age. This shows that over time, change is possible by focusing on the age of marriage. Very early childbearing and an absence of spacing increase risks to mother and child (Table 1). The risk of maternal deaths is about three times higher in girls aged 15–19 years and five times higher in those younger than 15 years as compared with women in their 20s. Diseases of RH that are predominantly infectious cause some two-thirds of women's deaths.

Table 1

Facts about Early Childbearing

Although fertility in the 15–19 age group is decreasing, a substantial proportion of teenagers are still coming under the childbearing age
Category
• 12 per cent of women are already mothers.
• 45 per cent of women are pregnant with their first child.
• In total, 16 per cent women have begun childbearing.

Source: National Family Health Survey-3 (2005–06).

Statistics also reveal that 57 per cent girls of 10–13 years age group and 30 per cent of 14–17 years age group were undernourished. Rural health services form the backbone of the public health system in India. But the latest National Rural Health Mission (NRHM)–2009 Report reveals that nearly 85 per cent of the country's primary health centres do not have a doctor. The condition of community health centres is equally appalling. In many areas, the primary health care facilities through which RH care services have been implemented are in a disorderly mess, making the people lose faith in the health care programme itself. 'Gender parity' is still being seen as an unaccomplished goal, in fact, a goal which is yet to be identified and accomplished. Attention is rather being paid to gender dimensions of other goals such as poverty eradication and combating HIV/AIDS. Many women simply do not use health care services at all; and it is women of reproductive age who are most likely to be left out with untreated conditions such as reproductive tract infections, that are chronic, contributing to greater disease and cost burdens at a later stage. Chief causes have been found to be – decision-making at the family level about accessing health care for childbirth, timely transport to a health facility, and kind of care and response available at the facility. Most mothers in rural India are not aware of their entitlements in RH programmes.

Neo-Malthusian Thinking and Its Impact on Health

In population and development programmes, the neo-Malthusian thinking has had a detrimental impact where it has restricted women's ability to exercise their reproductive and sexual rights. Economic reforms have been to the detriment of women's health more generally, not just to the health services they need (Nair et al., 2006: 179). In the absence of any other form of social security, women are the worst affected when neo-liberal economic policies and trade agreements are implemented.

The origin of Malthusian thinking goes back to Thomas Malthus, the noted English economist, who had articulated in 1798, through his doctrine, 'Malthusianism', that as population increases geometrically, the food supply increases only arithmetically (by a constant amount), given the scarcity of natural resources. Therefore, he advocates population control as a solution to these problems. Though he himself opposed abortion and deliberate birth control on moral grounds; nevertheless, his doctrine has become closely associated with the provision of contraception and abortion for the purposes of population control (Bandarage, 1997: 5). The overriding commitment to quantitative goals persists, despite the International Conference on Population and Development (ICPD) agenda's claim that empowerment of women should be an end in itself.

This thinking views women's education, welfare and programmes of women's empowerment, in which contraceptive provision can be a part, not as ends in themselves, but merely as a means to 'getting the numbers down'. Putting Reproductive Health and Rights at the centre of population policies has encouraged policy-makers to continue to think of women only as wombs to the neglect of the wider economic and social roles, and of the conditions that could advance the health of women. Although the POA does not contain the phrase 'population problem', it does not identify demographic factors as the principal causes of any problem, or seek many demographic changes, but a neo-Malthusian subtext still runs through it.

The POA together with the accompanying political organizing by international women's organizations and population groups, did not challenge neo-liberalism sufficiently, but endorsed it in several respects. It, thereby, undermined its ground-breaking principles and goals of reproductive health. Neo-Malthusian thinking is also detrimental when it acts through institutions that formulate and carry out economic development policies. One result of describing population policies in terms of reproductive health has been that the 'underlying agenda of fertility control becomes inconspicuous to the designated target audience'. Population policies should not have an ultimate goal of 'population stabilization', in which they regard women's empowerment and the elimination of social, cultural, political and economic discrimination against women, mainly as prerequisites for low fertility. Immigrants, the elderly, the disabled and those needing welfare have been added to the list of traditional population 'targets', such as women, indigenous peoples and people of colour. Those driving to create 'free' markets today by privatizing, undermining or abolishing public health and social services, and emphasizing individual responsibility consistently derive strengths from the goals of neo-Malthusianism. Neo-Malthusian thinking is as ingrained as ever in many development institutions, donor agencies and government departments. The implementation of neo-liberal economic and health policies over the past two decades, first by means of structural adjustment programmes (SAPs), and more recently, by international 'free' trade agreements and national-level policies, has had a negative impact on health (Nair et al., 2006).

The World Bank's neo-liberal approach indirectly was to the detriment of the reproductive rights agenda and the POA of the

ICPD, Cairo, 1994, went along all too readily with. The World Bank had in 1993, proposed that the public sector should only provide essential services as 'clinical packages' for the needy, and the governments should open up the rest to full global competition. The basic package of health services that many public health systems now attempt to provide – family planning, prevention and treatment of sexually transmitted diseases, child health, control of communicable diseases, and some curing of diseases – is much narrower than even the essential services outlined in the POA. And in many instances, the private health care sector does not provide a higher quality of care, nor is it economically responsible and efficient. One study concluded that 'economic reforms' were the 'paramount constraints in implementing the ICPD programme', particularly in expanding RH services (Sadasivam, 1999: 10).

Another result of neo-liberal economic policies is the privatization and lack of regulation of family planning services themselves, as corporations, non-governmental organizations and philanthropic bodies become more involved (Rao, 2004). British sociologist Frank Furedi (1995: 139) had conceded that promoting population policies through the rhetoric of women's health has become central to 'the marketing of fertility control'. This medicalization of population issues 'is seldom contested, because it appears to be entirely about the non-controversial subject of health'.

Health Financing and Expenditure: A Grim Picture

India spends only 0.6 per cent of its Gross Domestic Product on health, against the 6.5 per cent by the United States, 8.3 per cent by Germany and 6.4 per cent by Saudi Arabia. India has one of the lowest public spendings and among the highest out-of-pocket (OOP) spendings on health in the world. To add to the problems, the Union budget 2010–11 announced in early 2010, that the nationally run health programmes were not going to be under the focus of the government this year. This has come as a disappointment because the five-year internal review of the National

Rural Health Mission (2009) has revealed that it had brought significant benefits to many areas of primary health care provision in rural areas across India.

The problems of inadequate health-sector funding and the tendency to focus on programme-specific rather than comprehensive health care have been aggravated in the 1990s and 2000s by two more developments. The first is the increasing privatization of health care at all levels, but especially of tertiary, hospital based services. The second relates to the increasing clout of the international pharmaceutical industry in the post-liberalization period that has led, in the Indian context, to the successive erosion of price control for essential drugs including medications vital to the control of maternal mortality, and the constraints placed by the international Trade Related Intellectual Property Rights agreement that have pushed up the prices of many essential drugs. It is within this broad context that policy related to women's health has been formulated in India over the years (Narayanan, 2011: 41).

The national budget allocation tells us that though it is meant for 'health and family welfare', and has gone up steadily over the past few years, it is still just 2 per cent of the total budget. Overall health spending allocation remains just a little over 6 per cent of the country's gross domestic product and, further, the actual spending is far less: less than 1 per cent of the GDP. These statistics have to be further reviewed in light of two facts: one, that only around 17 per cent of all expenditure in the country is borne by the state, the rest is shouldered by the individuals concerned (Jan Swasthya Abhiyan, 2006); and two, that perhaps 12 per cent of the country's public-health expenditure comes from international sources and is ring-fenced for specific programmes.

In India OOPs are growingly contributing to a disproportionately large component of total health expenditure. The 60th round of National Sample Survey–2004–06 (2006) reveals that consumption expenditure of health care is higher in the rural than in urban population. The proportion is close to 33 per cent in rural areas (with indirect costs and income loss during the period of illness added) and 17 per cent in urban areas. This suggests that expenditure burden of what may be called 'day-to-day morbidities', (reference period of one year) is very high, especially in the rural areas. Private expenditure is higher than public expenditure in India (Table 2).

Table 2

Public and Private Expenditure on Health in India, 2001–02

Health Expenditure (in ₹ 000s)	*1,03,24,95,050*
Public Expenditure as a per cent of Total Expenditure	20.8
Private expenditure as a per cent of Total Expenditure	79.2
Per Capita Expenditure (in ₹) – Public	207
Per Capita Expenditure (in ₹) – Private	790
Per Capita Expenditure (in ₹) – Total	997

All India public expenditure including expenditure by the MOHFW central ministries and local bodies, while private expenditure includes health expenditure by NGOs, firms and households.

Source: National Health Profile 2006, Ministry of Health and Family Welfare, GOI.

As per the National Sample Survey Organization (NSSO), in 2004, a mere 21 per cent of people in rural and 19 per cent in urban areas utilized the public sector for out-patient services. Figures for inpatient treatment were 42 per cent and 38 per cent in rural and urban areas respectively. For in-patient care, from a 60 per cent utilization of public services in the 1980s, the rural and urban utilization has fallen to 42 per cent and 38 per cent respectively. In the absence of a strong public sector, poorer people are the worst affected when the utilization of in-patient public services decreases with an increase in the income quintiles.

A market-based or commercialized approach to health, not only drives up the costs of health care, but can also lead to lack of interest in poor RH and the factors that make women ill. It promises (falsely) that medical technology can fix only diseased people; that good health can be bought and sold in the market place rather than being something to promote or work for.

The Way Forward to Achieve Optimal Reproductive Health and Rights

The Health Policy of 2002 and the 10th Plan documents of India have expressed concern about the persistence of inequities in provisioning, use and health outcomes. Equity concerns were also given by the 11th Plan document (Approach Paper to the 11th Five-Year Plan) that took cognizance of several issues: the link between poverty and ill-health; the systemic weakness of public provisioning and the need for strong public provisioning in order to ensure affordable access; regulation of the private sector; concern about rising costs and its negative impact on the non-poor; greater attention to the needs of marginalized sections, especially women (GOI, 2006). Many of these concerns have been raised by civil society organizations for over two decades. Examples of these are the women's groups that have taken up issues on the choice of reproductive technologies, access to basic services; and banning of irrational and unsafe technologies. But the health care system is not geared to handle huge number of emergencies and complications. It is clear now that there are persisting gaps between health and gender equality. The goals of gender equality and empowerment have been conspicuously absent in various reforms of the health sector.

By undermining or privatizing public health services, 'free' markets are creating a burden on the poor by increasing their private expenditure and making them further poor. In a country like India, where women are amongst the most marginalized, a comprehensive regulation of the public and private sectors is required in provisioning and research on medical technology and pharmaceuticals. This is critical for controlling costs and improving quality and accountability. For example, according to the neo-Malthusian doctrine, contraceptives are being used merely to bring the population numbers down. The fact is, methods such as the condom and diaphragm that are under user's control help prevent the spread of sexually transmitted diseases, and have no adverse impact on breastfeeding.

Therefore, there needs to be adequate allocation in terms of research funds for improvement and increased distribution of such contraceptives in the ongoing Reproductive and Child Health (RCH) programme. Similarly specialized services and integrated management for ante-natal care, new-born care, adolescent-girls, reproductive health care, sexually transmitted infections, should be designed and implemented in such a way so as to meet women's broader health needs. Poor immunization coverage leaves mothers prone to health risks. Weak mothers give birth to weak children without adequate nutrition which increases the possibility of weak adolescent girls (who again get married early) being pushed into intergenerational cycles of poverty and ill-health.

If we have to implement reproductive and sexual rights, we will have to first confront macro-economic and neo-Malthusian agendas that perpetuate gender, race and class inequalities, and cause impediments from achieving those rights. For this it is necessary to view women's health problems in the context of the social constraints of their lives, food, security systems, minimum wages, freedom from violence, etc. The United Nations Millennium Development Goal Five (MDG 5) to improve maternal health and achieve universal access to reproductive health by 2015 is to be met by India. India bears a disproportionate share of worldwide maternal deaths, therefore health delivery systems must be strengthened so that facilities provide women with the quality services they need to stay healthy during and after pregnancy. In recent years, the government, through the programme, RCH-II, has taken steps to introduce and implement programmes specifically in women's health, in order to facilitate their welfare and empowerment. Janani Suraksha Yojana (JSY) programme has successfully raised the number of births that are attended by trained health care professionals for poor women in largely rural settings. The government's flagship National Rural Health Mission has contributed to improved health services in rural India by setting up village-level voluntary health and sanitation committees and employing Accredited

Social Health Activists (ASHA), who are tasked with, among other things, accompanying pregnant women to ensure they receive the services they need. The government has also initiated an insurance scheme, Rashtriya Swasthya Bima Yojana (RSBY) which is a hospital insurance scheme for families below the poverty line, as a protection from catastrophic expenses. These progressive and encouraging initiatives now need to be strengthened and replicated.

In addition to basic health care services, new life-saving technologies need to be made available to all Indian women. One such example is HPV (Human Papilloma Virus) testing that identifies high-risk types of this virus. The promise of HPV testing to prevent cervical cancer has already been demonstrated on 130,000 women in the state of Maharashtra, where a single round of HPV testing significantly reduced the numbers of advanced cervical cancers and deaths when compared to other screening methods. A version of HPV test has been developed for low resource settings in India and does not require highly trained personnel, running water or electricity (Pachauri, 2010).

Such technologies need to be actively integrated into our existing RH services, training of health care workers and be implemented as affordable and accessible services to women. These will help in promoting women's reproductive and sexual rights. There is an increasing need to integrate the women's agenda of empowerment and self-determination into the health agenda. In India, besides the government, several NGOs and popular movements are gaining momentum. We need to pave the way for Reproductive and Sexual Health and rights to be incorporated within the larger agendas of other social movements. As thinkers and activists, we need to build networks and alliances with each other, to make such movements effective.

References

Bandarage, A., *Women, Population and Global Crisis: A Political-Economic Analysis*, Zed Books, London, 1997.

Baru, R., A. Acharya, S. Acharya, A.K. Shiva Kumar and K. Nagaraj, 'Inequities in Access to Health Services in India: Caste, Class and Region', *Economic and Political Weekly*, Vol. 45, No. 38, 2010: 49–58.

Furedi, F., *The Numbers Game in Population and Development: A Critical Introduction*, Polity Press, Oxford, 1995: 139.

Government of India, *Four Years of National Rural Health Mission, 2005–2009: Making a Difference Everywhere*, Ministry of Health and Family Welfare, New Delhi, 2009.

——, *Approach Paper to the Eleventh Five-Year Plan*, Planning Commission, New Delhi, 2006.

——, *Morbidity, Health Care and the Condition of the Aged*, National Sample Survey 60th Round (January–June 2004), Report No. 507, NSSO, New Delhi, 2006a.

——, Central Bureau of Health Intelligence, National Health Profile, Ministry of Health and Family Welfare, New Delhi, 2006b.

——, *Reproductive and Child Health (RCH) Programme Phase I, 1997–2004 and Phase II, 2005–2009*, Ministry of Health and Family Welfare, New Delhi, 1998 and 2005.

Hodgson, D. and S. Cotts Watkins, 'Feminists and Neo-Malthusians: Past and Present Alliances', *Population and Development Review*, Vol. 23, No. 93, 1997: 469–523.

International Institute for Population Sciences (IIPS), *National Fact Sheet India (Provisional Data), National Family Health Survey (NFHS–3) 2005–2006*, IIPS, Mumbai, India, 2007.

Jan Swasthya Abhiyan, National Coordination Committee, *Women's Health: Towards the National Health Assembly II, Booklet–3*, October 2006, http://phm-india.org/pdf/nha2/Women_Health.PDF, accessed on 30 April 2011.

McIntosh, C.A. and J.L. Finkle, 'The Cairo Conference on Population and Development: A New Paradigm', *Population and Development Review*, Vol. 21, No. 2, 1995: 223–260.

Ministry of Health and Family Welfare, New Delhi, http://www.cbhidghs.nic.in, accessed on 8 December 2010.

Nair, S., S. Sexton and P. Kirbat, 'A Decade after Cairo: Women's Health in a Free Market Economy', *Indian Journal of Gender Studies*, Vol. 13, No. 2, 2006: 171–193.

Narayanan, H., 'Women's Health, Population Control and Collective Action', *Economic and Political Weekly*, Vol. 46, No. 8, 2011: 39–47.

Pachauri, S., 'Investing in Women: We Must Focus Attention on the Lacunae in Maternal Health in India', *The Times of India*, Hyderabad, 4 August 2010.

Rao, M., *Malthusian Arithmetic: From Population Control to Reproductive Health*, Sage, New Delhi, 2004.

Sadasivam, B., *Risks, Rights and Reform: A 50-Country Survey Assessing Government Actions Five Years after the International Conference on Population and Development*, Women's Environment and Development Organization (WEDO), New York, 1999.

Sen, G. and Aditi Iyer, 'Incentives and Disincentives: Necessary, Effective, Just?', *Seminar*, No. 511, 2002.

Vaidyanathan, K.E., 'Social Protection for Children, Women and Families: The Indian Experience', paper presented at the UNICEF Conference on 'Social Protection Initiatives for Children, Women and Families: An Analysis of Recent Experiences', New York, 30–31 October 2006, www.unicef.org/spanish/policyanalysis/files/Agenda_Social_Protection_Initiatives_for_Children_Women_and_Families_final.pdf, accessed on 18 April 2011.

World Bank, *World Development Report: Investing in Health*, Oxford University Press, New York, 1993.

CHAPTER 10

Unbelievable

The Case of HPV Vaccines

KALPANA MEHTA AND NALINI BHANOT

Market research, lobbying efforts, advertising, promotional offers – none of these are to any one buying a phone or a vehicle. This is exactly what we have witnessed in the case of Gardasil and Cervarix except that these are not consumer products but vaccines that are being promoted among girls of 9–14 years of age in more than a hundred countries. Some of the moves are outright illegal and some others are condemnable but nothing befitting a product which is meant to prevent women from getting cervical cancer.

India is getting out of the licence-permit Raj, centralized governance and is either handing over production and import to the private sector directly or is sharing its revenues and advantages with the private sector through the now popular buzz word Public Private Partnership (PPP). Social sector spending was curtailed in the early nineties with structural adjustment imposed by the International Monetary Fund (IMF) and the World Bank. Despite promises to the contrary and much discussion around adjustment with a human face, the situation is that India has one of the most privatised health care systems in the world. A recently released report by the World Health Organization (WHO) has shockingly revealed that even in 2008, general government expenditure on health was a mere 32 per cent of the total expenditure on health in the country. This is lower than the average for low income countries (40.5%) and also lower than the average for the South-East Asia region (41.3%). In India, about 68 per cent of the total expenditure on health is paid for by the people from their own pockets and this expenditure is pushing them, especially the poorest, below the poverty line.[1]

The government is ready to let the private sector benefit at the cost of the larger good. While instances of private acquisition of land, rivers, mining rights, and new legal provisions to facilitate these, are well known and are also being widely protested, what is probably not as well known is that in the field of health and medical care also, the government has been abdicating its responsibility towards the common citizens to favour a growing GDP which will be garnered by doctors, private sector facilities and pharma companies. As of today drug prices are unchecked, while licensing of new inadequately tested drugs has become easier and the future of cheap generic medicines has been subordinated to big multinational firms. Multinational companies are demanding and getting more than a fair playing field and are taking over domestic companies.

The path of multinational companies is being smoothened by foreign agencies including private foundations like the Bill and Melinda Gates Foundation, multilateral agencies like the WHO, donor agencies of the first world like United States Agency for International Development (USAID) and NGOs sponsored and supported by them. Foreign contribution to the health expenditure is just about 1.6 per cent of the total but these agencies sit on almost every decision-making body.[2]

As if this deregulation were not enough to burn a hole in the pockets of Indians, the thrust of the government is towards medical tourism (where foreigners get treated by our best doctors at a fraction of the cost in their home country); assisted reproductive technologies (rent a womb); and clinical trials (test drugs/vaccines on our people, even if we cannot afford these products). As and where needed, laws are being diluted to favour foreign capital. Whereas the issue of Intellectual Property Rights and product patent was noted by all those agitating against the World Trade Organization (WTO), changes in the Drugs and Cosmetics Act that have now made India an even more attractive location for testing new drugs/vaccines and dilution of regulations for introduction of new drugs/vaccines, made their appearance unnoticed in 2005. Needless to say, with doctors diverted towards the rich paying clientele and drug companies' research agendas, the poor will have reduced access to them. Medicines and treatment costs are spiralling and people will now be doubly exploited to become trial subjects and surrogate mothers.

One of the major growth sectors for drug companies has been the vaccine market. The year 2008 saw the closure of government facilities for vaccine production giving rather flimsy excuses. Domestic requirements started to be increasingly fulfilled using private suppliers. The logic of selective vaccination has been applied in the case of Hepatitis B, whereas in respect of polio, which was to have been eradicated more than ten years back, the efforts are still continuing at enormous cost to the already strained primary health care services. The hapless Indian population is now being exposed to dubious vaccines that have more to do with the health of pharma giants than with disease control. There are a number of vaccines on the anvil, for Malaria, HIV, Diarrhoea, etc. which will mean that other than immunization, the health workers will not be able to do anything else. Countries like India are attractive to pharmaceutical companies due to their large population, and people's faith in injections and vaccination.

Case of the Human Papilloma Virus (HPV) Vaccines

Pharma companies are known the world over for their aggressive marketing strategies, collusion with the medical fraternity, lobbying with politicians and conflict of interest with drug regulatory authorities. The case of marketing HPV vaccines the world over brings out these strategies adopted by them.

Marketing assumes greater importance than need, safety, or efficacy. In health care, actually the terms market, marketing, etc. are jarring as illness produces need and the discourse should be in terms of needs for prevention or treatment.

History

In the mid-1990s, the technology developed by National Cancer Institute, USA was licensed to two companies, Merck and GlaxoSmithKline, to develop HPV vaccines for widespread distribution.

HPV infection is very common. The virus has more than 160 known strains and it infects virtually everyone at some point of time or the other. Some 15 strains of this virus are believed to be associated with the development of cervical cancer (cancer that develops at the mouth/neck of the uterus). The main route of transmission of this infection is sexual contact. HPV infection is considered a necessary but not sufficient cause of cervical cancer. Most HPV infections of the cervix are asymptomatic and more than 90 per cent of them clear up on their own within 2 years. It is only when the infection persists for a long period that it is associated with an increased risk of cancer. Considering the prevalence of the infection, a minuscule minority is at the risk of getting cancer. This cancer is prevalent in women starting late forties and is very rare among younger women.

The vaccines marketed by Merck (called Gardasil) and by GlaxoSmithKline (called Cervarix) work against HPV strains 16 and 18, and Gardasil also protects against strains 6 and 11, which cause genital warts. Both these vaccines claim to offer protection against these particular strains. These vaccines are given as a series of three intramuscular injections over a six month period.

Merck's Gardasil was given fast track clearance by the United States Food & Drug Administration (USFDA) (manufacturer's home country) in June 2006 and was approved for use among healthy girls and women between the ages of 9–27 years. The focus was on school girls, who would be easily accessible through schools, and had the highest possibility of not having prior infection with HPV as the vaccine had no impact on existing infections. However, at the time of granting approval, most of the research with Gardasil had been done on women aged 16–23 years, and only a small sample of less than 1,200 girls aged 9–16 had been studied and that too only to see if they reached the same anti-body level for the HPV strains under consideration.

Do the Vaccines Work?

Even today, several years after being approved, there are a lot of unknowns about Gardasil as well as Cervarix, though it was claimed they are more than 90 per cent effective against strains 16 and 18. According to WHO, the minimum threshold of antibodies for disease protection is not known. It is also not yet known 'whether seropositivity (according to the thresholds used) correlates with clinical protection ... whether women who become seronegative are susceptible to disease'.[3] Since the level of required anti-bodies is still not known, it is also not known whether and when a booster shot will be needed to continue protection.

Other limitations and unknowns about the vaccines include:

- The vaccines protect against 70 per cent of high risk HPV strains but have no effect on the remaining 30 per cent of high risk strains associated with cervical cancer.
- All women (vaccinated or not) still need periodic screening such as pap tests, to guard against cervical cancer.
- The vaccines do not provide protection to those who were already infected with HPV 16 and 18 at the time of vaccination. In fact, in these persons, the vaccines could actually *increase* the risk of developing cervical cancer by 44 per cent (Gardasil) and 32 per cent (Cervarix).[4]

- The full range of side effects is not known, as these will become known only after extensive and long-term use of the vaccines. The carcinogenic or mutagenic potential of the vaccines has not been determined. Their effect on pregnancy has not been studied. The impact on breast-fed infants is not fully known and has not been studied.
- The effect on immunocompromised individuals is not known.

Although Gardasil was given fast track approval by the USFDA, the letter of approval had a number of stipulations:

The number of young girls studied by Merck before licensing was considered very small by the USFDA, so it asked Merck to follow up 44,000 vaccines for general short-term safety for sixty days post-vaccination and then for six months to find out if they developed autoimmune disorders, thyroiditis, etc. The final report on this follow up was to be submitted by 30 September 2009.

USFDA also asked Merck to do a long-term follow up in Nordic countries for 14 years, to assess the actual impact of the vaccine and also to answer whether administration of the vaccine will result in replacement of the disease due to vaccine genotypes by other non-vaccine genotypes. This query was vital because if other genotypes (strains) became more virulent then there would be no net advantage from vaccination.

Merck had claimed that Gardasil was 98 per cent effective in preventing pre-cancerous lesions, but the company's data itself showed this was true only for those women previously uninfected with the virus. Efficacy against pre-cancerous lesions in the general population fell to a range between 17 per cent and 44 per cent over the three-year period of follow up.[5]

It should be noted that fast track approval has little to do with immediate necessity of the product but with the extra payment made by the company to have its case taken up. It should also be noted that USFDA has a poor record of post-marketing study compliance by companies.

After getting approval for marketing, Merck launched a series of initiatives to promote sales ranging from lobbying with politicians to get vaccination made mandatory for school girls, launching award winning advertising (which concealed the risks of the vaccines but heightened those of cervical cancer), etc. At that time Gardasil was projected as a blockbuster for Merck with estimated sales of 1 billion dollars in the first year alone. This was to provide the company with much needed relief after withdrawal of its best selling drug Vioxx and the expiry of some patents. It also had to make an out of court settlement with the tax department and needed to put money aside for pending consumer law suits against Vioxx. However controversy erupted with Merck's push for mandatory vaccination, the emergence of serious side effects among those vaccinated, the publicizing of material showing lack of knowledge about the vaccine and parents insisting on the right to decide whether to vaccinate their children or not.

Since its approval in the US, many questions have been raised regarding the means adopted to smoothen the passage of Gardasil into the market and the continuing support it has received from the Centre for Disease Control (CDC). While criminal investigations were undertaken with respect to influencing the Nobel Prize given to Hausen for discovering the link between HPV and cervical cancer, conflict of interest has been established in the FDA expert panel, and the largest eye-opener has been the appointment of the ex-CDC chief to the position of Chief of the vaccine division of Merck in December 2009.

Yet the company is relentlessly continuing its marketing efforts and has got the vaccine approved for boys. However, its application to extend the vaccine for women up to 55 years of age, was denied for the third time by the USFDA in April 2011.

Cost of the Vaccines

These vaccines are the most costly in history. Priced at more than $300 for the recommended three doses, they are expensive even for developed countries and this price has nothing to do with the cost of R&D or production but with the assumed

Box 1

Safety issues acknowledged by Merck

According to the prescribing information prepared by Merck for the US,[6]

Common adverse reactions include headache, fever, nausea, dizziness, local injection site reactions such as pain, swelling and bruising.

Syncope, temporary loss of consciousness, was noticed post-approval and later added to the package insert. As this can result in fainting/falling with injury, it is now recommended that all girls be made to lie down and be observed for 15 minutes post-vaccination.

Anaphylaxis has been reported following vaccination with GARDASIL.

Post-marketing data (as provided by Merck in its prescribing information) indicated that the vaccine has an adverse impact on almost every system of the body, i.e. nervous system, immune system, musculoskeletal system, blood and lymphatic system, respiratory system, gastrointestinal system, and vascular system. Serious adverse effects such as anaphylactic shock, seizures, blood clots and even death were acknowledged. A vaccine that affects almost all systems of the body is unlikely to leave the delicate, maturing reproductive system of adolescents unaffected, but this has not yet been studied.

User experience with Gardasil showed a number and range of adverse events including seizures, chronic pain, paralysis, blood clots and death of young girls post-vaccination.

Some of the most worrying adverse effects are on pregnancy. Although pregnant women were not meant to be recruited in the trials of Gardasil, some pregnant women were included by accident. The prescribing information indicates that after being vaccinated, these women had a higher incidence of spontaneous abortions, and malformed babies. In the few women who were breast-feeding at the time of vaccination in trials, a higher number of breast-feeding infants developed acute respiratory illnesses within 30 days post-vaccination as compared to infants whose mothers were in the control group.

Box 2

Analysis by consumer groups – Opening the Pandora's box

There are many critics of safety such as Judicial Watch, National Vaccine Information Centre (US) who have drawn their data from the company's submission to the USFDA and the Voluntary Adverse Reporting System (VAERS) of the US government. In March 2010, a group of six women including the victims of Gardasil made a presentation to the USFDA.

Their analysis of the VAERS database from 1/6/2006 – 26/10/2009 compared 100 per cent of all reports filed for all 80 vaccines listed including UNKNOWN with 100 per cent of all identifiable HPV reports filed during the same time period. The results show disturbing differences.

- In the 3 and ½ years the Gardasil vaccine has been on the market, the total number of reports to VAERS makes up 21.7 per cent of ALL reports submitted on or after June of 2006 to present.
- 'Life Threatening' events for all other vaccines add up to a yearly trend of 27, whereas for HPV vaccine alone the corresponding figure is 90.
- Emergency room visits shows an annual trend of 86 per cent more reports for the HPV vaccines.
- Among reports for hospitalization, there is an increase of 220 per cent because of the HPV vaccines.
- For extended hospitalizations there is an annual trend of 38 more reports due to the HPV vaccines. This is an increase of 265 per cent.
- In the category of 'Did Not Recover', there was an increase of 203 per cent for only the HPV vaccine.
- In the category of 'Disabled', there is an increase of 372 per cent due to the HPV vaccines.
- Among 'Vaccines Deaths' there is an increase of 184 per cent due to only HPV.
- In these three and a half years, 73.3 per cent of participants that received Gardasil acquired a new medical condition; from flu-like symptoms to paralysis.
- Of the 6,533,460 persons who received at least one dose of Gardasil (HPV4), only 17.9 per cent received all three doses, indicating a very high drop out rate.[7]

In addition, there are case reports which link Gardasil to blindness.[8]

benefit to society and individuals due to reduced cancer burden. 'We based the price on a number of factors, most importantly the value Gardasil brings to individuals and society', says Jennifer Allen, a spokesperson for Merck. 'HPV-related diseases cost the US health care system about $5 billion every year, and we took that into consideration'. [9]

Interconnections

On the surface, GlaxoSmithKline and Merck appear to be competitors but as early as 2006 the two made a profit-sharing agreement. Royalty has not been shared between the two companies alone but also with the National Cancer Institute USA, CSL Ltd. Australia, and Universities of Rochester and Queensland.

While the first market to be skimmed by the two companies acting hand in hand were the well-off countries – USA, Britain and Australia but they also had their eyes set on the poorer nations. Within two years of being approved in the home country, Gardasil had been approved in more than hundred countries. In the very month that the USFDA approved Gardasil, Bill and Melinda Gates Foundation gave a five-year grant to a US based NGO, PATH to carry out research to look at the possibility of introducing the vaccines in the Third World. The specific countries targeted were India, Peru, Vietnam and Uganda.

Gardasil also became the first HPV vaccine to receive WHO pre-qualification which was also extended to Cervarix. WHO pre-qualification means that GARDASIL® is now eligible for procurement by the United Nations Children's Fund (UNICEF) and other United Nations (UN) agencies including the Pan American Health Organization (PAHO), for use in national immunization programmes. WHO pre-qualification aims to ensure that vaccines meet WHO standards of quality, safety and efficacy, which in conjunction with other criteria, is used by the UN and other agencies to make purchasing decisions. This process also happened simultaneous to getting the licences. One may point out that there is an all-pervasive conflict of interest involved here. The Bill and Melinda Gates Foundation (BMGF) which gave grants to PATH for the promotion of the vaccine had a major shareholding in Merck in millions of shares.[10] The same foundation also happens to be the largest source of funds for WHO giving it more money than G-20 governments put together.[11]

Needless to say that the grants to PATH (global health organization) and the WHO (World Health Organization) prequalification were meant to gain access to the large public health sector.

Does India Need Human Papilloma Virus (HPV) Vaccines?

These vaccines have generated intense debate across the globe, regarding their relevance and assumed benefit. The fact that cervical cancer is not among the top ten leading causes of death anywhere in the world (according to WHO data),[12] leads one to question the projected need and urgency with which these vaccines are being promoted. In developed countries, deaths due to cervical cancer have come down sharply due to early detection and treatment. For instance, in the US, between 1955 and 1992, the cervical cancer death rate declined by 70 per cent and continues to decline by nearly 3 per cent each year.[13] In developing countries, which account for 80 per cent of the global deaths due to cervical cancer, there are several competing and pressing health priorities. In these countries, even a combination of all cancers, does not figure in the list of top killers. Cervical cancer rates vary across classes and it is considered a disease of poverty. Besides, cervical cancer is curable. The high death rates in developing countries like India are due to detection at very late stages of the disease and a lack of screening and treatment facilities.

HPV vaccines are promoted as a way of overcoming these constraints. However, the vaccines are not a stand alone in the cancer prevention strategy. Assuming that they are effective in fighting off at least the two most prevalent carcinogenic strains of HPV, as stated before, they have no impact on the remaining thirteen high risk strains and even vaccinated girls and women will continue to require screening for abnormal pap smears as before. In so far as Indian public health system is concerned, it should be noted that there is not enough staff even to make child-birth safe leave alone to do consistent screening for cancer. In Andhra Pradesh where PATH undertook its study, there is not even a single government facility doing pap smear tests. After testing, localized treatment takes care of abnormal cells. This too is not available as there is dearth of specialists all over the country.

Whether the vaccines will provide lifelong protection is still unknown. Even then, the benefit of vaccination is not going to show for the coming forty years. The disease peaks at age fifty and the girls being vaccinated are just 10 year old. So focussing on the vaccine, which has limitations of covering only 70 per cent of the problem 35–40 years down the line, is extremely lopsided.

Apart from HPV, other factors are implicated in the development of cancer cervix. Among these are: having multiple sexual partners, long-term use of oral hormonal contraceptives, having had a tubectomy, poor nutrition and compromised immunity. But the government is doing all it can to promote hormonal contraception and female sterilization, thereby increasing the disease burden. And poverty reduction is not likely to happen given the economic policies of the government.

It is interesting to note that according to some studies, condom use deters persistent HPV infection[14] and can heal pre-cancerous changes in the cervix![15] If this is the case, then why not focus on the condom which will not only prevent HPV infection but also HIV and unwanted pregnancies.

In other words, there is no coherent or comprehensive strategy to deal with cervical cancer or health issues related to sexual practices. Extensive vaccination with an exorbitantly expensive vaccine can boost sales but is not likely to reduce cancer deaths because so many critical components are not being addressed.

Stranger than fiction – the case and course of HPV vaccines in India: In India the first moves were made in 2002 by WHO[16] to hold clinical trials while these vaccines were still investigational products. Then, in Dec 2005, Merck and Co., Inc. operating in India as MSD India and the Indian Council of Medical Research (ICMR), signed a memorandum of understanding (MoU) to study Merck's investigational cervical cancer vaccine, GARDASIL™ even before Gardasil was approved in the home country (US).

The plan at the time spanned a range of activities, starting with the design of a study to assess the use of Gardasil in the Indian population. In addition to assistance with the study design, Merck was to supply Gardasil for use in the study. Upon completion of the study, the two partners were to work together to assess the role of HPV vaccine in the population of India and identify ways of providing access to HPV vaccine. Merck wanted to work closely with fellow collaborators to establish a model in India that could be adapted for use in the many developing nations worldwide.[17] Since Indian initiatives to develop HPV vaccines were in infancy, India was going to initiate clinical trials with Gardasil.[18] From this, it is apparent that in 2005, Indian authorities were quite tentative about the HPV vaccine and were envisaging that clinical trials would provide data on which they could base future decisions. The plan was to conduct trials in two phases on women aged 17–18 years. The first phase was to take two years and the second four years. In other words, if trials were conducted properly the vaccine could not even have been licensed in India before 2011.[19]

An article written around the signing of this MoU stated,[20]

> Unlike western countries, where the vaccine was administered to young girls in clinical trials, in India it would be difficult to vaccinate adolescent girls due to ethical, social, and monitoring problems. 'Our social setting is such that it may not be possible to vaccinate healthy, young, unmarried girls', pointed out director general of Indian Council of Medical Research (ICMR), Nirmal Kumar Ganguly. Thus, the trial may

include married women in the 18–25 years age group, considering that premarital sex is low in India. Phase III trials will be preceded by smaller 'bridging studies' to test the safety and efficacy of the vaccine in local conditions.

Since pricing is critical for any future HPV vaccine in resource-poor settings like India, the Merck-ICMR agreement contains a clause on making the vaccine available at 'affordable' price for state-funded immunization programmes. 'We will negotiate the price, because unless it is affordable it will be of not much use', pointed out Ganguly.

Also in 2005, ICMR showed a bias towards HPV vaccines and claimed that they are 'expected to be cost-effective measure for prevention of cervical cancer'.[21] However, no Indian trials had been done to support this claim, nor had the price of procurement been fixed. Also till date there is no comprehensive national strategy for control of cervical cancer which includes screening and treatment facilities, – in other words costs are still not clear and effectiveness is impossible to achieve sans screening.

The pharma companies needed ICMR's support but were not ready to wait for the full range of trials to be done. So despite the MoU, MSD hired a contract research organization to do a 7-month trial on 110 subjects aged 9–15 in India, which just tested antibody levels and did no follow up.

In June 2008, based on the slim evidence of this incomplete and limited trial, the Drug Controller approved Gardasil for marketing in India. At this time, a Merck official claimed the approval had been granted on the basis of international experience together with the results of this Indian study. Moreover, the Drugs Controller approved use of Gardasil in the age group of 9–26 years when even the small trial had been done on only 9–15 years-old girls. Cervarix was approved for the age group of 10–45 years with only one trial having taken place on women between 18–35 years but none on children.

The inappropriateness of these actions has to be seen in the context of the regulatory framework of the country.

- According to Indian regulations, even if a drug is already approved/marketed in other countries, phase III trials must be done to confirm the efficacy and safety of the drug on Indian patients. This applies also to vaccines, except that the trials need to be conducted in a much larger number of subjects with vaccines.
- For clinical evaluation of a new drug the study in children should always be carried out after the phase III clinical trials in adults.

These trials are meant to determine if the diverse population of India reacts to the drug/vaccine under trial in the same way as the population in which it was tested for approval in the home country.

In violation of the law, the drugs controller approved Merck's Gardasil for marketing in June 2008, much before the mandatory Phase III trials. The trial in adults began recruitment only in 2009.

The trials done by Merck and GlaxoSmithKline are in the nature of immunobridging studies, which are done prior to Phase III trials, and not in lieu of them.

Once Gardasil and Cervarix were hastily licensed for use, all out attempts were made to create a market.

Promotion in the Private Sector

These two companies are known to have taken the help of associations of doctors in other countries also to promote their products. This has been well documented by Rothman and Rothman.[22] In India also, the Federation of Obstetricians and Gynecologists endorsed the products and GlaxoSmithKline rewarded them by sponsoring their annual report. Not only this, various city chapters of Federation of Obstetricians and Gynecological Societies of India (FOGSI) held meetings to make other doctors aware of the product in the guise of seminars on cancer cervix.

All such events are routinely sponsored by Pharma companies any way. Indian Society for Paediatrics also endorsed the two products. These moves were unwarranted because there was no Indian data to base their decisions on.

Behaviour of doctors was further modified by the companies by giving them huge discounts on purchases. Some doctors went to the extent of holding camps and offering early bird discounts to women coming forward for vaccination. The doctor is no longer just treating the patient but is directly benefiting from a specific approach to managing the disease. The patient suffers from lack of information regarding alternatives and is ignorant of the financial benefits accruing to the doctor.

Pediatricians really went overboard. Instead of limiting themselves to advising their young patients and their parents, they started promoting the vaccines to young mothers accompanying small children.

The companies did not stop at this but started holding workshops in elite schools. These workshops were targeting minors who would then pressurize their parents. Parents were in turn sent on a guilt trip through direct advertising for not acting fast enough to protect their daughters.

Direct advertising was totally misleading, as these vaccines were projected as vaccines against cervical cancer as opposed to vaccines against HPV infection. At any rate, Magic Remedies Act of India specifically prohibits advertising of remedies against cancer. The advertisements hyped the risk of cervical cancer. Though they were aimed at the paying segment of the market, undifferentiated rate of cervical cancer was used to instil fear, even though this cancer has been identified as a disease of poverty. No information was provided on the limitations of the vaccines and the ads of GlaxoSmithKline were purported to be issued in public interest, whereas it stood to profit from any sales generated as a consequence because of its profit-sharing arrangement with Merck. Huge half page ads ran in national dailies, on TV and hoardings also came up. Promotions in schools were not limited to workshops but school authorities were also asked to recommend the vaccines for their students. Some schools agreed but some refused to take this additional responsibility.

We have reports from Bengaluru that girl students in colleges were sent SMS messages advising them to take the vaccines and these messages left nothing to chance but also carried names of doctors who would administer them.

Attempts to Gain Access to the Public Sector

For the vast majority of Indians who cannot pay for such an expensive vaccine, access is possible only through the public sector immunization programmes. It also provides an assured and stable market to pharma companies. Introduction to Indian government programmes makes entry in other Third World countries easier, thereby multiplying the market many times over.

While no progress was made with trials, in June 2006 itself, as soon as USFDA approved Gardasil, PATH (Programme for Appropriate Technology in Health) signed an MoU with ICMR for their Evidence for Impact study which was to be done in 3 phases, for which it received a grant from BMGF. PATH's explicit role was to expedite the introduction of the vaccines in the public sector in India.

The first phase was their formative research. According to PATH: In this case, PATH and our partners used formative research to explore two primary questions:

- What important factors are most likely to result in a child receiving the HPV vaccine?
- What important factors are most likely to foster institutional decisions that result in successful vaccine delivery?[23]

In other words, carrying out market research and developing a lobbying strategy. Formative research was done in Gujarat and Andhra Pradesh with a view to understanding behavioural and attitudinal issues among potential vaccines, villagers, health workers as well as policy makers. Advocacy with policy makers succeeded to the extent that the vaccine was licensed for use, without research.

In the second phase, PATH carried out a population-based vaccination programme in the name of a demonstration project. 16,000 girls between the 10–14 years age group in three remote mandals in Khammam district including Bhadrachalam (a tribal area), Kottagudem (rural) and Tirumalayapalem (semi-urban) were a part of the pilot project.[24] In Gujarat, in three blocks of Vadodara District – Dabhoi, Kawant and Sinor – the project aimed to immunize every girl between the ages of 10 and 14 years.[25] Gardasil and Cervarix were used in Andhra Pradesh and Gujarat respectively. In this study, ICMR and the two state governments were partners with PATH.

Unmindful of ethics, PATH built the results of its formative research into its demonstration project. During the formative research, the villagers had wanted an assurance that such a vaccine was safe and that it was approved by the government, which has a long history of immunization. As it was to be administered to adolescents they also wanted additional assurance that the fertility of girls would not be adversely affected.

PATH incorporated all these elements in the second phase of its study. Project literature for the Khammam study pronounced the vaccine to be safe except for immediate reactions on the injection site. In getting the so-called informed consent, PATH, along with all its partners including ICMR and the State governments, as well as all agencies involved in approving the project including the ethics committees at various levels and the DCGI (Drugs Controller General of India), chose to ignore information in the package insert totally. Not just that, the project made claims about life long immunity and unimpaired fertility. The project documents and banners also used the popular logo of the National Rural Health Mission (NRHM), thus misleading the villagers into believing that it was a part of the government immunization programme. This is normally the strategy adopted by all sellers of consumer goods, but is by no means an ethical method of enrolling participants for medical study.

PATH has stated officially that in the other countries where it carried out a similar project it has even tried out different schedules of immunization, i.e. not stuck to the approved dosage of zero, two and six months.[26] One does not know how they can do this and on whose authority, and what will be the repercussions for the girls on whom these schedules were tried out.

Time and again the lack of ethics in research has been explained away by calling the PATH study a post-licensure study, an operations research project, etc. But the fact remains that the PATH-ICMR project has conducted bio-medical research with human subjects without any regard for the rights and welfare of the subjects.

The ethical guidelines for biomedical research state that persons who are economically or socially disadvantaged should not be used to benefit those who are better off than them. The PATH study in 3 remote mandals in Khammam district, is being done on economically or socially disadvantaged children who will never be able to afford the vaccine (and the government does not have the capacity to provide it to them). In this regard, a recent article in *Asian Age* titled 'Vaccine demonstrated to govt on tribal girls'[27] says,

> That Dr V.M. Katoch, director-general, ICMR, has his own objections to this programme. 'The cost of the vaccine is about ₹ 9,000 (all three doses). How many tribal parents can afford such an expensive vaccine? It is beyond their means. Therefore, I have failed to understand how this rural population can benefit from this vaccine. He says cervical cancer has many causes and this vaccine will prevent two strains of virus. The government needs to develop an indigenous vaccine which should be distributed widely. He pointed out that the project was kick-started in 2006 prior to his appointment as ICMR director general.

WHO is also playing a role in facilitating public sector introduction. As stated earlier, they gave pre-qualification to the vaccines. Then, they initiated a trial for cost cutting. This trial would find out if 2 doses of the vaccine would suffice to give immunity instead of the 3 doses being given at present. If this study has any scientific basis, then one has to assume that either the millions of girls vaccinated so far have been overdosed, or the 10,000 subjects of this study will be unprotected.

The concerned pharma companies are waiting neither for PATH nor for WHO. Their medical representatives have already started approaching government functionaries at state and district level for direct purchases.[28]

The Campaign

We were alerted to the 2nd phase of the PATH project in July 2009. A fairly comprehensive memorandum signed by more than 60 organizations working on women's and health issues was sent to the Health Minister on September 30, 2009. In addition to the technical and programmatic issues, it also raised objections about cost effectiveness and unethical advertising. By October, we had managed to get some information from the field by way of publicity literature, informed consent form and news of the first death in Khammam. Always preoccupied with women's health it took some time to sink in that we were now dealing with the question of child rights. Children are protected especially under the Drugs and Cosmetics Act but the project seemed to be violating their rights on three counts:

1. No trial had been undertaken in India with Gardasil among adults before foisting it on children.
2. The objective of the exercise was not clear as the vaccine was unaffordable. Covering all girls in the 10–14 age groups in the country with Gardasil would have amounted to spending two and a half times the annual health budget. When there could be no plan to go ahead, such a large scale vaccination only meant that the girls were being used as guinea pigs.
3. The girls were being chosen from socio-economic strata that just could not afford the vaccine at the market price. The project was just for two years and the requirements of booster doses were not known. The longest known effectiveness at the time was four years and the ten-year-olds would not even be at risk during this time. This was the other way in which they were being used as guinea pigs.

These issues were raised before the National Commission for Protection of Child Rights (NCPCR) in November 2009, and groups working on child rights were also drawn in the campaign. The Minister had not responded to the memorandum for more than two months, and it was during this time that the aggressive media advertising blitz took off by the pharma companies. It was decided to hold a public meeting on the matter and all players were invited to answer questions related to their role and responsibility. The two drug companies, Health Ministry, Drugs Controller, NCPCR, ICMR and PATH were sent an advance list of questions which included the question of allowing advertising in violation of the laws. Only after these letters went out, the Drugs Controller, for the first time, asked the companies to stop advertising. The ministry refused to respond and the drug companies refused to show up. One media representative from PATH did come to the meeting but had no answer to any questions raised by us. The complaint to the NCPCR did evoke a response in that it was sent to the government of Andhra Pradesh for a reply.

The government's silence continued till April 2010, when the results of a fact-finding undertaken by Sama and Janwadi Mahilla Samiti were released at a press conference on World Health Day. A whole host of adverse effects and ethical violations were reported from the field. Ms Brinda Karat raised the matter first in the Parliamentary Standing Committee on Health and Family Welfare and then in Rajya Sabha itself. By then six deaths among vaccinees were admitted. The government was forced to set up an enquiry committee and suspend the trials. But the programme had completed most of the vaccination by then.

Organizations had also written to the Andhra Pradesh government to do exhaustive review of the health status of the girls, since the study protocol was to recruit only healthy girls. They also demanded compensation for death and debility, and treatment for any new conditions.

A memorandum was also submitted to the DCGI to suspend the licence of the two vaccines due to various anomalies in their introduction in the country without trials and demanding the completion of WHO studies before allowing further sale of vaccines. This again did not draw a response. RTIs were filed with the Drugs Controller but no response was forthcoming and trial results were falsely claimed as being company trade secrets and due to this the Drugs Controller denied permission to part with information. This is indeed a mockery of justice where citizens have no rights but the drug companies can conduct trials and not be obliged to share results. According to Dr C.M. Gulhati, the pharma companies are now lobbying for data exclusivity rights and denial of information may become a legitimate limitation for patient rights.

But the real eye-opener was the reply of the Andhra Pradesh government to NCPCR which was forwarded to us in April 2010. The State government stated that as the PATH study was a post-licensure study they were not looking into problems suffered by the girls. They also stated that the question of beneficial impact (of vaccination) was not relevant! The reply was definitely not drafted by the Andhra Pradesh government as instead of 'vaccine' in singular it used 'vaccines' a plural as if an agency spanning both the states was replying. Later we found same explanations (verbatim) on PATH website. The essential theme of the reply was to skirt around the issues of safety and responsibility but to harp on the fact that the vaccines were approved by more than a hundred countries and endorsed by professional associations. If this was enough, then what is the relevance of the National Drug Authority and the apex Research body ICMR?

The power of the companies held sway over media reporting also. For a few months the journalists had to desist from mentioning the names of the company as the owners of the press were worried that the companies would take them to court. This spell was broken only as the media personnel were cajoled into visiting the field and seeing things for themselves.

The enquiry committee set up by the government was to give its report in June 2010 but came out with it only in February 2011. Even then, the report is not available in the public domain. We got a copy of part of the report (titled Final report of the Committee appointed by the Govt. of India (vide notification No. V. 25011/160/2010-HR dated 15th April 2010) to enquire into 'Alleged irregularities in the conduct of studies using Human Papilloma Virus (HPV) vaccine' by PATH in India, 15 February 2011).

This enquiry was not looking at the totality of violations with respect to the two HPV vaccines, but its terms of reference was limited to enquiring into the deaths and ethics of the PATH project. At the outset, the experts concluded that the study which had been carried out was indeed a clinical trial regardless of the claims of PATH, ICMR and others in this regard. With regard to deaths the committee found that there was a long delay before deaths were reported and post mortem had been done in only 2 of the 7 deaths. For the remaining deaths, the information provided was very sketchy. There was severe under reporting of even minor adverse events. While Merck's data on the Indian study showed 83 per cent reporting of minor side effects, the PATH data showed this incidence as less than 2 per cent. Based on this, the experts felt that serious adverse events were also seriously under reported. Regarding informed consent, the committee found many irregularities such as, incomplete forms with signatures and dates missing, no consent of the participant in writing, and above all, issuing circulars to school authorities to sign consent forms.

But the report made some very alarming revelations:

- PATH had insured itself for the project but had not insured the children.
- In violation of laws of the land the DCGI had extended the indications for use of Gardasil for women up to the age of 45 years while the home country authorities (USFDA) has refused this extension thrice. In fact, according to a Merck press release, dated 6 April 2011, 'An indication for adult women was not granted; instead, the Limitations of Use and Effectiveness for GARDASIL was updated to state that GARDASIL has not been demonstrated to prevent

HPV-related CIN 2/3 or worse in women older than 26 years of age'.[29]

- Financial data regarding the study was not provided to this committee and it is interesting to note that the committee took no exception to this non-cooperation. But there were indications that NRHM funds were used to subsidize the project, whose beneficiaries were going to be multinational firms and not the people for whom NRHM was meant.
- The enquiry committee was also of the view that in taking free vaccines from the manufacturers there was a conflict of interest.
- In using the NRHM logo PATH had blurred the distinction between the government's routine immunization programme and the research study.

The report glossed over the fact that false reassurances were given to the trial subjects about safety and efficacy of the vaccine and that they were used as guinea pigs. It did not look into the question of GlaxoSmithKline being given a licence for use among children without any research on children. Hence, the committee concluded that since both products were licensed for use among children there was nothing wrong in this.

Unfortunately, the committee commented on lack of data about side effects and deaths but did not call either health groups or affected girls and their families to make a deposition, even though they could have provided a more complete picture.

Despite there being problems at every level the committee refused to hold PATH accountable and said that the deficiencies were minor in nature. One may question if false information, consent by coercion, not recording adverse events following vaccination, not insuring children, not worrying about their welfare during and after the project are minor, then what would constitute a major violation which would merit action against erring officials and the Project Director?

The most valuable recommendation made by the committee is to bring together formulation of Good Clinical Practice, ICMR's guidelines on research on human subjects and Schedule Y under statutory status. A bill is already on the anvil in this regard.

Issues Thrown up by the Case

The power of multinational pharma companies and their hold over decision-making bodies directly and indirectly is increasingly becoming a cause for worry. NGOs promoted by foundations that have an interest in profits can really play havoc and are not accountable to anyone other than their donors.

The behaviour of the Government of India as well as that of the State Governments is unacceptable and unconstitutional. The government is duty bound to protect the life and health of its citizens and has to do it within a policy framework that offers optimal programme strategies as opposed to single-mindedly pursuing a course which is so uncertain. In this very case, the interest of the citizens was disregarded, right from the stage of licensing and permitting false propaganda. It is unfortunate that this is not happening in India alone but all over the world.

No bio-medical research on humans can be allowed without proper ethical safeguards, compensatory mechanisms and continued medical care being built into it. This cannot only be a statement of intent but the government should take disciplinary action such as blacklisting of NGOs, charge sheeting errant officials, and above all, compensate all the girls who participated in the trials since they were meant to be selected only if they were healthy as per the inclusion criteria.

The government has to contain its tendency to measure and assess everything in terms of growing GDP which is eroding the health infrastructure of the country. This alone can stop the growing menace of medical tourism, clinical trials and surrogacy which are diverting precious resources away from those who most need them.

Lastly, it is interesting to know that Bill and Melinda Gates Foundation seems to have come out the only winner, as it sold off Merck shares in 2009 before vaccine injury cases are taken up by courts.

Notes

1. World Health Organization, World Health Statistics 2011. Table 7 Health Expenditure.
2. Ibid.
3. World Health Organization, 'Human Papillomavirus and HPV Vaccines: Technical Information for Policy-Makers and Health Professionals', 2007, p. 20.
4. See in FDA Pressured to Consider Expanding HPV Vaccines to 'Older' Women, http://www.prlog.org/10990882-fda-pressured-to-consider-expanding-hpv-vaccines-to-older-women.html
5. John Carreyrou and Keith Winstein, 'Medical Journal Questions Efficacy of HPV Vaccine', *Wall Street Journal*, 10 May 2007, p. D3, http://www.forums.pharma-mkting.com/showthread.php?t=496
6. http://www.merck.com/product/usa/pi_circulars/g/gardasil/gardasil_pi.pdf, Full prescribing information, accessed on 22 May 2011.
7. http://truthaboutgardasil.org, FDA Webinar documents, http://www.scribd.com/doc/28357750/03–12–10-FDA-Script-for-Presentation–1
8. F.J. DiMario Jr., M. Hajjar and T.A. Ciesielski, 'A 16-Year-Old Girl with Bilateral Visual Loss and Left Hemiparesis Following an Immunization against Human Papilloma Virus', *Journal of Child Neurology,* Vol. 25, No. 3, 2010, pp. 321–327, http://Jcn.Sagepub.Com/Content/25/3/321.Abstract
9. 'Why is the HPV Vaccine So Expensive?', *Discover Magazine*, 11 June 2007, http://discovermagazine.com/2007/jun/hpv
10. 'Gates Foundation Sells Off Most Health-Care, Pharmaceutical Holdings', *Wall Street Journal,* 15 August 2009, http://online.wsj.com/article/SB125029373754433433.html
11. 'Journal Critique on Bill and Melinda Gates Foundation Grant Pattern', *The Hindu,* 10 May 2009, http://www.hindu.com/2009/05/10/stories/2009051055151000.htm
12. World Health Organization, 'The Top 10 Causes of Death', Fact Sheet No. 310, Updated October 2008.
13. http://www.cancer.org/Cancer/CervicalCancer/DetailedGuide/cervical-cancer-key-statistics
14. Rachel L. Winer et al., 'Condom Use and the Risk of Genital Human Papillomavirus Infection in Young Women', *N Engl J Med*, Vol. 354, No. 25, 22 June 2006, pp. 2645–2654.

15. Ibid.
16. 'Can Condoms Help Clear HPV?', Wiley Online Library.
17. http://caonline.amcancersoc.org/cgi/content/full/54/2/69
18. 'WHO Team to Identify Centres for Trial of Cervical Cancer Vaccine', http://articles.timesofindia.indiatimes.com/2002–11–30/chandigarh/27304768_1_cervical-cancer-hpv-cytology-and-preventive-oncology, accessed on 25 May 2011.
19. 'Merck and the ICMR Announce a PP Partnership on HPV Vaccine', http://www.moneycontrol.com/news/business/merck-icmr-announcepp-partnershiphpv-vaccine_194974.html
20. http://icmr.nic.in/annual/2005–06/hqds/ncd.pdf, p. 94.
21. 'Merck, ICMR to Conduct Joint Trials on Cervical Cancer Vaccine', http://www.medindia.net/news/view_news_main.asp?x=6507, accessed on 27 May 2011.
22. Dinesh C. Sharma, 'India Opens Up to Clinical Trials of Papillomavirus Vaccines', *The Lancet Infectious Diseases*, Vol. 6, 2006, p. 76.
23. 'Strategies for Control of Cervical Cancer in India', 6th INCTR Annual Meeting, Chennai, India, 10–13 December 2005.
24. Ibid.
25. See in Charlotte Haug, 'The Risks and Benefits of HPV Vaccination', *JAMA*, Vol. 302, No. 7, 2009, pp. 795–796.
26. PATH and National AIDS Research Institute (NARI), *Shaping a Strategy to Introduce HPV Vaccines in India: Results from the HPV Vaccines: Evidence for Impact Project*, PATH, Seattle, Washington, 2009, http://www.rho.org/files/PATH_FRTS_India.pdf
27. 'Pilot Program for Vaccination against Cervical Cancer Launched', *The Hindu*, 10 July 2009.
28. 'Gujarat Launches Cervical Cancer Vaccine', *Press Trust of India*, 13 August 2009.
29. 'Immunogenicity of Alternative Schedules of Gardasil® in 11–13-Year-Old Girls in Vietnam', K.M. Neuzil, D. Cahn, V. Thiem, V. Huong, D.N.T Nguyen, Y. Tang, A. Janmohamed, D.S. LaMontagne.

CHAPTER 11

Mental Health

A Fringe Issue in the Prostitution or Sex Work Debate

SUNEHA KANDPAL

Mental health is an integral and essential component of health. The WHO constitution states: 'Health is a state of complete physical, mental and social well-being and not merely the absence of disease or infirmity'. An important consequence of this definition is that mental health is described as more than the absence of mental disorders or disabilities.

Mental health is a state of well-being in which an individual realizes his or her own abilities, can cope with the normal stresses of life, can work productively and is able to make a contribution to his or her community. In this positive sense, mental health is the foundation for individual well-being and the effective functioning of a community.

Mental health promotion involves creating living conditions and environments that support mental health and allow people to adopt and maintain healthy lifestyles. It entails promotion and protection of basic civil, political, socio-economic and cultural rights. In the public health debates and literature, prostitution is an essential area of intervention. There is a spectrum of implications for public health and health service provision; yet sex work is typically stigmatized and often criminalized. Particularly, in developing countries like India, where there is an ongoing debate on the issue of decriminalization or legalization of prostitution, the focus in the prostitution/sex work debate is somewhat restricted to the physical health or legal rights perspective. In terms of services rendered and the laws pertaining to the same, mental health again takes a back seat. The present paper will discuss with understanding the mental health implications of prostitution/sex work and an abysmal response to it in the public health discourse. The paper will also provide an overview of the existing literature/research and field experiences in the context of the mental health issues on women working as prostitutes/sex workers.

Sex work/prostitution is an interesting intersect of sex, marriage, sexuality, patriarchy interplaying and impacting notions of morality, women's autonomy and feminism. Sex work, or prostitution, is the provision of sexual services for money or its equivalent. Sex workers may be male, female, or transgendered, and the margins of prostitution/sex work range from erotic displays without physical contact with the client, to high risk unprotected sexual intercourse with numerous clients. Individuals may occasionally and/or opportunistically render sexual services or may engage more or less full time in commercial provision of sex services. From being looked upon as an outcome of capitalism by Marxists or as a degrading form of violence on women by radical feminists, to being asserted as a right to work, this issue has come a long way.

Prostitution/sex work has far-reaching social, psychological, and medical consequences for those involved in it, especially women owing to their gender location. Studies of prostitution, world over, have focused largely on understanding the public health implications of this behaviour. Additionally, prostitution is often linked with socio-demographic disadvantage (e.g. minority ethnic status, low income, homelessness, low education level).[1,2] Due to its complexity and multifaceted nature, prostitution poses a significant challenge to professionals, clinicians and researchers alike. Within India and other industrialized or developing nations, studies have been focused largely on the prevalence, health hazards, HIV and AIDS and other aspects pertaining to their lifestyles, etc. Although this work provides a rich foundation for understanding prostitution as it exists in totality, nonetheless, a broader understanding of the effect of prostitution/sex work on the mental and physical health of men and women is needed. Although the traumatic effects of rape and other violence to women who are not in prostitution/sex work are well established, the same trauma is not well understood among women in prostitution/sex work. There is a real dearth of research in this particular area, particularly in India. We need intensive, longitudinal, ethnographic studies to find out what affects their health and mental health over a lifetime as they either stay or leave prostitution/sex work. Despite recognition of prostitution/sex work as a public health issue, research remains limited in scope. In addition, a comparative study with different groups of population could also aid in determining to what extent prostitution influences health after accounting for other common risk factors.

The locational and circumstantial contexts of sex work are important in estimating the potential health hazards of prostitution, hence, let us have a look firstly, into the different forms of prostitution or sex work that exists;

1. Street or other public place when used for sex work/prostitution is referred to as 'direct' prostitution and is probably the most widespread type of prostitution globally. Large numbers of street-based sex workers can be an indicator of socio-economic breakdown[3] in developing and war-torn countries.[4] In developed countries sex workers are more likely to solicit publicly if legislation denies them access to indoor venues, they are drug dependent, or there is an employment crisis.[5] Many sex workers regard street work as undesirable because of the danger of violence and other forms of social hostility.[6] Even so, some prefer the relative autonomy and unregulated conditions of outdoor work.[6]

Instead of waiting for fleeting clients, some sex workers actively approach the male-dominated site such as pubs, clubs, hostels or hotels.[7] Others frequent transport hubs or highways.[3,8] Between public and indoor prostitution is doorway and window prostitution. Commonly, sex workers in many parts of the developing world or poorer European suburbs solicit from the doorways of small brothels or their own homes.[9] Indoor sex work is typically brothel prostitution. Brothels vary enormously in their size and their administration. They range from individual 'houses' to fully staffed enterprises supervised by madams and pimps. The human rights and working conditions of brothel prostitutes vary too, but brothels generally offer greater security than the street, in terms of personal safety and provide some health care and education. Another widespread form of indoor prostitution is escort prostitution which may operate internationally also, where sex workers are contacted by phone and travel to the clients' premises. Operating covertly they are under less scrutiny of law enforcers and the community at large. However, escort sex workers are also potentially exposed to violence from clients without a proper redressal mechanism. Sex workers working alone or in small groups from 'residential' premises are emerging as a significant sector in India and many other parts of the world.[10, 11, 12] Private sex workers in developed countries, unlike doorway prostitutes, require the potential clients to make appointments by phone. Thus, although they often work alone, are able to control their work environment and pre select their clients to a considerable degree. It is, however, difficult to measure the sexual health and other welfare parameters of private workers because, like escorts, they work covertly.

2. Prostitution/sex work is not always the sole or primary source of income for individuals, but can provide additional income for many,[6] which may not be recognized as prostitution/sex work. Consequently, the personal and public health risks may be greater than in the 'direct' sex industry.[13] There are some indirect sexual services

(telephone sex, internet (virtual) sex, bondage and discipline, lap dancing, massage) that involve little or no genital contact and, therefore, have little sexual health risk.[14] These services are mostly confined to wealthier countries. Other forms of indirect prostitution involve genital intercourse, but only after a previous transaction, such as the purchase of beer, or a massage, or some form of entertainment, has occurred.[15, 16, 17] These and other forms of opportunistic sex, including sex for drug exchanges, can have major public health implications.[18] In 'Long time' arrangements, where a sex worker is engaged as a live-in companion (Bali, Philipines), 'minor wife' (Thailand), or 'outside wife' (sub-Saharan Africa)[12,19,20] the client may believe he has avoided the risks of 'commercial' sex by the arrangement, and the sex worker more of a concubine and at worst a sex slave. These arrangements reflect stark socio-economic disparity and power play between the sex worker and the client.

Apart from the locational factors, other cross cutting factors also influence the health and welfare of sex workers. An important variable is the number of clients a sex worker sees during a typical working hour. High number of clients over relatively short periods are linked to high levels of Sexually transmitted diseases (STD) and other poor health outcomes,[21,22] which can be reduced by consistent usage of condoms resulting in more earning.[11,23,24] High numbers of clients often associated with low income prostitution produces much worse outcomes and in turn is related to a number of factors. In developing countries most of sex workers work in filthy, vulnerable and impoverished hamlet for paltry amount of money which marginalizes them further. They have no say in choosing the clients, defining the working hours and having consistent access to condoms and health services. Pimps and traffickers to enhance their profit often force them to service large numbers of clients. Even without overt coercion, the constant debt and other expenses slapped on sex workers such as make-up, tips to the police, etc. push them to do so. Many sex workers for example very young and older sex workers, illegal immigrant, homeless, mobile, and/or physically and socially isolated sex workers have to see more clients because they are unable to command a larger amount for their service and the strata of the client being catered to also make a difference.

Literature Review

Now looking at the available literature about prostitution in the medical and social sciences, it fails to address the sexual violence and psychological harm, which both precede and are intrinsic to prostitution (Farley and Kelly, 2000). In the literature between 1980 and 1998 most authors have extensively focussed on HIV and AIDS, STI and have rather failed to deal with the violence in prostitution. Although HIV is a critical public health crisis but the violence and human rights violations in prostitution have also posed a matter of grave concern for sex workers. According to Farley et al., 2000 the literature review of the material on prostitution shows that it revolved around these three categories: (1) STD/HIV, (2) other harmful consequences of prostitution, (3) legal/demographic/psychoanalytic. The first category, STD/HIV, included those references which discussed means of transmission and infection rates of STD and various approaches to HIV prevention. The second category (other harm) included discussions of non-HIV-related harm of prostitution. Citations included discussions of sexual and physical violence in prostitution, and antecedent harm, such as juvenile prostitution and childhood sexual assault. The third category included demographic descriptions of those in prostitution (e.g. number of arrests, gender differences), (b) psychoanalytic theorizing about the origin of prostitution behaviour which did not discuss trauma, (c) discussions of legalization or decriminalization which did not discuss harm to those being prostituted, and d) historical accounts of prostitution (Farley et al., 2003). This systematic neglect of the mental health or psychologically has had its fall outs on the laws and interventions planned for them. Cotton and Forster (2000) surveyed psychology of women textbooks and found that eleven of fourteen texts published since 1995 failed to mention prostitution. When prostitution was mentioned, it was usually addressed as a 'feminist debate' or as 'work' rather than as violence. Much of the health sciences literature assumed the normalcy of prostitution as vocational choice for women (Green et al., 1993). It was often suggested that prostitution could be a safe activity. However, this perspective seemed only to consider safety from HIV. Hence, a very limited literature is found on the subject of mental and physical health of sex workers.

Psychological Implications

People in prostitution/sex work suffer from post-traumatic stress disorder (PTSD). Symptoms are anxiety, depression, insomnia, irritability, flashbacks, emotional numbing and hyperalertness. Farley et al., (1998) interviewed 475 prostituted people in 5 countries (South Africa, Thailand, Turkey, USA, and Zambia) and found that 67 per cent met diagnostic criteria for PTSD, suggesting that the traumatic squeal of prostitution were similar across different cultures. Since there have been studies which, in fact, show that there is no difference found in the incidence of PTSD and depression in the legalized and 'street' types of prostitution, suggesting that the emotional experience of prostitution is intrinsically traumatizing, regardless of its location and decriminalization (Farley, et al., 1998). Hence, regardless of legal status, prostitution/sex work has devastating effect on women's overall well-being, especially psychosocially. In addition, as a result of trauma of prostitution/sex work, multiple psychological dysfunctions are experienced by these women, which inadvertently also spill over to their overall functioning and well-being.

Dissociation is the psychological process of banishing traumatic events from consciousness (Herman, 1992). It is an emotional shutting-down which occurs during extreme stress among prisoners of war who are being tortured, among children who are being sexually assaulted and among women being battered or raped or prostituted. Ross et al. (1990) noted dissociative symptoms in women in strip club prostitution. Belton (1998) reported that depression as well as dissociative disorders was common among prostituted women.

Herman (1992) described the result in personality changes due to the violence of prostitution, the constant humiliation, the social indignity and misogyny which have been as complex post-traumatic stress disorder (CPTSD). Symptoms of CPTSD are changes in consciousness and self-concept, changes in the ability to regulate emotions, changes in systems of meaning, such as loss of faith, and an unremitting sense of despair. One of the long-lasting effects of CPTSD involves changes in relations with other people, including changes in perception of the perpetrator of abuse. Under conditions of control and captivity the emotional bond between those prostituted and pimps is very complex. The sex worker is dependent on the pimp for security and money and feels extremely helpless. This emotional bonding to an abuser under conditions of captivity has been described as the Stockholm syndrome. Attitudes and behaviours which are part of this syndrome include: (1) intense gratefulness for small favours when the captor holds life and death power over the captive; (2) denial of the extent of violence and harm which the captor has inflicted or is obviously capable of inflicting; (3) hyper vigilance with respect to the pimp's needs and identification with the pimp's perspective on the world (4) perception of those trying to assist in escape as enemies and perception of captors as friends; (5) extreme difficulty leaving one's captor/pimp, even after physical release has occurred. Ironically, women in prostitution may feel that they owe their lives to pimps and gave them an alternative to them to survive.

One of the myths that 'high-class' call-girl prostitution/sex work is vastly different and much safer than street prostitution has not been verified by research. One study reported that there was no difference in the incidence of post-traumatic stress disorder experienced by those prostituting on the street and those prostituting in 'high-class brothels' (Farley et al., 1998). Parriott (1994) found no differences in health problems reported by women in massage brothels, escort services, strip clubs, bars, and street prostitution. Boyer et al. (1993) reported that women in all forms of prostitution (escort, strip club, street, phone sex, and massage brothel) were subject to sexual violence. Domination and power are the central themes of prostitution/sex work where one person socially, legally or economically enjoys the power to employ persons, mostly women to be an object sexual gratification.

In all prostitution/sex work there is *commodification* of the woman's body resulting in internalizing this belief, where the prostituted woman begins to see sexually objectified parts of her own body as separate from, rather than integral to her entire self. In an attempt to defend the self and blank out the overwhelming distress they face during their working hours, women may make a conscious decision to disconnect from parts of the body. Eventually, this disconnect of the body results in somatoform dissociation and numbing in the same way that traumatic affects and memories are repressed into dissociated consciousness. This disconnection between the parts or whole from the self is common among survivors of extreme trauma. Vanwesenbeeck noted that '*dissociative proficiency*' contributed to the professional attitudes among women in prostitution in the Netherlands (1994: 107). For example, many women would state 'I become numb, don't feel anything' otherwise, it would be difficult for them to work since the feelings of pain, shame, and anger can be overwhelming. Most women who have been in prostitution for a long time also experience sexual dysfunction and mistrust even with their chosen partners. Since feelings are disconnected from sexual acts with the clients and pimps, it becomes difficult for sex workers to differentiate between their partners and their clients and engage in healthy sexual behaviour. Not surprisingly, women involved in prostitution report an increased incidence of *depression*, report lifetime suicidal ideation and self-destructive behaviour. Some even report feeling 'alive' after cutting or hurting themselves.

The social invisibility and stigmatization of prostitution/sex work come in the way of understanding deep psychological implications on the people engaged in it. If we do not recognize or perceive the harm then it would be difficult to formulate the interventions at least for those who do not want to be a part of it. In addition, it is commonly assumed that the greater the legal tolerance of prostitution, the easier it is to control public health (Green et al., 1993). 'Public health' in this context again refers primarily to HIV/STD, rather than to the mental and physical health of sex workers. Unfortunately, due to the lack of in-depth understanding of mental health issues, closely entwined with human rights, legal and public health discourses, translates into grossly inadequate or absent laws and services for this marginalized population. This becomes even more emphatic when we talk about empowerment of sex workers and achievement of political or legal rights while ignoring the psychological rights of the women.

Conclusion

Therefore, a broader understanding of how prostitution affects mental and physical health is needed. In particular, the study of prostitution among individuals in substance use treatment would improve efforts to provide comprehensive treatment. Overall, prostitution presents before us complex clinical profile with co-morbidity of substance abuse and suicidal ideation. Findings suggest that prostitution, whether seen as a proxy for complex mental health issues or a risk factor for exposure to interpersonal trauma, warrants an effort to design tailored treatment to this population. The formulation of the programmes ought to be considered at three levels: (1) after the raid or rescue operation, (2) during the course of their work and (3) during the process of rehabilitation. Developing appropriate interventions also entails a comprehensive picture of the shape and location of local sex industries and the conscription process. In addition, the support group for them and their children can also prove to be immensely helpful in facilitating them to adopt healthy patterns for coping and survival and management of mental and physical health symptoms related to involvement in prostitution. Emerging literature has also begun to explore interventions like peer networking, social support systems, social assistance to assist women attempting to leave prostitution[25] combining it with the de-addiction programme.[26] These approaches have been characterized as a nonjudgmental harm-reduction model and typically include a peer-support element.[25] In due course, a comprehensive mental health and trauma-related literature may allow for the development of truly comprehensive interventions. Ultimately, research could contribute to empirically informed and more effective intervention for this population.

Notes

1. M.A. Medrano, J.P. Hatch, W.A. Zule and D.P. Desmond, 'Childhood Trauma and Adult Prostitution Behaviour in a Multiethnic Heterosexual Drug-Using Population', *American Journal of Drug and Alcohol Abuse*, Vol. 29, No. 2, 2003, pp. 463–486.
2. G. Gilchrist, L. Gruer and J. Atkinson, 'Comparison of Drug Use and Psychiatric Morbidity between Prostitute and Non-Prostitute Female Drug Users in Glasgow, Scotland', *Addiction Behaviour*, Vol. 30, No. 5, 2005, pp. 1019–1023.
3. S.O. Aral, J.S. Lawrence, L. Tikhonova et al., 'The Social Organization of Commercial Sex Work in Moscow, Russia', *Journal of Sexually Transmitted Diseases*, Vol. 30, 2003, pp. 39–45.
4. C.A. Hankins, S.R. Friedman, T. Zafar et al., 'Transmission and Prevention of HIV and Sexually Transmitted Infections in War Settings: Implications for Current and Future Armed Conflicts', Editorial Review, *Journal of AIDS*, Vol. 16, 2002, pp. 2245–2252.

5. J. Allen, *Sex and Secrets: Crimes Involving Australian Women Since 1880*, Oxford University Press, Melbourne, 1990, pp. 189–194.
6. C. Harcourt, I. van Beek, J. Heslop et al., 'The Health and Welfare of Female and Transgender Sex Workers in New South Wales', *Australian and New Zealand Journal of Public Health*, Vol. 25, 2001, pp. 84–89.
7. C.A. Blackmore, K. Limpakarnjanarat, J.G. Rigau-Pe´rez et al., 'An Outbreak of Chancroid in Orange County, California: Descriptive Epidemiology and Disease-Control Measures', *Journal of Infectious Diseases*, Vol. 151, 1985, pp. 840–844.
8. Y.N. Singh and A.N. Malaviya, 'Long Distance Truck Drivers in India: HIV Infection and Their Possible Role in Disseminating HIV into Rural Areas', *International Journal of STD AIDS*, Vol. 5, 1994, pp. 137–138.
9. C. Asamoah-Adu, N. Khonde, M. Avorkliah et al., 'HIV Infection among Sex Workers in Accra: Need to Target New Recruits Entering the Trade', *Journal of AIDS*, Vol. 28, 2001, pp. 358–366.
10. A. Wade and G. Mateljan, 'Research Fieldwork among Sex Workers', in R. Perkins, G. Prestage, R. Sharp et al. (eds), *Sex Work and Sex Workers in Australia*, UNSW Press, Sydney, 1994, pp. 292–300.
11. H. Ward, S. Day and J. Weber, 'Risky Business: Health and Safety in the Sex Industry Over a 9 Year Period', *Journal of Sexually Transmitted Infections*, Vol. 75, 1999, pp. 340–343.
12. K. Ford, D.N. Wirawan and P. Fajans, 'AIDS Knowledge, Risk Behaviours and Condom Use among Four Groups of Female Sex Workers in Bali, Indonesia', *Journal of Acquired Immune Deficiency Syndrome and Human Retrovirology*, Vol. 10, 1995, pp. 569–576.
13. L. Jackson, A. Highcrest and R.A. Coates, 'Varied Potential Risks of HIV Infection among Prostitutes', *Journal of Social Science and Medicine*, Vol. 35, 1992, pp. 281–286.
14. R. Blain, 'A Female Sex Worker's View', in R. Perkins, G. Prestage, R. Sharp et al. (eds), *Sex Work and Sex Workers in Australia*, UNSW Press, Sydney, 1994, pp. 113–125.
15. M.R. Josoef, M. Linnan, Y. Barakbah et al., 'Patterns of Sexually Transmitted Diseases in Female Sex Workers in Surabaya, Indonesia', *International Journal of STD AIDS*, Vol. 8, 1997, pp. 576–580.
16. N.T.T. Thuy, V.T. Nhung, N.V. Thuc et al., 'HIV Infection and Risk Factors among Female Sex Workers in Southern Vietnam', *Journal of AIDS*, Vol. 12, 1998, pp. 425–432.

17. H.B. Leng, 'Cambodia', in T. Brown, R. Chan, D. Mugrditchian et al. (eds.), *Sexually Transmitted Diseases in Asia and the Pacific*, Venereology Publishing, East-West Centre, Thai Red Cross, Armidale, NSW, 1998, pp. 62–71.
18. J.A. Inciardi, 'Crack House Sex and HIV Risk', *Archive of Sexual Behaviour*, Vol. 24, 1995, pp. 249–269.
19. A. Larson, 'Social Context of Human Immunodeficiency Virus Transmission in Africa: Historical and Cultural Bases of East and Central African Sexual Relations', *Reviews of Infectious Diseases*, Vol. 11, 1989, pp. 716–731.
20. S. Peracca, J. Knodel and C. Saengtienchai, 'Can Prostitutes Marry? Thai Attitudes toward Female Sex Workers', *Journal of Social Science and Medicine*, Vol. 47, 1998, pp. 255–267.
21. B. Donovan, 'Medico-Social Aspects of a House of Prostitution', *Medical Journal of Australia*, Vol. 140, 1984, pp. 272–275.
22. P. Jha, N.J.D. Nagelkereke, E.N. Ngugi et al., 'Reducing HIV Transmission in Developing Countries', *Science*, Vol. 292, 2001, pp. 224–245.
23. J. Vioque, I. Herna´ndez-Aguado, E.F. Garcia et al., 'Prospective Cohort Study of Female Sex Workers and the Risk of HIV Infection in Alicante, Spain (1986–96)', *Journal of Sexually Transmitted Infections*, Vol. 74, 1998, pp. 284–288.
24. B. Donovan and C. Harcourt, 'The Female Sex Industry in Australia: A Health Promotion Model', *Journal of Venereology*, Vol. 9, 1996, pp. 63–67.
25. N. Hotaling, A. Burris, B.J. Johnson, Y.M. Bird and K.A. Melbye, 'Been There Done That: A Peer Leadership Model among Prostitution Survivors', in M. Farley (ed.), *Prostitution, Trafficking and Traumatic Stress*, Haworth Maltreatment and Trauma Press, New York, 2003, pp. 255–266.
26. S.C. Timpson, M.W. Ross, M.L. Williams and J. Atkinson, 'Characteristics, Drug Use and Sex Partners of a Sample of Male Sex Workers', *American Journal of Drug and Alcohol Abuse*, Vol. 33, No. 1, 2007, pp. 63–69.

References

American Psychiatric Association, *Diagnostic and Statistical Manual of Mental Disorders*, 4th edition, Washington, DC, 1994.

Belton, R., 'Assessment, Diagnosis and Treatment of Prostitution Trauma', American Psychological Association, San Francisco, 1998.

Boyer, Debra, Chapman, Lynn and Marshall, Brent, 'Survival Sex in King Country, Helping Women Out', North West Resource Associates, Seattle, 1993.

Cotton, A. and Forster, C., 'Pornography and Prostitution: A Survey of Psychology of Women Texts'. Paper Presented in Association of Women in Psychology, 25th Annual Meeting, Saltlake City, Utah, 2000.

Dworkin, A., *Prostitution and Male Supremacy in Life and Death*, Free Press, New York, 1997: 131–151.

Farley, M., 'Prostitution and the Invisibility of Harm', *Women and Therapy*, Vol. 26, No. 3/4, 2003: 247–280.

——, 'Bad for the Body, Bad for the Heart: Prostitution Harms Women Even If Legalized or Decriminalized', *Journal of Violence against Women*, Vol. 10, 2004: 1087–1125.

Farley, M., I. Baral, M. Kiremire and U. Sezgin, 'Prostitution in Five Countries: Violence and Post-Traumatic Stress Disorder', *Journal of Feminism and Psychology*, Vol. 8, 1998: 415–426.

Farley, M., A. Cotton, J. Lynne, S. Zumbeck, F. Spiwak, M.E. Reyes, D. Alvarez and U. Sezgin, 'Prostitution and Trafficking in 9 Countries: Update on Violence and Post-Traumatic Stress Disorder', in M. Farley (ed.), *Prostitution, Trafficking and Traumatic Stress*, Haworth Press, Binghamton, New York, 2003: 33–74.

Farley, Melissa and Vanessa Kelly, 'Prostitution: A Critical Review of the Medical and Social Sciences Literature', *Women and Criminal Justice*, Vol. 11, No. 4, 2000: 29–64.

Green, S.T. et al., 'Female Street Worker Prostitute in Glasgow: A Descriptive Study of their Life Struggle', AIDS Care 5 (3): 321–325, 1993.

Harcourt, C. and B. Donovan, 'The Many Faces of Sex Work', *Journal of Sexually Transmitted Infections*, Vol. 81, 2005: 201–206, retrieved on 1 November 2010 from sti.bmj.com

Herman, Judith, *Trauma and Recovery*, Basic Book, New York, 1992.

Kramer, L., 'Emotional Experiences of Performing Prostitution', in M. Farley (ed.), *Prostitution, Trafficking and Traumatic Stress*, Haworth Press, Binghamton, New York, 2003: 187–198.

MacKinnon, C.A., 'Prostitution and Civil Rights', *Michigan Journal of Gender and Law*, Vol. 1, 1993: 13–31.

Parriot, R., 'Health Experience of Twin Cities Women Used in Prostitution', Survey initated by WHISPER, Minneapolis, 1994.

Ross, C.A., G. Anderson, S. Heber and G.R. Norton, 'Dissociation and Abuse among Multiple Personality Patients, Prostitutes and Exotic Dancers', *Hospital and Community Psychiatry*, Vol. 41, 1990: 328–330.

Vanwesenbeeck, I., *Prostitutes' Well-Being and Risk*, VU University Press, Amsterdam, 1994.

Wallace, B., 'Prostitution Raids in 4 San Francisco Homes', *San Francisco Chronicle*, 23 January 2004, retrieved on 10 December 2010 from http://sfgate.com/cgibin/article.cgi?file=/chronicle/archive/2004/01/23/MNGTA4GD2K1.DTL

Wallace, B. and J.H. Zamora, 'Sex Trafficking Ruthless, Lucrative: Brothels Proliferate Despite Crackdowns', *San Francisco Chronicle*, 24 January 2004, retrieved on 10 December 2010 from http://www.sfgate.com/cgi-bin/article.cgi?file=/c/a/2004/01/24/MNGU84GUJ01.DTL

Weitzer, R., 'Flawed Theory and Method in Studies of Prostitution', *Journal of Violence against Women*, Vol. 11, 2005: 934–949.

CHAPTER 12

Colonizing Distress

The Violence of Normalization and the Normalization of Violence

CHINA T. MILLS

> They didn't believe things I was saying, they said it was all in my head but I tried to tell them it was real to me.

> One needs to recognize that there is a continued role of unmodified/direct ECT for treatment of severely ill (violent, suicidal, treatment unresponsive cases) patients.[1]

This paper is concerned with what governs and sanctions the recognition of some acts as 'violence', and others as 'treatment'. Writing the paper stems from my growing unease with many of the violent and intrusive psychiatric and medical procedures, purportedly carried out in children and adult's 'best interests'. As a lens through which to explore the violence of normalization and the normalization of violence in the name of 'treatment', I will draw upon research I carried out in the UK with people who heard voices as children; and the tenuous beginnings of my research in India on the intersections of mental distress and the market. I draw on this research to focus on how the framing of a whole category of children and adults as 'outside' normality; as 'irrational', pathological and incompetent; results in these people being subjected to 'treatment' that would in other circumstances be constituted as violence. Taking this further, the paper will engage with how the dual mobilization of India as a 'poor country', and of people who are distressed as 'irrational' and 'dangerous' or 'violent', work to sanction acts of normalization 'outside' of normative judgments of violence; framing them as 'treatment'. Here the violence enacted on the bodies and minds of certain people is sanctioned by the law, as 'humanitarian violence', violence that prevents and pre-empts further violence.[2] Violence constructed as normal, and necessary. Violence not recognized as violence.

Drawing upon post-colonial theory, with a particular focus on the work of Homi Bhabha and Ashis Nandy, the paper will move between and through intersecting layers of violence, to explore some tenuous links between the violence of normalization and the violence of colonization. This will centre on how the colonial relation is mobilized within psychiatric treatment, and how thinking through the violence of colonialism may enable a rethinking of contemporary forms of psychiatric violence. Finally, I will explore the mobilization of the desire to be 'normal' and to 'fit in' as a kind of colonialism that we do to children and to ourselves.

This paper will follow Yep in recognizing that '[n]ormalization is a symbolically, discursively, psychically, psychologically, and materially violent form of social regulation and control'.[3] I will explore how normalization in the name of psychiatric 'treatment' operates at multiple levels of violence; the epistemic or symbolic violence of representation and of non-representation; the 'primary violence' of living under terms imposed by others (Butler, 2009); the hegemonic violence of being rendered illegitimate and irrational; the material violence of surgery, medication and Electro-Convulsive Therapy (ECT); and the subtle violence of delimiting our very desires for what children should be like, the normative judgments written into the chemicals of psychiatric medication.

Psychiatric 'Treatment' and Hearing Voices

Dominant medical and psychiatric frameworks for understanding the experience of hearing voices tend to conceptualize these experiences as 'symptoms' of an 'illness'. Such frameworks, given medical legitimacy in the Diagnostic and Statistical Manual (DSM IV-TR), used by GPs and psychiatrists to diagnose mental health problems, construct the experience of hearing voices as 'auditory hallucinations', seen to constitute the 'psychotic dimension' of 'positive symptoms' of schizophrenia.[4] However, many young people who hear voices (with whom I interviewed and within survivor literature from the UK) did not understand their experiences in this way. Sometimes, young people had always heard voices and to them the experience was 'normal'.

> At first I thought everyone shared this experience, but when I talked to a friend about it she said she had not had this experience and she thought I was strange ... At the same time, I thought she was strange because to me hearing a voice was normal.[5]

Many people reported that they understood hearing voices as a coping strategy, an aid to survival in an unequal and often abusive adult world. In one interview, Pete explained that his voices reminded him he should tell someone about the abuse he had experienced.

Ellie said that 'far from being some sinister psychiatric symptom, the phenomenon was probably no more than my own externalized thoughts ... it was a useful indicator to me of how I was really feeling'.[6]

However, the people with whom I spoke, frequently reported having their experiences framed by adult professionals as pathological, as an illness and as a 'problem', when for some children the voices were far less frightening than the 'real' world. This might be partly explained by the dominance of psychiatry and the pharmaceutical industry to mediate particular experiences within a specific medical framework of intelligibility, 'where individual actions come to read as 'signs' of a more enduring problem' and thus of a pathology.[7] One young woman described how *these very ordinary feelings of adolescent insecurity were immediately interpreted as symptoms of a diseased mind.*[8]

The reactions and responses of adults, then often affected how young people went on to understand and frame their own experience of hearing voices. As one interviewee said, 'the voices are not (always) the problem, its other people's reactions'.[9] Children and young people's understandings of hearing voices highlight a major paradox within psychiatry. Here voices which may actually be a coping strategy (even though sometimes distressing) and which have enabled the voice hearer to survive, are framed by psychiatry as in need of eradication through procedures constructed as 'treatment'. This highlights the dominance of bio-medical frameworks for judging and recognizing violence, and for understanding children's behaviour; medicalizing and depoliticizing children's experiences; leading us to question what counts as violence and what counts as 'treatment'.

Electro-Convulsive 'Therapy'

It was a brilliant cure but we lost the patient (Ernest Hemingway)

One such 'treatment' that has sparked numerous debates, is Electro-Convulsive Therapy (ECT). ECT involves passing an electrical current through the brain, eliciting a seizure. This seizure is characterized by convulsions, caused by the stimulated brain activity due to the electrical current. Generally, a muscle relaxant is administered to minimize muscular contractions, which can cause bone fractures and dislocations. However, the muscle relaxant paralyses the respiratory muscles, and so the person undergoing ECT is artificially ventilated during the procedure.[10] Recent reports from the USA document the use of modified ECT for 'correcting the behaviour problems' associated with autism,[11] telling the story of an eight-year-old boy who self-injured and who was thus given 15 sessions of ECT. The fact that this reduced his self-injury is thus seen as a justification to develop this 'therapy' for use on more children with autism. But why is self-injury constructed as an act of violence while ECT is constructed as 'treatment', despite injuries such as bone fractures, dislocations and memory loss caused by ECT? Seemingly then, the irony of conceptualizing ECT as a 'treatment' to stop self-harm is lost. This calls into question what can be recognized and defined as violence, and who decides?

In 2001, Saarthak, an NGO working for people with mental illness in India, filed a petition to the Supreme Court of India highlighting their concern that 'mentally ill persons are being subjected to some of the most inhuman and callous treatment in State and private institutions'.[12] A key area of their concern was with the use of direct (unmodified) ECT.[13] This is ECT without the use of an anaesthetic; and is widely practised in India.[14] The petitioners highlighted some of the problems associated with direct ECT, including bone fractures and dislocations due to uncontrollable motor seizures; and memory loss (both temporary and permanent).[15] Thus, the petitioners called 'to prohibit direct ECT, making it a penal offence'.[16]

However, in response to Saarthak's petition, the Delhi Psychiatric Society filed for impleadment to the Supreme Court, saying that 'there are certain situations where it becomes imperative, for the health and well-being of the patient himself/herself that he/she cannot be given modified ECT because the patient cannot be administered anaesthesia'.[17] The 'certain situations' constructed by the Delhi Psychiatric Society, fall loosely into two threads; the construction of the 'violent' patient, and the argument that India is a 'poor country'. Thus, the Delhi Psychiatric Society argues that, 'if the patient is so violent, an intravenous injection of anaesthetic can't be given' because the patient 'is continually disrupting the procedure ... it is not an easy task to give an injection in the veins to a violent patient'. They go on to say that:

> 'Suicide is a common complication of depression ... hence, it is a serious medical emergency for severe depressed patients. Suicidal patients, therefore, require active, intensive and

> prompt care so that their lives can be saved, this direct ECT would save the life of the patient. Thus, one needs to recognize that there is a continued role of unmodified/direct ECT for treatment of severely ill (Violent, Suicidal, treatment unresponsive cases) patients.[18]

Alongside these 'violent, suicidal' and 'treatment unresponsive cases', literature justifies direct ECT in India because anaesthetists are not always available and anaesthesia raises the cost of ECT. Therefore, direct ECT is the most 'cost effective' and cheapest form of psychiatric treatment.[19] Pathare (2003) calls into question the argument 'that there is a special case for permitting direct ECT in India because of the lack of facilities for anaesthesia and to reduce the costs of treatment'.[20] It is thus argued 'that in a resource poor setting, we have to compare existing alternatives, use the cheapest means available for cure, and not go for the most ideal. If the choices were between no ECT and direct ECT, then direct ECT is considered to be the more 'ethical alternative'.[21] Here then, the issue is not whether India is or is not a poor country, but what the mobilization of it as a 'poor country' serves to legitimate and justify. As the Centre for Advocacy in Mental Health, at the Bapu Trust in India, point out:

> On the basis of the argument that India is a 'poor country' and the poor need quick alternatives, justifications have also existed for various invasive and undignified 'treatments', such as mass sterilization, and hysterectomies, in the case of mentally challenged girls.[22]

The image of the 'poor country' also invokes the colonial construction of 'the madness of native India', the maddening colonial encounter that 'induce[s] madness, they are madness itself'.[23] Pathare (2003) also highlights that the routine prescription of direct ECT in India, based on the 'poor country argument', works to prevent the development of alternative psychological and community-based resources and services.[24] Also, the debate becomes limited to the pros and cons of direct versus modified ECT, silencing debates about the ethics and indeed scientific validity at all of ECT as a form of psychiatric treatment. But how do these 'certain situations'; the tropes of the violent individual and the poor country, work to enable ECT to be justified as ethical, 'imperative' and 'life saving'?[25]

Leonard Roy Frank, a survivor of ECT asks,

> Why is it that 10 volts of electricity applied to a political prisoner's private parts (genitalia) is seen as torture while 10 or 15 times that amount applied to the brain is called 'treatment'?

In fact, the Convention for the Prevention of Torture (2002) recognizes and prohibits the use of electric shocks as a form of torture. Thus, it would seem that the evocation of the 'poor country', and the 'violent, suicidal' and 'treatment unresponsive' individual work alongside each other to change our normative recognition of violence, and to legitimate and sanction violence in the name of 'treatment'. 'Noah' – a survivor of ECT from India – describes this experience; 'I was bundled into the car and driven off to a government psychiatric facility. A long and unending night of torture in the name of treatment awaited me'.[26] Thus, the 'violent' individual works as a powerful device in changing direct ECT from a method of torture into what the Delhi Psychiatric Society justify as 'a necessary evil'.[27]

Once constructed as 'mentally ill', of 'unsound mind' and as 'dangerous', people seem no longer to be regarded as subjects, they are 'humans who are not conceptualized within the frame of a political culture in which human lives are underwritten by legal entitlements, law, and so humans who are not humans'.[28] Drawing similarities with Weizman's exploration of justifications for military attacks, psychiatry's use of ECT (both direct and modified) are often presented as a kind of violence that is necessarily employed to *reduce* violence. A 'humanitarian violence', sanctioned by the law, to pre-empt and prevent further violence.[29] Violence constructed as 'normal', 'necessary' and 'legitimate'.[30]

The mobilization of the interrelating tropes of the 'poor country' and the 'violent patient' work then to change our recognition not only of what counts as violence but also of who counts as human, evoking the colonial discourse of the 'human and not wholly human'.[31] In fact, if ECT is 'necessary' and 'life-saving', if it reduces violence, then we are prevented from seeing it as violent at all, and thus unable to recognize those who undergo it as being violated. This works to prevent 'victims of direct ECT' from being 'considered as victims of medical torture and brought within human rights and medico-legal jurisprudence'.[32]

This helps us to understand how violence against those labelled as 'mentally ill' in the name of 'treatment' can coexist alongside the strong push for human and children's rights, through a process of framing hearing voices and self-injury as 'psychotic', as outside the realm of 'normal' experience and thus outside the parameters of human and child rights. Here labels of 'irrationality' and 'violence', along with hearing voices and self-injury act as tropes in which humans undergo a suspension of their ontological status as humans. Schrag and Divoky note, in reference to Attention Deficit Hyperactivity Disorder (ADHD) in children that consequentially; 'millions of children are no longer regarded as part of the ordinary spectrum ... but as people who are qualitatively different from the 'normal' population.[33]

This has links to constructions of non-Europeans (and women) in the language of colonialism, which Helen Carr illustrates as either;

> 'ripe for government, passive, child-like ... needing leadership and guidance, described always in terms of lack-no initiative, no intellectual powers ...; or on the other hand, they are outside society, dangerous, treacherous, emotional, inconstant, wild, threatening, fickle, sexually aberrant, irrational, near animal, lascivious, disruptive, evil, unpredictable.[34]

Thus, colonial constructions of the Orient as 'backward' and 'wild', populated by irrational, primitive natives in need of civilizing and rescue, for their own good, has its parallels with psychiatry's construction of particular people as 'irrational', 'violent' and 'dangerous'. This is particularly so as both work to construct a set of people as 'outside' normality, and outside humanity; a set of people who can be intervened with, rescued and 'treated' by others in their 'best interests', with or without their consent. In constructing certain children and adults as 'outside' the parameters of childhood and humanity, professionals can then intervene in that person's life, outside of the normative recognition of violence.[35] People are then subjected to treatment' that, outside of this psychiatric 'state of exception', would be constituted as legal battery and, in the case of children, child abuse.[36]

Collateral Damage

The violent, suicidal patient also figures in pharmaceutical companies' justification for clinical trials and in the promotion of drugs. For example, 'physicians speaking for Glaxo (Smith-Klein) exhort doctors to detect and treat depression on the basis that treatment will reduce risks of suicide'.[37] However, David Healy documents how psychiatric drugs trialed on children were actually found to increase suicidal behaviour and yet remained unpublished. Internal company documents, not made public, showed that in one trial, 9 per cent of children given the anti-depressant Zoloft made suicidal acts.[38] While in Glaxo's trials of Paxil (another anti-depressant), there was a 5 per cent suicidal act rate, compared to 1 per cent in children taking the placebo.[39]

Here anti-depressants are evoked as humane violence, violent interventions that reduce suicide. The fact that children are actually likely to be more violent after having taken medication, and more likely to attempt and commit suicide, is then not considered as knowledge, and is subsequently not made public. In the process of publication of trial results, arbitrary numbers and percentage levels are used to establish what pharmaceutical companies will count as relevant. Thus, in one publication of the Zoloft trial, with its 9 per cent of suicidal behaviour in children, the authors decided that they would only report on side-effects that occurred at a rate of 10 per cent or more.[40]

It is in these banal calculations of what count as side effects and how many suicide attempts are seen as statistically significant; the considerations as to what counts as acceptable collateral damage that psychiatric violence has its political effect. Here a statistical, 'normalized, everyday, 'rational' and bureaucratized violence'[41] is perpetrated; a banal violence that renders certain children's lives as necessary collateral damage within pharmaceutical research. Increasingly, this includes the testing of pharmaceutical drugs, including psychiatric drugs, on children and adults in countries of the global south, such as India, where whole (usually poor) populations come to be constructed as 'test' subjects, guinea pigs; with increasing numbers of people considered collateral damage.

In this way, those constructed as 'outside' not only normality, but 'outside' the market economy, are rendered invisible and disposable. Giroux describes how the category 'waste' includes no longer simply material goods but also human beings, particularly those rendered redundant in the new global economy; those who rely on others for care and those who cannot or will not 'fit' current neoliberal employment structures.[42] These populations, constructed as 'outside' the market economy, are reified as disposable, as 'leftovers in the most radical and effective way: we make them invisible by not looking and unthinkable by not thinking'.[43]

However, Giroux and Bauman's conceptualization of such people as 'outside' the market does not entirely seem to fully grapple with the dual construction of people with mental illness as both an 'economic burden' (in Government and World Bank portrayals), and an 'emergent' or target market for the pharmaceutical industry's marketing of psycho-pharmaceuticals. Although the label of 'irrationality' can cast you 'outside' normality, there is another market in abnormality, and in normalization, making money out of people's desires to be 'normal'. In fact, in India, there is a large private market in providing ECT,[44] not to mention in medication.

However, this market is itself somewhat irrational. Amita Dhanda (2008) points out that in a so-called logical market, psychiatrists would be seen to have the skills to treat people with mental health problems and so logically these people would voluntarily seek this treatment.[45] However, within the psychiatric market, when the 'mentally ill' do not seek psychiatric 'treatment' willingly, psychiatrists label them as incompetent – meaning, people must be coerced or forced into 'treatment' in their 'best interests'. Therefore, if you don't want 'treatment' such as ECT, you must be mad! And, in fact, on April Fool's Day in Pune, India (2007), Chaitanya Mental Health Care Centre, organized an event to 'eradicate foolish myths and phobias on ECT', displaying large posters saying 'Nothing Shocking about Shock'.[46] Here, a persons' desire to avoid ECT is constructed as a 'phobia', depoliticizing resistance through constructing it as an 'illness'.

Colonizing Affect

Pharmaceutical colonization and medicalization of our everyday lives is particularly worrying because the huge commercial incentive to construct particular experiences as 'mental illness' changes our view of what it means to be human; and, also, changes our normative frameworks for recognizing and responding to violence. Thus, such treatments affect and reshape how we understand and interpret our world and our selves. These frameworks of emergence also set parameters on how adults can respond to children, often preventing them from believing in children. Hadjimatheou (2009) recounts how, '[t]he doctors told the other staff not to pay attention to me when I spoke about the voices; they said it would be playing into my delusions.'[47] The violence of having one's reality dismissed as irrational, and 'unreal', emerged within my interviews, through children's desire to be believed. 'They didn't believe things I was saying, they said it was all in my head but I tried to tell them it was real to me, that was what was happening'.[48]

'I tried to tell people but I was never believed about the abuse. And I sort of shut up and I stopped talking about them. Because nobody was believing me, I stopped talking about the voices'.

I think I'd have liked them to believe me about everything ... The abuse and the voices because its real to me. I mean I'm not saying they have to say 'Oh aye we hear them as well' but if they said well you know 'Well I can understand that must be frightening'.

For a number of people, the voices they heard actually only became distressing after telling others about them, as one man I interviewed said, *'quite often people have no issues with the voices until they disclose'*.[49] This was, as one young man said, because his voices 'were worried the doctors were gonna medicate them away'. He felt that before taking any medication he first needed to understand what the voices were trying to tell him and why they were there in the first place.

Psychiatric framings also delimit what adults can feel in their interactions with children; limiting their available affective responses to children who are distressed or different. In relation to medication, Healy points out that 'the drugs used to treat ADHD are the same (chemically) as Speed and cocaine. We react with horror to the idea that our kids would use such drugs, but don't react about drugs such as Ritalin being given to them', by doctors.[50]

This raises important ethical questions around what governs our affective responses to different forms of violence against children and what regulates, when we will and when we will not feel horror. According to Judith Butler, "[h]orror" and "outrage" are differentially distributed' and we thus need to ask '[w]hat are the social conditions and abiding interpretative frameworks that make horror possible in the face of certain kinds of violence, and when and where is it 'ruled out' as an affective response'?[51] I would argue that while adults may react with horror at children who are distressed and who hear voices or self-injure, constructing them as pathological; acts constructed as psychiatric treatment operate to 'rule out' horror as an available affective response. Simultaneously limiting what we can recognize as suffering and who we can see as being violated.

Once framed within medico-legal understandings as lives that are, in Butler's terms, 'already lost',[52] children are then subjected to often aggressive medical and surgical interventions justified in the name of 'treatment'. While the image of the 'normal child' operates within prenatal testing, impacting on which children are actually born,[53] assumptions of life worth living also impact on decisions around death. In a human rights memorandum to the Government, Scope (a UK charity) recount a story of a young disabled man who was admitted to hospital with pneumonia. When his parents arrived at the hospital their son had not been given oxygen and 'Do Not Resuscitate' had been written on his notes.[54] Within this normative framework, even death may be considered in a disabled child's 'best interests'.

Thus, we might fleetingly glimpse how psychiatry, medicine and 'the law (are) never impartial but always caught up with strategies of power and with a discursive violence that seeks to grasp and domesticate the troublesome other'.[55] In this way, medico-legal judgments work to domesticate those 'troublesome' children who do not easily 'fit', often through psychiatric 'treatment' and medical interventions; physically colonizing bodies and rendering them docile. Appeals to the principle of working in children's 'best interests' and 'for their own good' may serve as 'an additional adult veto to children's decision-making in the name of protection, diverting attention from the maintenance of adult interests and inequality'.[56] Thus, it is on the bodies of these children, framed as mentally ill or disabled, where developmental psychology, psychiatry and biopower converge and interweave, becoming a technology of normalization that is translated into material, physical violence (such as surgery, forced medicating and Electro-Convulsive Therapy).

It seems such frames of pathologization and medicalization are given coherence through assumptions of a normal developmental trajectory for children. Thus, those children who do not 'fit', who do not meet the developmental milestones described (and prescribed) within developmental psychology are constructed in deficit, and often pathologized.[57] This trope of the 'normal' child then becomes the standard by which all childhood is judged, constructing normative boundaries on what it means to be a child, to be 'normal', and of what requires 'treatment' in the first place.

Sly Normality

But is there space for children to resist such treatment in the name of the normal? The following story was told to me by a young woman who I interviewed about her experiences within the psychiatric system:

> Marie heard voices for a long time; they helped her and comforted her while her parents sexually abused her. However sometimes they caused her distress, usually a sign for her that she was getting stressed or a reminder that she should tell someone about the abuse she experienced as a child and kept secret for a long time afterwards. After a particularly distressing experience she found herself sectioned, face to face with a psychiatrist. She found the courage and told him for the first time she had ever told anyone that she was abused as a child. He told her 'she was saying that because she was ill'. She made a decision, she knew 'that this wasn't somewhere she'd get well', so she pretended to comply, pretended to agree, nodded her head to whatever the psychiatrist said, in order to get out as fast as she could.[58]

Marie's story highlights the political significance of delegitimating someone's experiences through rendering them 'irrational' and 'pathological'. When we consider that many children who hear voices have experienced physical and sexual abuse,[59] we are lead to question how the right to their bodily integrity (UN Convention on the Rights of the Child (UNCRC)) is violated yet again through forced 'treatment' and detainment by medical professionals, repeating previous traumas that children may have experienced.

However, Marie's story also highlights young people's resistance to violent attempts to normalize them; the infrapolitics by which subordinate groups employ a politics of disguise and deception, while outwardly appearing, in power laden situations, to willingly consent.[60] Therefore, such '[L]ies, secrets, silences and deflections of all sorts are routes taken by voices or messages not granted full legitimacy in order not to be altogether lost'.[61]

Drawing on postcolonial theory, and particularly on the work of Homi Bhabha, to read this story may enable the subversive potential of pretending to be 'normal', mimicry of the norm, to be glimpsed (if fleetingly) as it disturbs our normative conceptions of what it means to be a 'normal' child. Here, we might say that Marie mimicked 'illness acceptance', 'treatment compliance' and 'recovery' in order not solely to survive, but as a form of camouflage. Reading Marie's story alongside the 'sly civility' performed by colonized peoples,[62] we could say that Marie enacted 'sly normality'. Marie made herself invisible; she became almost normal but not quite; the psychiatrist could see her, but only partially. It is this partial presence, the 'area between mimicry and mockery, where the reforming, civilizing mission (in this case psychiatry) is threatened by the displacing gaze of its disciplinary double'.[63]

Thus, such 'secret arts of invisibleness' and 'sly normality' may be resistant because they enable children to be less visible to a normative gaze, through appearing 'almost the same'; almost normal but not quite. But, according to Bhabha, these strategies do more than veil resistance, they 'change the very terms of our recognition of the person'.[64] They create a crisis in the representation of personhood and 'at the critical moment, initiates the possibility of political subversion'.[65] This is because invisibility 'erases the self-presence of the I' demanded by traditional concepts of political agency and narrative mastery of the unitary rational subject.[66] The subaltern instance of the slyly normal, thus intercuts boundaries of rationality and normality, and 'wreaks its revenge by circulating, without being seen'.[67]

The performance of sly normality as a subaltern instance can be further engaged with through the genre of art known as the 'trompe l'oeil'. Such art 'fools the eye' by imitating the depicted object so convincingly that the viewer is momentarily seized by an inability to tell the difference between original and copy, reality and representation.[68] Marie also 'fools the eye' by imitating normality so convincingly that for a moment it becomes impossible to tell the difference between normality and abnormality. In pretending to agree and in acting 'normal', in being *almost* normal 'but not quite', Marie, therefore, highlights an ambivalence and produces a slippage that does not only "rupture' the discourse, but becomes transformed into an uncertainty which fixes the colonial subject as a 'partial presence'.[69] These 'secret arts of invisibleness', the infrapolitics of subordinate groups, thus do more than veil resistance, they 'change[s] the very terms of our recognition of the person'.[70]

Attending to these moments of imitation and struggle against normalization in young people's lives, it would seem there is a mismatch between children's lived realities and this 'normal' child conjured by developmental discourse,[71] the 'inevitable misalignment between expectation and realization, and between image and referent.[72] But, Homi Bhabha asks, 'where do *we* stand in that uncanny echo between what may be described as the attenuation of identity and its simulacra?'[73]

Drawing upon the experience of colonized peoples in India, Bhabha illustrates how such 'mimic men' are 'the effect of a flawed colonial mimesis, in which to be Anglicized is emphatically not to be English'.[74] In being 'slyly normal' and 'almost normal but not quite', Marie then highlights an ambivalence at the heart of the model of the 'normal child', where her imitation highlights the limits of the model of normality and that which supposedly makes it imitable. Her story emerges between mimesis and mimicry, mocking 'normality' and mocking its power to be a model; the very power that supposedly makes it imitable.[75]

This exposes the 'normal' child as a fiction; developed from statistical analysis that strips children from all that tied them to their context and render their lives into abstraction. Images of 'normal' childhoods operate as a space where the norm is in force with no reference to reality. Here, the 'normal' child functions as a simulacrum, a 'model with no basis in reality', a 'map that precedes the territory'.[76] Simulacra do not mask reality or its absence, they bear no relation to any reality at all, and, in fact, they call into question the existence of any so-called reality. This alludes to how our cultural imaginaries of what is 'normal' in society are produced by models and statistical hypotheses.

Marie's story puts us as readers, 'professionals' or academics in a strange place. She dislocates the penetrative psychological or psychiatric gaze by looking back, from a place that can barely be seen. These 'disembodied eyes' of the subaltern that speak and see forms where they are not, disrupt and subvert both the presumed unitary 'I' of the child, and the surveillant, disciplinary 'eye' of psychiatry. In looking back, unseen, Marie could be read post-colonially as subverting the perverse satisfaction of the rational, ableist, psychiatric gaze that denies her experiences and delegitimizes her presence, by looking back through a counter gaze that turns the discriminatory and delegitimizing look back on psychiatry itself.

Appearing within psychiatry or the law as 'mentally ill' or as disabled, children enter into specific realms of appearance and frameworks of recognition that delimit and foreclose what sort of subject that child can be and how that child can come to understand their experiences. Young argues that the textuality of law, and I would add psychiatry, has been occupied by a visual order of representation, where 'judgment becomes an aesthetics of appearance', 'a conversion of writing (and statistics) into a specular image'.[77] Thus, psychiatry and the law reconstruct the 'real' of mental illness and disability in the order of vision, 'where judgments is governed by the desire to see'.[78] This decontextualizes the image, stripping it of its political significance, preventing meaningful engagement with the social context of children's lives, meaning the very reasons they may hear voices or self-injure are overlooked.

Thus 'children are regulated and measured ... in relation to fictitious norms elaborated by dominant models'.[79] We might read this as a form of violence in itself, a sort of Orientalism. Just as with knowledge production around the 'child', Western constructions of the Orient established a whole apparatus for seeing the Orient that bore no relation to people's lived experiences. These images were then used 'to further colonize the 'real' people of the region', silencing their voices.[80] Might we understand images and statistics of the 'normal' child as operating in a similar way? These images bear no relation to most children's diverse and multiple lived realities and yet are used as models in which children must 'fit', colonizing children's minds and bodies.

Sly Normalization

To appear within psychiatric or legal discourse involves the child entering a specific realm of appearance governed by norms that 'condition and orchestrate the subject who can and does appear' (Butler, 2009: 140). In this way, the child is given over to frameworks and social terms that are never its own. Thus, we might draw on Butler to explore how such terms (as psychotic, disabled) institute a primary violence where the child is vulnerable to terms that it never made.[81] It thus becomes possible to see how those who occupy marginal positions in society, particularly those children with labels of mental health problems or disability come to occupy 'quasi colonial status' in current neoliberal society.[82]

In this way, those constructed as 'outside' not only normality, but 'outside' the market economy, are rendered invisible and disposable. Giroux describes how the category 'waste' includes no longer simply material goods but also human beings, particularly those rendered redundant in the new global economy; those who rely on others for care and those who cannot or will not 'fit' current neoliberal employment structures.[83] These populations, constructed as 'outside' the market economy, are reified as disposable, as 'leftovers in the most radical and effective way: we make them invisible by not looking and unthinkable by not thinking'.[84] For Bhabha there is something particularly feminist in this representation of invisibility as a form of subversion, in mimicry as a 'secret art of revenge'.[85] However, the social and political invisibility of certain groups may render them invisibly colonized, as techniques of normalization operate slyly and invisibly too.

We cannot then ask questions around how to recognize or represent children or violence if we do not query and contest how power operates to differentiate between those subjects who will be eligible for recognition and those who will not; those who are constructed as normatively children and those who are not; and those actions constructed as violence and those that are not. The emergence of such subjects and the recognition of particular types of violence are governed by the social frameworks that regulate the possibility of emergence.

Currently, the pharmaceutical industry operates as a monopoly of such possible frameworks and images, governing and delimiting the emergence of non-medicalized and non-pathological frameworks for understanding children's experiences and distress. In this way, the pharmaceutical industry establishes parameters of what can count as 'publicly recognizable violence' and of what and who counts as a child. Just as with colonialist knoweldges, currently psychiatric and bio-medical knowledge and definitions about what it means to be human are imposed as impartial 'truths',[86] restricting what sort of child the medication can 'restore' children to be. In fact, pharmaceutical marketing of drugs such as Ritalin for ADHD, often does not promise a new self or a better child, they mobilize the desire to get your child back again, 'it is through the drug that the self is restored to itself' (Rose, 2007: 214). As such, Ritalin is sometimes described by pharmaceutical companies, parent groups funded by the pharmaceutical industry and children themselves not as coercive or constraining, but as 'restoring the child to his or her true self again' (Rose, 2007: 211). In this way, anti-psychotics and stimulants, such as Ritalin, are entangled with certain conceptions of what children can or should be, norms and judgments are internalized in the molecular make-up of these drugs, and 'the drugs embody and incite particular forms of life in which the 'real me' is both 'natural' and to be produced' (Rose, 2007: 222).

This points to how we might read the mobilization of the desire to be 'normal' and to 'get your child back' as a form of colonization. Ashis Nandy points to two types of colonialism; the physical conquest of territory, and the more covert colonization of minds.[87] The forced normalization of children's bodies, using Electro-Convulsive Therapy and the 'Ashley Treatment' (both discussed in this paper) provide examples of how normalization through psychiatric treatment and surgery can physically colonize the bodies of those children who do not 'fit'. However, normalizations, as with colonial missions to civilize, are not solely based on force. Just as psychiatric and medical intervention in children's lives is often justified as being in their 'best interests', colonialism was often justified as a civilizing mission; 'the disinterested purveyor of cultural enlightenment and reform'.[88] Nandy describes how a colonial system perpetuates itself through inducing the colonized to accept new categories and norms through psychological and economic rewards. He points to the 'more dangerous and permanent' inner rewards, 'the secondary psychological gains and losses from suffering and submission under colonialism'.[89] This second type of colonization is more covert and dangerous because colonized peoples learn to view it as a 'prerequisite for their liberation'.[90] Indeed, children and adults' compliance in taking medication often seems to be a 'prerequisite for their liberation', or at least for them to be legally framed as competent, and to be released from psychiatric in-patient units (as we saw in Marie's story). Indeed, this is often how pharmaceutical companies advertise psychiatric drugs in America – direct to consumers. Thus, Astra Zeneca's current (2010) advert for Seroquel X R promotes the drug as a way to 'get your life back'; as a way to be free.[91] Here, we can glimpse the seductive power of such marketing, working up people's desire to be 'normal' and to be 'themselves again', and mobilizing the colonized's complicity in the colonial condition.[92]

Gruzinski points out that although colonization rarely destroys all creativity and resistance, 'it does succeed more than often in weaving indissoluble ties between indigenous cultures and the imported ones'.[93] However, if a key strategy of resistance involves complying with what the doctors say, taking your medication with no fuss, performing sly normality, then we encounter some serious problems. How 'sly' can you be when you are so heavily medicated that you're like a 'zombie', when you can't think anymore and find it exhausting to speak?[94] Thus, while resistance may be sly, so too can be the monopoly of bio-psychiatry as it weaves indissoluble ties between children labelled as mentally ill and medication. Ties that are socially and biologically hard to break.

Therefore, it seems that if we assume that some violence is justified by the law, the state and by psychiatry (and even as necessary for them as disciplines), often under the guise of being in children's 'best interests', then normative judgments about what can be understood as violence and as 'treatment', and who counts as human, are built into our very definitions of 'violence' and of 'treatment'. Some of the terms in which violence, normality and the child can be conceptualized then may 'dispose us in advance towards certain kinds of moral responses and normative conclusions'.[95]

This raises questions of how we can conceptualize contemporary forms of violence. How will we negotiate these different forms of violence, and should they all be understood as violence? By what ethical frames can we conceptualize, recognize and respond to the ordinary, everyday manoeuvres of violence, the banality of violence within psychiatric 'treatment', violence constructed as normal, necessary and legitimate;[96] how we can compare and judge such forms of 'violence'.[97] Does this violence secure the ground for wider, more pervasive violence? And how can we recognize our own complicity? This calls for new conceptual tools with which to explore the violence of normalization, and the normalization of violence.

Acknowledgements

This paper is the product of a collective (re)thinking of issues of colonization, normalization and violence. While I may be the author, many voices are whispering throughout, particularly, the voices of those I interviewed about their experiences of hearing voices (and the voices those people hear); the voice of Erica Burman – forever supportive and inspiring; the voices of those who attended the session on 'New Markets and Interlocking Inequalities' at the Indian Association of Women's Studies Conference in Wardha, 2011 (and particularly Sudeshna Mukherjee) – for whom this paper was written; Bhargavi Davar and the whispering of the archives at the Centre for Advocacy in Mental Health, in Pune; and the voices of those who made it possible for me to share my work at Ambedkar University Delhi (particularly Anup Dhar) – where discussion rendered me literally speechless, due to the wonderful suggestions of the participants and a simultaneous throat infection.

Thank you all.

Notes

1. Delhi Psychiatric Society.
2. Eyal Weizman, 'Forensic Architecture: Only the Criminal can Solve the Crime', *Radical Philosophy*, Vol. 164, November/December, 2010.
3. Gust A. Yep, 'The Violence of Heteronormativity in Communication Studies: Notes on Injury, Healing and Queer World-Making', in Gust A. Yep, Karen E. Lovaas and John P. Elia (eds), *Queer Theory and Communication: From Disciplining Queers to Queering the Discipline(s)*, Harrington Park Press, New York, 2003, p. 18.
4. Diagnostic and Statistical Manual IV-TR, American Psychiatric Association, Arlington, 2000, p. 299.
5. Comment from a young girl at the Children's Hearing Voices Conference, Amsterdam, 1993. Report available on request to the author.
6. C. Campbell, 'The Terrifying Ordeal of a Brilliant Student Who Started Hearing Voices and Then Fell into the Abyss of Insanity', *The Daily Mail*, 7 February 2008.

7. Maggie MacLure et al., *Becoming a Problem: How Children Develop a Reputation as 'Naughty' in the Earliest Years at School*, Full Research Report, Economic and Social Research Council, 2008, p. 3.
8. Campbell, op. cit.
9. Quote from an interviewee in research by the author in 2008.
10. Chittaranjan Andrade, Electro-convulsive Therapy, no date.
11. http://www.indianpsychiatry.com/ECT.htm, accessed on 3 February 2011.
12. D. Chieco, 'Case Study Suggests New Therapy for Autism', *The John Hopkins Newsletter*, 26 February 2009.
13. Writ Petition No. 562, Saarthak vs. Union of India, 2001, p. 14.
14. The petition also called for changes in the use of physical restraint and single isolation cells in State Mental Hospitals.
15. A.K. Agarwal, C. Andrade and M.V. Reddy, 'The Practice of ECT in India: Issues Relating to the Administration of ECT', *Indian Journal of Psychiatry*, Vol. 34, No. 4, 1992, pp. 285–297.
16. Bhargavi Davar, 'ECT: The Need for Ethical Debate', *India Together*, 2003.
17. http://www.indiatogether.org/2003/apr/hlt-ect.htm, accessed on 10 March 2011.
18. Writ Petition, p. 16.
19. Delhi Psychiatric Society represented by Dr Utpal Goswami filed for impleadment on 4 March 2002 for Writ Petition No. 562 of 2001, p. 9.
20. Ibid., pp. 10–11.
21. See C. Andrade, 'Unmodified ECT: Ethical Issues', *Issues in Medical Ethics*, Vol. 11, No. 1, 2003, pp. 9–10; and P. Tharyan, P.J. Saju, S. Datta, J.K. John and K. Kuruvilla, 'Physical Morbidity with Unmodified ECT: A Decade of Experience', *Indian Journal of Psychiatry*, Vol. 35, No. 4, 1993, pp. 211–214.
22. S. Pathare, 'Beyond ECT', *Issues in Medical Ethics*, Vol. XI, No. 1, January–March 2003, pp. 11–12.
23. 'ECT (Electro-convulsive Therapy): Need for Debate', Centre for Advocacy in Mental Health, Pune, no date, p. 14.
24. Ibid., p. 20.
25. Ania Loomba, *Colonialism/Postcolonialism: The New Critical Idiom*, Routledge, London and New York, 1998, p. 117.
26. Pathare, op. cit.

27. Leonard Frank Roy, 'Testimony of Leonard Roy Frank at a Public Hearing on Electro-convulsive 'Treatment' before the Mental Health Committee of the New York State', 2001, http://www.idiom.com/~drjohn/LFrank.html, accessed on 28 January 2001.
28. 'Noah', in Tina Minkowitz and Amita Dhanda (eds), *First Person Stories on Forced Interventions and Being Deprived of Legal Capacity*, World Network of Users and Survivors of Psychiatry, Odense and Bapu Trust, Pune, 2006, p. 44.
29. Delhi Psychiatric Society, op. cit.
30. Judith Butler, *Precarious Life: The Power of Mourning and Violence*, Verso, London and New York, 2004, p. 77.
31. Weizman, op. cit.
32. Anup Dhar, 'Survival of Violence: Violence of Survival', *Identity, Culture and Politics*, Vol. 5, Nos 1 and 2, 2004, pp. 60–85.
33. Lord Rosebery (1900), cited in Homi Bhabha, *The Location of Culture*, Routledge, Abingdon, 1994 (2005), p. 122; and Centre for Advocacy in Mental Heath, 'Direct ECT: A Shocking Matter', *Aaina*, Vol. 3, No. 2, 2003, p. 7.
34. In reference to ADHD; Peter Schrag and Diane Divoky, *The Myth of the Hyperactive Child and Other Means of Child Control*, Penguin, Harmondsworth, 1981, p. 36.
35. Helen Carr, 'Woman/Indian, the 'American' and His Others', in F. Barker, P. Hulme, M. Iversen and D. Loxley (eds), *Europe and its Others*, Vol. 2, University of Essex Press, Colchester, 1985, pp. 46–60 and p. 50.
36. Alison Young, *Judging the Image: Art, Value, Law*, Routledge, Abingdon, 2005, p. 87.
37. Helen Spandler and Tim Calton, 'Psychosis and Human Rights: Conflicts in Mental Health Policy and Practice', *Social Policy and Society*, Vol. 8, 2009, pp. 245–256.
38. David Healy, 'The Latest Mania: Selling Bipolar Disorder', *PLoS Med*, Vol. 3, No. 4, 2006, p. 23.
39. Ibid.
40. Martin B. Keller, Neal D. Ryan and Mitcet Strober et al., 'Efficacy of Paroxetine in the Treatment of Adolescent Major Depression: A Randomized, Controlled Trial', *Journal of American Academy of Child and Adolescent Psychiatry*, Vol. 40, No. 7, 2001, pp. 762–772.
41. David Healy, 'Shaping the Intimate: Influences on the Experience of Everyday Nerves', *Social Studies of Science*, Vol. 34, No. 2, 2004, p. 20.

42. Erica Burman, 'Between Justice and Pathologization: Juxtapositions of Epistemic and Material Violence in Transnational Migration and Domestic Violence Research', in John F. Schostak and Jill Schostak (eds.), *Researching Violence, Democracy and the Rights of People*, Routledge, London and New York, 2010, p. 47.
43. Henry A. Giroux, 'Violence, Katrina and the Biopolitics of Disposability', *Theory, Culture and Society*, Vol. 24, Nos. 7 and 8, 2007, p. 308.
44. Zygmunt Bauman, *Wasted Lives: Modernity and its Outcasts*, Polity Press, Cambridge, 2004, p. 27; and Centre for Advocacy in Mental Health, op. cit.
45. Amita Dhanda, 'Mental Health Law: On the Road to Freedom', *Aaina*, Vol. 8, Nos 1 and 2, March and July 2008.
46. See report of this event at http://www.mindfreedom.org/kb/mental-health-abuse/electroshock/pune-india., accessed on 15 January 2011.
47. Chloe Hadjimatheou, 'Embracing the Dark Voices Within', *BBC World Service*, 2009, accessed on 17 September 2010, http://news.bbc.co.uk/1/hi/health/8232555.stm
48. This and the following two quotes are taken from interviews from my research in 2008 (Funded by RIHSC, MMU).
49. Excerpt from an interview as part of my research in 2008.
50. David Healy, cited in G. Fowler, 'Turning Children into Mental Patients: ADHD in the UK', *Asylum*, Vol. 17, No. 2, 2010, p. 21.
51. Judith Butler, *Frames of War: When is Life Grievable?*, Verso, London and New York, 2009, p. 159.
52. Butler, 2004, op. cit.
53. See Ruth Hubbard, 'Abortion and Disability: Who Should and Who Should Not Inhabit the World?', in *The Disability Studies Reader*, Routledge, New York and London, 1997, p. 187. This also links to wider debates about the prenatal testing and abortion of girl babies in countries such as India and China.
54. Human Rights Joint Committee, Memorandum (2009) submitted by Scope, Parliament.co.uk., accessed on 5 June 2009.
55. Magrit Shildrick, 'Transgressing the Law with Foucault and Derrida: Some Reflections on Anomalous Embodiment', *Critical Quarterly*, Vol. 47, No. 3, 2005, p. 31.
56. Brenda A. Lefrancois, ''It's Like Mental Torture': Participation and Mental Health Services', *The International Journal of Children's Rights*, Vol. 16, 2008, p. 213.

57. MacLure, op. cit.
58. Story told to me during research, RIHSC, MMU, December 2007–March 2008.
59. Marius Romme et al., *Living with Voices: 50 Stories of Recovery*, PCCS Books, Ross-on-Wye, UK, 2009.
60. James C. Scott, *Domination and the Arts of Resistance: Hidden Transcripts*, Yale University Press, Yale, 1990.
61. B. Johnson, *A World of Difference*, John Hopkins University Press, Baltimore, 1987, p. 31.
62. Bhabha, op. cit., pp. 132–144.
63. Ibid., p. 123.
64. Ibid., p. 67.
65. Ibid., p. 79.
66. Ibid.
67. Ibid.
68. Maggie MacLure, Rachel Holmes, Liz Jones and Christina MacRae, 'Silence as Resistance to Analysis: Or, on Not Opening One's Mouth Properly', *Qualitative Inquiry*, Vol. 16, No. 6, 2010, p. 496.
69. Bhabha, op. cit., p. 123.
70. Ibid., p. 47.
71. MacLure et al., p. 10.
72. Nikolas Rose, *Governing the Soul: The Shaping of the Private Self*, 2nd edition, Free Association Books, London and New York, 1989.
73. Bhabha, op. cit., p. 77.
74. Ibid., p. 125.
75. Ibid.
76. Jean Baudrillard, *Simulacra and Simulation*, Sheila Faria Glaser (trans.), The University of Michigan Press, Michigan, 1988, p. 1.
77. Alison, op. cit., p. 79 and p. 86.
78. Ibid., p. 93.
79. Erica Burman, *Developments: Child, Image, Nation*, Routledge, East Sussex, 2008, p. 176.
80. Gaile Sloan Cannella and Radhka Viruru, *Childhood and Postcolonization*, Routledge Falmer, New York, 2004, p. 66.
81. Judith Butler, *The Psychic Life of Power*, Stanford University Press, Stanford, California, 1977.
82. W.E.B. Du Bois, 'Human Rights for all Minorities', in Phillip S. Foner (ed.), *W.E.B Du Bois Speaks: Speeches and Addresses 1920–1963*, Pathfinder, New York, 1945 (reprint 1970), p. 183.

83. Giroux, op. cit.
84. Bauman, op. cit., p. 27.
85. Bhabha, op. cit., p. 80.
86. Cannella and Viruru, op. cit.
87. See Ashis Nandy, *The Intimate Enemy: Loss and Recovery of Self under Colonialism*, Oxford University Press, Oxford, 1997.
88. L. Gandhi, *Postcolonial Theory: A Critical Introduction*, Oxford University Press, New Delhi, 1998, p. 14.
89. Nandy, op. cit., p. 174.
90. Ibid., p. 170.
91. Seroquel X R advert campaign for bipolar disorder, advert made by Saatchi and Saatchi for Astra Zeneca.
92. Gandhi, op. cit.
93. Serge Gruzinski (1988), cited in Majid Rahnema with Victoria Bawtree (eds), *The Post-Development Reader*, Zed Books, London and New Jersey, 1997, p. 169.
94. Reported by Pete in an interview as part of my research in 2008.
95. Butler, 2004, op. cit., p. 156.
96. Dhar, op. cit.
97. Ibid., p. 159.

References

Butler, Judith, *Frames of War: When is Life Grievable?*, Verso, London and New York, 2009: 159.

Dhanda, Amita, 'Mental Health Law: On the Road to Freedom', *Aaina*, Vol. 8, Nos 1 and 2, March and July 2008.

Hadjimatheou, Chloe, 'Embracing the Dark Voices Within', *BBC World Service*, 2009, accessed on 17 September 2010, http://news.bbc.co.uk/1/hi/health/8232555.stm

Pathare, S., 'Beyond ECT', *Issues in Medical Ethics*, Vol. XI, No. 1, January–March 2003: 11–12.

Rose, N., *The Politics of Life Itself: Biomedicine, Power and Subjectivity in the 21st Century*, Princeton University Press, Oxford, 2007.

CHAPTER 13

Reproductive Technologies

New Market and Emerging Inequalities

SUDESHNA MUKHERJEE

In the last two decades the use of reproductive technologies (RTs) has become an inevitable and often indispensable part of women's lives. On one hand, the increased knowledge and availability of a wide range of RT options has redefined 'traditional' notions of conception and procreation. On the other, the introduction of each new device or technique has served to renew a growing flux in the way reproductive choice is understood. The right to bodily integrity – defined as the inalienable right of women to have control and autonomy over their bodies – has been central in the feminist understanding of choice. Women have expanded access to reproductive technologies (RTs), including abortion, is an essential corollary to this argument. Access to certain types of RTs have indeed saved women's lives and often provided them with expanded choice with regard to reproductive decision-making. However, there is a continued need to evaluate the role of RTs and examine their role in providing women with real choice. This need becomes particularly acute in the face of the growth of the non-medical use of RTs to satisfy individual and socio-cultural needs (Mallik, 2002).

For obstetricians, reproduction is an area of professional specialization, defined in terms of pregnancy and childbirth.

Reproductive technology offers these physicians a means of entry into the high-pay, cutting-edge circle of high-technology medicine, therefore, enhancing their professional prestige. To patients, reproduction means the ability to procreate – to create a new life in their bodies; they focus exclusively on the biological aspects of the reproductive process. Feminists see reproduction as a potential source of women's power, since it is a uniquely female ability, and also as the historical justification for the limitation of women's power. Thus, each group's attitude toward the issue of procreative technology is imbedded in a world view which gives reproduction a distinct meaning, and in each case, the meaning attributed to the reproductive process is central to the group members' self-definition (Strickler, 1992).

Since the advent of the feminist movement, one of the most important issues confronted by the feminists is their attempt to gain control over the female body. For centuries, their bodies and reproductive capacities were used to control and oppress women. Feminist movement led by Radical feminists sought to liberate women from being prisoner of their bodily capacities. Right to abortion was an important step towards this end. Radical feminists like Shulamith Firestone believed that women with the help of the emerging new reproductive technologies can exercise more choices and will liberate themselves from oppressive and restrictive reproductive practices. But many believe these choices, especially in case of surrogacy, opens up newer areas of Patriarchal, capitalistic, societal control and exploitation over women through their reproductive capacities.

Scope of Artificial Reproductive Technology (ART)

Definition of ART includes 'all fertility treatments in which both eggs and sperm are handled. In general, ART procedures involve surgically removing eggs from a woman's ovaries, combining them with sperm in the laboratory, and returning them to the woman's body or donating them to another woman.' According to CDC (The Centers for Disease Control and Prevention, 1992), 'they do not include treatments in which only sperm are handled (i.e. intrauterine or artificial insemination) or procedures in which a woman takes medicine only to stimulate egg production without the intention of having eggs retrieved' Procedures are mainly fertility medication, as well as ART techniques that use more substantial and forceful interventions, of which is in vitro fertilization (IVF) and expansions of it.

In vitro fertilization (IVF) is the technique of letting fertilization of the male and female gametes (sperm and egg) occur outside the female body. Techniques usually used in vitro fertilization include:

- *Transvaginal Ovum Retrieval* (OCR) is the process whereby a small needle is inserted through the back of the vagina and guided via ultrasound into the ovarian follicles to collect the fluid that contains the eggs.
- *Embryo Transfer* is the step in the process whereby one or several embryos are placed into the uterus of the female with the intent to establish a pregnancy.

The following Assisted Reproduction techniques do not necessarily involve IVF.

In *Gamete Intrafallopian Transfer* (GIFT) a mixture of sperm and eggs is placed directly into a woman's fallopian tubes using laparoscopy following a transvaginal ovum retrieval.

Sex selection is the attempt to control the sex of offspring to achieve a desired sex. It can be accomplished in several ways, both pre- and post-implantation of an embryo, as well as at birth. Pre-implantation techniques include Pre-implantation genetic diagnosis (PGD), but also sperm sorting.

Artificial Insemination (AI) is when sperm is placed into a female's uterus (intrauterine) or cervix (intracervical) using artificial means rather than by natural copulation. This can be a very low-tech process, performed at home by the woman alone or with her partner.

The Surrogacy Practices

Surrogacy is a practice, where a woman agrees to become pregnant and deliver a child for a contracted party. It may be her own genetic child, or a child conceived through in vitro fertilization or embryo transfer using another woman's ova.

Surrogacy is basically of two types. One is altruistic where the surrogate mother is not compensated by way of money in return of her efforts; and the other one is commercial where the motive to deliver an infant is earning money. Commercial surrogacy is a debated issue as it has many moral and legal complications and is illegal in many other countries.

The laws relating in other countries differ to what is being presented in India. In UK, no contract or agreement relating to surrogacy is legally binding. All expenses must be justified to the courts, which can intervene and ask for proof if the expenses incurred by the genetic parents are too high. In most US states, commercial surrogacy is either illegal or unenforceable. In Australia, arranging commercial surrogacy is a criminal offence and any surrogacy agreement giving custody to others is void. The surrogate mother is deemed to be the legal mother of the child. In Canada and New Zealand, commercial surrogacy has been illegal, but altruistic surrogacy is allowed. In France, Germany and Italy, surrogacy whether commercial or not, is unlawful. Renting a uterus for money is illegal in South Africa.

The starting point for tackling the question of surrogacy is in recognizing that this new technology splits up older notions of natural reproduction into three parts – 'social' parents, a gestational mother, and the genetic matter that links the first two. The 'stakeholders' thus created, often have conflicting interests – the 'commissioning' parents; the surrogate mother; her family, if any; the new baby; and the commercial sperm banks and ART clinics.

The market, though a domain of exchange, is also facilitators of interaction between various actors that govern its functioning, and are involved in the production and purchase of goods and services and also have a lasting impression on functioning of social life. The entry of reproductive technologies is met with the same kind of processes that the market exerts on any product. This can predominantly be seen in the transformation of the items transacted or produced into commodities.

For example, in the sale and purchase of services of a surrogate, a woman sells her reproductive labour to an individual or a couple who purchases this at a price against a signed contract which is legally binding. Surrogate, here, is being treated as labourer selling her reproductive labour against a price determined by the supply and demand policy of market. But the situation is not always as simple as these transactions are not under the purview of well-defined and implemented guidelines, and perceived gap in the socio-economic status of buyer and seller increases the scope of exploitation of the latter in the hand of the former.

Surrogacy and Legality in the Indian Context

The Supreme Court legalized commercial surrogacy in 2008 in the case of baby Manji Yamada, daughter of Ikufumi Yamada and Yuki Yamada (the couple got divorced shortly before the child was born) in an agreement with Preeti Patel, the surrogate mother observing that 'commercial surrogacy reaching industry proportions is sometimes referred to by the emotionally charged and potentially offensive terms wombs for rent, outsourced pregnancies or baby farms'. It is presumably considered legitimate because no Indian law prohibits surrogacy. But then, as a retort, no law permits surrogacy either. Surely, the proposed law will usher in a new rent-a-womb law, as India is set to be the only one to legalize commercial surrogacy.

The Indian Council for Medical Research has given guidelines in the year 2005, regulating Assisted Reproductive Technology procedures. The Law Commission of India submitted the 228th report on Assisted Reproductive Technology procedures discussing the importance and need for surrogacy, and also the steps taken to control surrogacy arrangements. The following observations had been made by the Law Commission:

1. Surrogacy arrangement will continue to be governed by contract amongst parties, which will contain all the terms requiring consent of surrogate mother to bear child, agreement of her husband and other family members for the

same, medical procedures of artificial insemination, reimbursement of all reasonable expenses for carrying child to full term, willingness to hand over the child born to the commissioning parent(s), etc. But such an arrangement should not be for commercial purposes.

2. A surrogacy arrangement should provide for financial support for surrogate child in the event of death of the commissioning couple or individual before delivery of the child, or divorce between the intended parents and subsequent willingness of none to take delivery of the child.
3. A surrogacy contract should necessarily take care of life insurance cover for surrogate mother.
4. One of the intended parents should be a donor as well, because the bond of love and affection with a child primarily emanates from biological relationship. Also, the chances of various kinds of child-abuse, which have been noticed in cases of adoptions, will be reduced. In case the intended parent is single, he or she should be a donor to be able to have a surrogate child. Otherwise, adoption is the way to have a child which is resorted to if biological (natural) parents and adoptive parents are different.
5. Legislation itself should recognize a surrogate child to be the legitimate child of the commissioning parent(s) without there being any need for adoption or even declaration of guardian.
6. The birth certificate of the surrogate child should contain the name(s) of the commissioning parent(s) only.
7. Right to privacy of donor as well as surrogate mother should be protected.
8. Sex-selective surrogacy should be prohibited.
9. Cases of abortions should be governed by the Medical Termination of Pregnancy Act 1971 only.

The Union Cabinet is, therefore, in the process of examining a Draft Assisted Reproductive Technology ART (Regulation) Bill, 2010. But, what prompts India to take a lead in adopting a legislation which is not fostered in many developed countries? The proposed ART legislation can be summarized as:

1. The Draft Bill gives gays, singles the legal right to have surrogate babies. It defines a 'couple' as two persons living together and having a sexual relationship. After the Delhi High Court verdict on homosexuality, even two gay men can claim to be a couple. But after recent (December 2013) supreme court verdict homosexual couples cannot apply as couples but they can do so as individuals.
2. A woman in the age-group of 21–35 can become a surrogate mother. She will be allowed five live births, including her own children. She will not be allowed to undergo embryo transfer more than three times in her life to the same couple. If implemented properly this provision will check the malpractice which compromise with the health of both mother and the child.
3. In case of a single man or woman, the baby will be his/her legitimate child. If the surrogate mother is married, consent of her spouse is mandatory. The commissioning parents will have to accept the child's custody irrespective of any congenital abnormality.
4. A child born to an unmarried couple using a surrogate mother and with the consent of both parties shall be the legitimate child of both of them.
5. During the gestation period, the couple will bear the surrogate's expenses and give monetary help to her. The couple may enter into an agreement with the surrogate. Clinics will have to keep surrogates identity strictly confidential.
6. Foreign couples must submit two certificates – one on their country's surrogacy policy and the other stating that the child born to the surrogate mother will get their country's citizenship. This provision is formulated keeping in mind a recent case of twins born to a German couple in January 2008 to a surrogate mother in India who were rendered stateless as they did not get the citizenship of either India or Germany. After a two-year long legal battle, the Supreme Court got them exit permits in May 2010.
7. Foreign couples have to nominate a local guardian who will take care of the surrogate during gestation.

8. ART banks, accredited by the government, will maintain a database of prospective surrogates as well as storing of semen and eggs and details of the donor. Any ART bank or clinic cannot send Indian citizens abroad for surrogacy.
9. State boards will give accreditation to ART banks – private and government. The board will have a registration authority which, in turn, will maintain a list of all in vitro fertilization (IVF) centres and monitor their functioning.
10. The draft bill also entails provision for live in couples who can go for IVF only if the woman cannot biologically bear a child or if it is too risky for her. No ART clinic is allowed to carry a surrogacy for patients for whom it may normally be possible to conceive a baby. This provision also rules out the fear of use of commercial surrogacy by women who opt for it due to their busy career life.
11. The Law Commission of India (2009) described ART industry as a '₹ 25,000-crore pot of gold'. It recommended only altruistic surrogacy arrangements and not commercial ones. The report in its conclusion largely supports surrogacy but its commercialization is something that has been an issue in the mind of the law commission. But the Draft Bill legalizes commercial surrogacy as well.

The Draft Bill contains several landmark proposals to streamline surrogacy practices in the country since there were no rules earlier regarding the rights of the surrogate, minimum age, and details about the contracts, informed consent and adoption requirements. In these times of globalization and market-driven economies, there is a considerable demand for outsourced babies from India. The Bill is appropriate, considering the exponential growth that commercial surrogacy is going to be witnessed in India in the coming years.

Critique of the ART Bill 2010

In spite of being tabled in 2010, the Bill has not been passed by the parliament till date. Thus, there is a very strong recommendation for its implementation as early as possible, despite there being several anomalies in the Draft Bill which has raised several objections from various quarters. They are:

- There is a need for establishment of National Regulatory Body to monitor ART practices, predominately provided by private players and to ensure health and well-being of the women and children. The Draft Bill in its present form focuses only on IVF clinics and semen banks, but ignores gynecologists offering infertility 'treatments' and intrauterine insemination (IUI) procedure. The Draft Bill also does not take into consideration other consultancies, organizations, agents, private agencies and travel agencies involved in promoting IVF/ART techniques, egg donation and surrogacy. The Draft Bill does not adequately dwell on the regulation and monitoring mechanisms for the public hospitals offering these technologies. The Draft Bill should ensure that the ART clinics provide all relevant and correct information to the individuals. All technical terms and details must be explained and all written information must be read out to non-literate persons in a language understood by them.
- Compensation of the surrogate is the grey area. It is, therefore, not clear who is actually compensating the surrogate. The Draft Bill does not mention the details of administration of the contract between the surrogate and the couple: who makes the contract and monitors so that it is not breached? How would the money transaction actually take place? In case the surrogate is directly hired by the couple, how would the semen bank come into the picture and what would be the significance of the surrogate's contract with the semen bank? Modalities of payment are also an issue. In western countries, where commercial surrogacy is permitted, maximum part of the payment is paid during signing the contract, whereas here the maximum payment is paid only after successful transaction of product, 'the baby'. It ignores the risk associated with surrogacy.
- It is not clear where the screening and testing of donors would take place. Also, since the semen banks are not equipped to conduct oocyte retrieval, the Draft Bill does not specify how they would equip themselves for the purpose.

- The Draft Bill appears narrow in its approach by trying to regulate only a specified number of procedures. For example, the Draft Bill mentions procedures of: Artificial Insemination (AIH/AID), Intra Uterine Insemination (IUI-H/IUI-D), In vitro fertilization and Embryo Transfer (IVF-ET) and associated techniques of, Gamete Intra-fallopian Tube Transfer (GIFT) or Tubal Embryo Transfer (TET), Intra Cytoplasmic Sperm Injection (ICSI) and ICSI with MESA/PESA/TESA/TESE, Oocyte donation or Embryo Donation and Cryopreservation of Semen, Embryos, Oocytes and Ovarian Tissue. However, the clinics also offer facilities of assisted hatching, blastocyst culture and transfer, laser hatching, ovarian drilling, in vitro maturation, etc. PGD by PCR/FISH techniques have also been introduced in some of the IVF clinics. The Draft Bill does not mention any of these procedures in the entire draft.
- The Draft Bill allows couples to advertise for surrogates without mentioning 'details relating to the caste, ethnic identity or descent of any of the parties' and prohibits ART clinics from seeking surrogates for its clients [Clause 34(7)]. However, advertisements for egg donors or surrogates by advertisement agencies, tourism departments, surrogacy agents, women's magazines, medical tours and travel agencies are not covered in the Draft Bill at all. (Imrana Qadeer and Mary E. John, 2008)
- Draft Bill too supports these trends by asking for the surrogate's colour of skin, hair, eyes [Form M2 (34, 35, 36)], which is completely pointless since her oocytes would not be used in the procedures. As she only gestates the child, it is unnecessary to record her genetic characteristics. They only encourage eugenic tendencies and lead to discrimination against people belonging to particular religions, castes and with low educational and economic status.
- The Draft Bill also falls short in the measures taken to ensure the welfare of the children born through ARTs. In fact there is no section in the Draft Bill, which talks about the welfare of the child. The only points mentioned in this regard are those granting legitimacy to the children born though ARTs

and the right of the child to have non-identifying information about his/her genetic parents (Qadeer and John, 2008). Surrogate children are often denied their claim over breast-feeding. There is also an in-built bias against the newborn baby as the surrogate mother is constrained to underplay her bond with the growing baby from the beginning. Early separation is at the cost of the baby's immunological and psychological health. The baby is denied the right to breast-feeding even for three months. This aspect is completely ignored with the burden of surrogacy being shifted to one who cannot protest. Every child born through ART, whether disabled or one of a multiple pregnancy must have the same rights of survival and care as any other child. The proposed right of social parents to ask for 'pregnancy reduction' goes against this (ibid.).

- The Draft Bill does not adequately emphasize on adoption. Considering the fact that these technologies do not 'treat' or cure infertility, and keeping the potential risks for the mother and child in mind, a responsible legislation regarding infertility and ARTs must encourage adoption and present it as a course of action as significant as ARTs. Rather, this Draft Bill mentions adoption only twice in the whole document, suggesting that adoption is an option if and when ARTs fail for a particular couple. This clearly demonstrates the endorsement of the desire for a 'biological' child or 'genetic make' in an official document.
- 'No woman shall donate oocytes more than six times in her life, with not less than a three-month interval between the oocyte pick-ups'. However, the maximum number of cycles (which may be 6 or more) has not been mentioned. Also the mechanism to record and monitor the number of times a woman is making donations has not been mentioned. The three-month interval between the donations stipulated by the Draft Bill is very inadequate. The potential of exploitation of women for their eggs is as great as for their wombs. Since the sourcing of both egg donors and surrogates is through semen banks, the risk of commercialization is similar. The flow of payment to the egg donor is not quite clear in the Draft Bill (Qadeer and John, 2008).

- While the Draft Bill advises a studied recommendation of foetal reduction for multiple gestations, it does not mention the morbid risks of fetal reduction. Risks associated with ART procedures were not discussed at all.
- The Draft Bill has left a substantial void in the regulation process by not specifying the maximum permissible age of women for undergoing ART procedures. Considering the serious health implications whose magnitude increases with the age of the women, this lacuna needs to be addressed. There have been cases where women as old as 60 years or above have been made to conceive through ARTs with serious implications to their health.
- Regulation of surrogacy must be preceded by an examination of the context within which it is proliferating in India. There should be a separate format for the agreement between the surrogate and the foreign couple. The Draft Bill must prohibit the entry of intermediaries in the process of surrogacy arrangement and clearly prohibit acceptance of consideration for arranging the services of a surrogate or making such offers by making it punitive. (Sama, 2010), The Draft Bill prohibits the surrogate from being the egg donor. 'Success rates of pregnancy are generally higher for artificial insemination than for IVF, and therefore by extension, genetic surrogacy is generally more successful than gestational surrogacy'.
- The Bill mentions that 'No woman shall act as a surrogate for more than 3 successful live births', [Clause 34(5)] irrespective of the number of earlier pregnancies although the medical risks of frequent childbirths without adequate spacing are well known (ibid.). Restricting surrogacies in terms of successful live births is futile if the number of cycles is not specified. The document allows three successful live births along with permitting 3 Embryo transplant (ETs) for a particular couple. Therefore, the surrogate may legally undergo 9 cycles, may result in hazardous consequences for her health. Moreover, she may be donating oocytes and may also have had children of her own. These coupled with a lack of record keeping and a

subsequent failure to trace a woman's reproductive history may have hazardous consequences on her mental and physical (especially reproductive) health. (Sama, 2010),

- The Draft Bill must ensure that the intended parents understand and agree to the fact that the surrogate has a right to physical integrity and bodily autonomy, i.e. she cannot be forced to abort the foetus, go through foetal reduction or made to follow a certain diet. These decisions are for the surrogate, and no one else, to make. The Medical Termination of Pregnancy (MTP, 1971) Act guarantees women in India the right to abortion, while international human rights legislation guarantees her physical integrity. However, no sex-selection should be allowed even with the consent of the surrogate. The surrogate's right to privacy and physical integrity should be acknowledged in the Draft Bill. Every human being, without distinction of any kind, has a right to life, health, physical integrity, privacy, and a right to make decisions concerning reproduction free of discrimination, coercion and violence (ibid.).

India and Fertility Tourism

India is fast becoming a favoured destination for medical tourism. It has become the Mecca for all treatment options for infertility and thereby opened new avenues for reproductive medical tourism or better known as the fertility tourism.

The key drivers for its growth is the increasing number of infertility cases in the country due to myriad socio-cultural and environmental reasons like women's education, employment and subsequent delay in marriage and conception, sedentary lifestyle, environmental pollution and so on.

There is a growing number of people from abroad who flock to India seeking high-end treatments that come at a fraction of the price that they have to pay abroad. It is the economic practicality that drives surrogacy market in India. According to the 228th Report of the Law Commission of India, 'Need for Legislation to Regulate Assisted Reproductive Technology Clinics As well As Rights and Obligations of Parties to a Surrogacy' the usual fee for surrogacy in India is $25,000 to $30,000, which is almost one-third to what it would cost in USA.

The other reason behind surrogacy boom in India can be due to the ease of procedure. After the legalization of commercial surrogacy the whole issue has become a lot less hassle free, at least legally. Also, the draft Bill recognizes surrogacy agreements under the Indian Contract Act, 1872 and also provides for single parents who wish to have kids. Since a single male parent cannot adopt a child in India, surrogacy seems to be a good option to such single parents.

The liberal guidelines of ICMR (Indian Council for Medical Research), allowing egg donation and surrogacy have facilitated this. The easy availability of egg donors and surrogates in India has also encouraged international patients to consider India as one of the suitable countries to pursue their treatment. Additionally, India is also equipped with some of the finest international IVF centres and highly qualified IVF doctors. And finally, it is the abject poverty and desperation for money that compels a poor Indian woman an easy target to be chosen to act as a surrogate.

Further on, benefits associated with fertility tourism are numerous. To name a few, fertility tourism brings in more income, creates jobs, improves lives and contributes to overall economic development. It has also showcased India as a progressive and developed nation erasing the Third World image.

Conclusion

Therefore, the introduction of this new product, i.e. ART in the market are transforming the moral and ethical dimension of the society. Women are pitched against women as commodities and consumers. The presumably dubious moral nature of the surrogate agreement has been considered as exploitative. Surrogacy is criticized for its commodification, morality and objectification. It reifies the notion of biological parenting over social parenting. Today, ART markets as well as the state emphasize relationships of blood and the genetic basis of paternity, marginalizing the essential social and biological contribution of nurturing children in an enabling environment. Long silence over the Bill which is preventing it to become law is reflection of state's apathy in this regard.

Ethical practice must take its cue from the experiences of surrogate mothers, who – motivated primarily by a shortage of personal income – often endure the social stigma associated with surrogacy. They may leave their homes, lie about the parentage and claim the death of the baby after it has been handed over. The danger is obvious: economic exigency may force some women to enter surrogate agreements when they might otherwise never have entertained the idea.

'Reproductive engineering' is liberating not only of women with fertility problems but also of other groups. For lesbians who utilize sperm banks and artificial insemination to achieve biological pregnancy without heterosexual sex, such technologies are a critical tool of reproductive freedom. The majority of poor and working class women in both developed and developing countries still have no access to amniocentesis, IVF and the rest, although they have the highest rates of infertility and fetal impairments. Along with constructive criticisms against reproductive technology, we need to demand that all women have access to the knowledge and resources to judge its uses and to use it wisely, in keeping with their own particular needs.

References

Birke, L., S. Himmelweit and G. Vines, *Tomorrow's Child: Reproductive Technologies in the 90s*, Virago Press, London, 1990.

Corea, G., *The Mother Machine*, Harper and Row, New York, 1985.

Fraser, N., 'Struggle Over Needs: Outline of a Socialist-Feminist Critical Theory of Late Capitalist Political Culture', in *Unruly Practices, Power Discourse and Gender in Contemporary Social Theory*, Polity Press, Cambridge, 1989: 161–187.

Gimenez, M.E., 'The Mode of Reproduction in Transition: A Marxist-Feminist Analysis of the Effects of Reproductive Technologies', *Gender and Society*, Vol. 5, No. 3, 1990: 334–350.

Kurinczuk, J.J., M. Hansen and C. Bower, 'The Risk of Birth Defects in Children Born after Assisted Reproductive Technologies', *Curr Opin Obstet Gynecol*, Vol. 16, No. 3, 2004: 201–209.

Mallik, R., 'Sex Selection: A Gender-Based Preference for a Pregnancy', *Reproductive Health Matters: Elsevier Science*, Vol. 10, No. 19, 2002: 189–190.

Menon, N., 'The Impossibility of 'Justice': Female Foeticide and Feminist Discourse on Abortion', *Contributions to Indian Sociology*, Vol. 29, Nos 1 and 2, 1995: 369–392.

Petchesky, R.P., 'Reproductive Freedom: Beyond a Woman's Right to Choose', *Signs: Journal of Women in Culture and Society*, Vol. 5, No. 66, 1980: 1–85.

Qadeer, Imrana and E. Mary John, 'Surrogacy Politics', *Kafila*, 25 December 2008, http://kafila.org

Rowland, R., 'A Child at Any Price? An Overview of Issues in the Use of the New Reproductive Technologies and the Threat to Women', *Women's Studies International Forum*, Vol. 8, No. 6, 1985: 539–546.

Sama, Resource Group for Women and Health, Annexure, New Delhi, 2010.

Srinivasan, S. (ed.), *Making Babies*, Zubaan, New Delhi, 2010: 126–138.

Stickler, Jennifer, 'The New Reproductive Technology: Problem or Solution', *Sociology of Health and Illness*, Vol. 14, No. 1, 1992.

The Indian Council for Medical Research Guidelines, 2005.

228th Report of The Law Commission of India on Assisted Reproductive Technology Draft ART Bill, 2010.

CHAPTER 14

Beauty and the Market

A Critical Perspective

BIKRAM KESHARI MISHRA

The female body is a contested terrain the world over constructed differently in different contexts, though the body is intensely personal. While interrogating the issue of 'body', one encounters two apparent facets. At one level, one witnesses a constant onslaught on the feminine body which is reflected in the form of foeticide, sexual harassment, domestic violence and the like. At another level, one discovers an organized and aggressive display of the body dictated by the logic of commerce and consumerism. This is most conspicuous in fashion shows, advertisements, modelling, beauty contests and the like. In fact, a different form of commerce is mushrooming that capitalizes on women's body and that hinges on its ability to manufacture their beauty. Beauty pageants represent nothing but the domination of market over body, bazaar over beauty. The idea that is often put forth about the annual beauty pageants held the world over (even in small towns and cities) is none other than that of the empowerment of women. Starting from the grassroots organizations, business houses, the academic communities, media channels, to the macro-level women's organizations and other civil society bodies, there is a plethora of viewpoints about the promising potential of the event for women's empowerment.

The event evokes multiple reactions that are at times intriguing, ambiguous, exciting and illuminating. Both optimists and skeptics carp at each other with regard to the contribution of beauty contests to women's life. It is very difficult to remain insouciant to the following conundrums.

To begin with, how does beauty contest impact women? Has it anything to do with altering the real life concerns of women of the society? Does it really seek to address and annihilate the question of commodification of women, their perpetual devaluation and subjugation in the patriarchal set-up? Or is it merely an annual carnival manifestly intended to glorify the grandeur of womanhood, feminism and to take the credit of championing the cause of women? Does it intend to challenge the attempt by the market/patriarchal forces that seek to treat women as commodity and propagate a dogmatized impression that woman is a sexual/sensual being whose worth lies in her appealing beauty to attract men? Does it really empower women? No wonder, from academic institutions to the global levels, the phenomenon of beauty contest has been an all-pervasive annual carnival. Here, the question that arises is twofold: does this beauty game lead to women's empowerment, or does it lead to their further enslavement?

Beauty: The Key Conundrums

The notion of beauty predominates one's consideration while judging the entire personality of a woman. The very fact of attaching the idea of 'beauty' to gauge women's worth gives rise to a spate of queries in public imagination. What is beauty? Is it something God–given, not man-made? Or, is it something that is subject to negotiation and manipulation? Is it a package consisting of desirable face, figure, features, curves and curls, hair, grooming, health and skincare items? Why is there a penchant for looking beautiful, sexy and ever young? How far beauticians, beauty parlours, costumes and cosmetics, designers, fitness centres succeed in producing 'beautiful' women? Is it imperative for every woman to 'appeal' necessarily be beautiful in order to be evaluated as a woman of worth, talent, intellect and high personality? Can beauty really be manufactured, cosmeticized and designed? Are beauty pageants organized only to choose the most beautiful woman of the soil? Or do they reflect something more? Can a woman without certain 'basic good looks' compete successfully in a beauty race? Shall a woman without an apparent/appealing beauty appear as a woman of substance in public perception?

The point that is intended to be raised is that the very phenomenon of beauty itself has turned out to be a fetish in our imagination. The contemporary world has started witnessing a growing cult of 'beauty-worship' that has almost engulfed the mankind. No wonder, in recent times, 'beauty' has started flourishing as an industry, as a domain offering a series of career opportunities, as a profession, as a consumerist status symbol, as an anxiety, as a passion, as a game, as a fetish and as a postmodern 'hypochondriac psychosis'. Thus, it requires a great deal of research, contemplation and sociological imagination to grapple with this booming phenomenon – the postmodern totem we call beauty and its corresponding ramifications.

The knowledge of our times spells out a metamorphic message. That is, the very understanding of the 'individual' has undergone a historic shift. Far from viewing the individual in terms of his/her total personality and achievement, the entire focus has now centred on his/her body, appearance, looks and apparel. Even more than body, things like costumes and cosmetics, at times, prove to be important for defining one's beauty and asserting their aggressive victory over the body in their battle of beauty. In other words, body image has come to be seen as an indicator of one's (especially a woman's) worth, identity and personality. To borrow Joanne Finkelstein's view, spending time, energy and money on 'appearance', pastimes and indulging in consumerist exercises is taken in modern society as a sign of blessed fortune and an emblem of social prestige.[1] For example, as has been mentioned earlier, it is not surprising that while thinking of women, the idea that ineluctably strikes one's imagination irrespective of their achieved or ascribed positions is 'beauty'.

Beauty Contest: Body, Beauty and Market

To penetrate deeper into the enigma of beauty, let's interrogate the phenomenon of 'beauty contest'. From the national as well as the international levels at the top, down to the city, university and college level, the phenomenon of 'beauty contest' has been an all-pervasive annual carnival. Here is a demonstrative opera wherein each woman competes to look beautiful, attractive, glamorous and sexy. Far from using the greater equality between the sexes to determine their own sexual image, we witness woman reaffirming the notion that what is most important to a woman is her sexual allure. Madonna is often held of as the young women's icon of self-defined female sexuality: Can we say, beauty contest is a show to select world's most all-round talented woman of the year? Or if we think that it is a show to select world's most beautiful woman, we have to think again. Perhaps it has been unavoidable as well as an inseparable manifestation/repercussion of the culture of aggressive consumerism, market and postmodernism. No wonder, there has been a growing tendency to apply the sexualized, marketized as well as the consumerist parameters of beauty to gauge women of all walks of life. For instance, once Indira Gandhi was branded as one of the 100 sexiest Indian women of the 20th century.[2] Critically speaking, beauty contests are not about beauty, but about commerce. It flourishes on the basis of exploiting women's physical attributes. In the beauty race, each woman has got a competing urge to look beautiful, attractive, gorgeous and nonetheless, sexy. The entire interpretation of beauty gets sexualized. The preference for short-cut garments/clothes to expose the body without being completely nude, the passionate initiative to maintain an anorexic pattern of diet-intake and body weight, the investment to maintain a sexy, attractive body shape and size and remain continually young without growing old despite one's chronological age. All these aspects explain that the relationship between woman and beauty, between woman and market, between beauty and market, between body and beauty, between sexuality and identity and nonetheless, between beauty and identity has undergone a paradigm shift. With the tendency of patriarchy to trivialize women's individual identity remaining deeply entrenched in society, it is almost impossible for a woman to claim herself as the master over her own body, beauty and sexuality. In views of Catharine MacKinnon, women are walking embodiments of men's projected needs and are reduced to attractiveness to men and sexual availability on men's terms. In short, to be a female implies attractiveness to men, which means sexual attractiveness, which means sexual availability on male terms. MacKinnon further avers, a woman is a being whose sexuality exists for someone else. And this sexuality is the capacity to arouse desire in that someone.[3] Propagating a consumerist, corporeal, distorted, cosmetic, sexualized, packaged notion of beauty, the market has driven women out of their private spheres of family, placed them in the public domain and made them act according to the tunes of a marketized version of the beauty race. It has given a swift boost to couture and fashion industries. The *Delhi Times* pages of the *Times of India* and the *HT City* pages of the *Hindustan Times* bring glossy images of designers and semi-clad models across their pages in a bid to grab men's attention. Even, nowadays, it is difficult to imagine a marriage ritual without an expensive trousseau and wedding *lehngas*. This is suggestive of the kind of 'constitutive relationship' that exists between beauty and market. In other words, market has discovered a new industry in the domain of 'beauty' to cash in on. Correspondingly, human (woman's) body has been a terrain for the entire practice of experimentation as well as commerce in order to expedite the running of the beauty industry and foster the cult of beauty-worship in society. As Sabala aptly argues, the consumption of the body (for male pleasure) forms the basis of the market manipulation of women's bodies. Whether it is the women dancing in bars or women depicted in serials and films, the objectification of women's bodies for male gaze has been a part of the body agenda.[4]

Judging from another angle, 'beauty' as an industry has been beneficial to certain sections of the population in a number of ways. For example, it has opened up a plethora of opportunities to profess, practice, propagate and advertise 'beauty' and 'fitness'. This explains the logic behind the mushrooming of beauty parlours, weight-loss centres, fitness-clinics, skincare and body-care enterprises, beauticians, models and model-turned actresses. In other words, like Information Technology (IT), beauty industry itself has been capable of providing livelihood to thousands of individuals in the form of opening up a series of career avenues. It appears, the beauty industry has been the fastest growing one that has revolutionized the service sector. Today's women have a growing concern for their skin, hair, body, colour, looks, weight, curve and curl. Lauren Langman is of the view that by the end of the 20th century, popular culture valorized, idealized 'bodies' as sites of commodified as well as sexualized forms of health, beauty and fashion, promising glamour identities and ecstatic sexuality.[5] This corporeal obsession with remaining ever gorgeous has multiplied their desire and demand for health and skin care services/products. This anxiety for looking young/beautiful, staying slim, appearing sexy has gradually been leading to the evolution of a new society that consists of people suffering from 'beauty hypochondria'. The reason why companies like Hindustan Lever, Colgate, Palmolive (India), Dabur India, Fa, etc. invests heavily on beauty/cosmetic products are quite revealing. The craving for 'looking sexy' has started engulfing mankind, inciting everybody to fall in love with this 'beauty race'. To say that there is nothing 'bazaar' about the show appears bizarre.

Beauty is never viewed with indifference. As Scruton opines, beauty can be consoling, disturbing, sacred, and profane; it can be exhilarating, appealing, inspiring, and chilling. It can affect us in an unlimited variety of ways.[6] Beauty is no longer viewed in terms of one's worth, essence or personality. It has metamorphosed into a commercial as well as a consumerist article that can be bought, sold, exploited, negotiated, procured, used, shaped, reshaped, consumed, reproduced, advertised, exposed and sexualized according to the tunes of market economy and that of the patriarchy. Beauty has come out to mean one that appeals, which can be transformed by surgery, cosmetic manipulation (make-up and costumes). For example women, today, are desired to possess a hairless body. As Merran Toerien and Sue Wilkinson would put it, the norm of feminine body tells that hairlessness is the appropriate condition for the feminine body.[7] Beauty purports the appeals of one's 'complexion', sexy curves and curls. The very characterization of beauty has transcended regional, cultural and national boundaries. It is not astonishing to find Madonna wearing a *bindi*, using *henna* or *kajal*, or it is no more surprising to find Russian Tennis star Anna Kournikova wearing a *saree* and promoting the cause of the Sahara Group. On the contrary, with the use of the Indian feminine *saree* dwindling over time, younger women are more prone to using mini-skirts and like garments. The very definition of what is a typical Indian feminine look (in appearance and apparel) is in a state of flux. Post-modern beauty does not lay in a chiffon-clad, traditionally coiffed middling young woman. Rather, it is seen as a package consisting of face, figure, features costumes and cosmetics, skin and surgery. In other words, the 'physical body' is increasingly viewed as the birthplace of beauty. That is, beauty lies in one's demeanor, ostentatious appearance and appealing looks. It has assumed the form of a postmodern totem, a symbol of propitiation. No wonder, beauty and beauty queens are reified and beauty has been symbolic of one's affluence, mobility, cultural capital, elitism and cosmopolitan outlook. People may not remember you if you are a Vice-chancellor, UN's Secretary General, Scientists/Nobel laureate or Army Chief; but the whole country remembers you, imitates you and aspires to fall in love with you if you are a sexy/attractive model, a model-turned actress or an appealing sex symbol. You discover yourself as the fantasy of many human beings.

Empowerment or Enslavement?

Beauty is no longer defined in terms of the ideals of truth, essence, genius or bliss. It has metamorphosed into a booming global industry that treats beauty and woman's body as commercial terrains. Today's woman is trapped in a consumerist culture that values 'being beautiful' as the highest accolade for her. Perhaps, Baudrillard is right when he holds that what is important about contemporary consumerism is 'what is we consume'. It is the image, then, that is 'consumed', valued, quantified and desired; the image in which we have libidinal investment.[8] What does this beauty race point to? Does it mean women's empowerment? Or, does it imply their further enslavement? The answer is, perhaps it means both. First, let's scrutinize the perspective of empowerment. It is empowerment in the sense that it has offered a space for women in public domain, which had hitherto been a taboo for each female being. Not solely that, women are exposed to a wide range of vocations like fashion designing, modelling, advertising, acting, painting, and a series of careers relating to beauty and fitness. These careers render quick money, glamour and recognition. These career opportunities stand distinguished from all other occupations in that they provide instant and handsome returns. Women in large number are increasingly joining such career that not only enables them to be economically self-sufficient but also helps them give concrete meaning to their artistic as well as creative talents. Needless to mention, it has freed a number of women from the four-walls of the kitchen and driven them out to intervene in the public career domain and earn equally as compared to their male counterparts. Here lies the triumph of beauty for the cause of women in society. Besides, it is argued that improving one's looks is an aspect of personality development, that in a contest the art of presenting oneself, pose, poise, panache and intellect are also taken into account.[9]

On the other hand, it also implies enslavement in the sense that beauty contests are not about beauty, that is, to choose the most beautiful woman on the soil or to choose the most talented woman of the world; but it is about exploitative commerce and aggressive consumerism. It thrives on the basis of using women's body, reducing them into commodity, moulding them and their physical body into an article of advertisement and exploiting their physical attributes. Media is the biggest representation of the female body. Women's bodies are sexualized and objectified for the male gaze and market. Competition in the beauty race implies commodification of the body, subjection of the body to multiple cosmeticization, that of femininity to patriarchy, subjugation of personality/appearance/apparel to sexual allure. The identification of women with their physical bodies is the root cause of their oppression.[10] To argue in line with Eric Fromm, the modern women has been transformed into a commodity, which is subject to multiple manipulation, investment and trivialization and which promotion as well as definition has solely been contingent upon the forces of market and patriarchy.[11] It also means reduction of a woman to her biology, body to an object for experimentation that can be bought/sold/advertised for the profit of consumeristic culture. Today the cosmetic industry promotes the notion of the 'ideal' body type.[12] Thus, 'beauty' has taken a reductionist view of women that ignores one's psychological, intellectual, moral or spiritual endowments. It seeks to evaluate a woman on the basis of her 'looks' alone, and not in terms of her all-round personality.

Glorification vs. Trivialization

The debate cited above is not free from its own imbricating queries that require serious intellectual reflection for their meaningful resolution. To begin with, what is the contribution of this 'beauty industry' to the cause of women's movement in society? Does it glorify women? Or, does it trivialize them? Moreover, does it seek to distort the meaning of 'beauty' for mankind? These are certain questions that need to be contemplated upon and scrutinized by every sensitive intellectual – feminist or a non-feminist. For example, today's notion of beauty does not refer to something real, inner, absolute or the truth. Anita Anand, a leading feminist scholar, argues that the mundane obsession for skin-centric beauty is increasingly fascinated by a universalistic beauty game that seeks to urge every woman to fit herself into the game.[13] The so-called beauty contest ignores one's intellectual and other endowments; it defines woman by her skin and looks. Besides, it is also argued that beauty contests imply the conception of women merely as things for enjoyment instead of ends in themselves.[14] Thus, the entire gauging of one's all-round beauty remains partial, selective, cosmetic, fragmented and distorted. Our contemporary game of beauty seeks to use women's appealing body for the cause of market economy and not for the cause of women themselves. It wishes to treat women as a 'commodity' for the promotion of another commodity. It seeks to subject feminism to cosmeticism. Here lies the victory of ensemble over image and surrender of womanhood to the ideology of patriarchy in the sense that women are competitively striving to prove their feminine attributes (viz. features, contours, shape, eye, glamour, beauty ...) by which they were traditionally defined. In other words, in the beauty game each woman competes with the other to attract male attention.

Today's woman has nothing to challenge the traditional notion that being sexually desirable is the ultimate source of power for a woman. As Alison Jaggar puts it, as like wage workers for 'top dollars' woman of our times is in a competition with other woman for male's gaze, approbation and approval.[15] It appears, as if a woman's worth/beauty lies in her (sexual/sensual) allure to draw male gaze. On one hand, feminism as a women's movement strives to debunk all patriarchal shibboleths; on the other, the consumerist cult of beauty-worship reurges every woman to reinvent, remake up and cash in on her female-like physical attributes to remain continually sexy as well as attractive in order to be a desirable, fitting and an appealing woman to suit the taste of patriarchy. The delirious celebration of beauty and the body and the tendency to keep women constantly captive in a state of 'becoming beautiful' at the great expense of time, energy and money is a direct contradiction of all the gains of the women's movement. Rosi Braidotti rightly explains that women have been forced with a structural need to posit themselves as female subjects: that is to say, not as disembodied entities, but rather corporeal and consequently 'sexed' beings.[16]

Today, there is hardly any boundary between 'looking beautiful' and 'looking sexy'. Thus, the aggressive campaign of 'beauty race' and that of the market that seeks to reduce woman to a mere bodily sexual being and that attempts to gauge her worth only in terms of her 'apparent looks' need to be resisted. An alternative set of questions should better be posed: Is it not possible for a non-sexy woman to be beautiful? Or, is it necessary for a woman to appear sexy and appealing in order to be branded as beautiful? Does a woman actually need a certificate from the market or the public domain in order to be viewed as a beautiful woman? Is it true that only the apparently beautiful women carry worth and talent? Does talent follow one's bodily beauty? Are the non-beautiful, non-attractive or the bodily ugly women bereft of any worth, talent or intellect? Is one's skin-centric appearance the defining criterion of one's beauty? Are the so-called bodily ugly, the bodily non-sexy, the non-beautiful women bereft of any beauty? These are certain queries that need to be critically interrogated before any attempt is made to establish the meaning of beauty and reify its race.

Notes

1. For details see Joanne Finkelstein, 'Fashion, Taste and Eating Out', in *The Polity Reader in Cultural Theory,* Polity Press, Cambridge, 1994, pp. 277–283.
2. *The Times of India* rules that Indira Gandhi was not only sexy but also had all the attributes of sexy women. And the sexiness lies in her eyes, curve of her waist and her lips. Refer 'Meri Eyes Bhi Sexy, Mera Pout Bhi Sexy', *The Times of India,* 16 January 2000, p. 1.

3. See Catharine MacKinnon, 'Feminism, Marxism, Method and the State: An Agenda for Theory', in Diana Tietjens Meyers (ed.), *Feminist Social Thought*, Routledge, New York, 1997, pp. 64–73.
4. In an era of globalization the images around us of 'ideal' feminine beauty and the pressure to emulate these ideals operate as reflections of patriarchy and capitalism, largely through the use of diets and consumer products designed to 'enhance' women's faces, hair and bodies. Patriarchy and capitalism are two of the socio-economic structures that play a large part in the conception of female sexuality. There is a blatant marketing of good looks with everyone following it blindly. For a critical interrogation, see Meena Gopal and Sabala, 'Body, Gender and Sexuality: Politics of Being and Belonging', *Economic and Political Weekly*, 24 April 2010, p. 43.
5. The scholar opines that with globalization, the question of identities imbricate bodies that can be gendered, racialized, eroticized, surveilled, disciplined and decorated. Every culture is interested in body images and practices. This may include ideals of beauty, bodily exposure and display. For an immense analysis refer Lauren Langman, 'Culture, Identity and Hegemony: The Body in a Global Age', *Current Sociology*, Vol. 51, No. 3/4, May–July 2003, pp. 223–247. Available at http://www.sagepublications.com
6. We have differing judgments of beauty. There can be no such thing as absolute judgment on it. Our experience of beauty is rationally founded, and beauty is a real and universal value. Scruton shows how our sense of beauty has an indispensable part to play in the way we shape our world. For an engaging discussion, see Roger Scruton, *Beauty: A Very Short Introduction*, Oxford, New Delhi, 2011.
7. These scholars argue that such hairlessness serves both to demarcate the masculine from the feminine and to construct the 'appropriately' feminine woman as primarily concerned with appearance. For an immense exposition of the topic read article by Merran Toerien and Sue Wilkinson, 'Gender and Body Hair: Constructing the Feminine Women', *Women's Studies International Forum*, Vol. 26, No. 4, July-August 2003, pp. 333–344.
8. Discussed in article by Scott Lash and John Urry, 'Postmodern Sensibility', in *The Polity Reader in Cultural Theory*, Polity Press, Cambridge, 1994, pp. 134–140.
9. The selection of Indian girls indicates social advancement of women in India. For details, see Satya Deva, 'Beauty Contests or Marketing Gimmick?', *Economic and Political Weekly*, 26 November 1994, p. 3002.

10. In the Indian context, the woman's body is a space where culturally coded and socially sanctioned norms of the desirable woman are inscribed. The socialization of the girl child is a complex process, the main purpose of which is to inculcate in girls the appropriate codes of conduct including self-effacement and self-denial and to train them to see their life primarily in terms of service to others. The rules for the presentation of bodily self in everyday life are clearly defined and they are socialized into conformity from a very early age. The identification of women with their bodies thus becomes the root cause of their oppression in a patriarchal culture. For an exciting debate on the issue, see Kanchan Mathur, 'Body as Space, Body as Site: Bodily Integrity and Women's Empowerment in India', *Economic and Political Weekly*, 26 April 2008, p. 54.
11. For further details, see Eric Fromm, *The Art of Loving*, Aquarian Press, London, 1993, pp. 72–77.
12. For a lucid explanation, see Maithreyi Krishnaraj, 'Women, Embodiment and Personhood', *Economic and Political Weekly*, 24 April 2010, pp. 39–42.
13. For extensive discussion, refer Anita Anand, *The Beauty Game*, Penguin, New Delhi, 2002.
14. Deva (op. cit.) argues that instead of indicating advancement, beauty contests denote continued exploitation of the worst kind, and that, in any case, they place in educational institutions since beauty is mainly inherited and not achieved by personal effort.
15. Jaggar proposes that a woman's body does not belong to her; it becomes an object/article of consumption in the hands of men. She is restricted with respect to the control over her own body that is female sexuality. Her sense of fulfilment hinges upon men's approval. Thus, a woman in herself is an alienated being. For further comprehension see, Alison Jaggar, *Feminist Politics and Human Nature* Roman and Littlefield Publications, Sussex, 1984, p. 353.
16. Rosi Braidotti, 'Becoming Woman: Or Sexual Difference Revisited', *Theory, Culture and Society*, Vol. 20, No. 3, June 2003, pp. 43–64.

Index